EVALYN WALSH McLEAN

Wearing the Hope Diamond and the Star of the East

FATHER
STRUCK
IT RICH

Evalyn Walsh McLean
with Boyden Sparkes

FirstLight
PUBLISHING

Father Struck It Rich
by Evalyn Walsh McLean

Published by:

FirstLight Publishing
1813 E. Mulberry St.
Fort Collins, CO 80524

Printed in the United States of America

ISBN 1-889459-00-3

cover design by Christy Trapp

To my father, who was the fairest and squarest man I ever knew, and to my mother — a gallant lady, shy, loveable and brave.

Foreword

As I read over the proofs of this book of mine, which has come into print only through collaboration with Mr. Boyden Sparkes, whose untiring efforts I most fully realize, I have come to feel that, in telling what has happened to me, the whole emphasis has been on events rather than on my impression of what life actually is and what I have attempted to get out of it.

Now for a few honest, plain facts about myself: Why should I at forty-one suddenly break up my home, walk out of three beautiful places, give back the private Pullman car to my husband, and, knowing it would be bitterly hard, start life over again? I have noticed that most women do not get a divorce unless they are ready to marry again or want large alimony. In my case, it was neither of these reasons. It was to try to save my three lovely children. Home life was growing so difficult; and I knew they would be affected, perhaps ruined by it; so I packed up one morning and moved quickly.

Little did I dream at the time how hard it would be, because I was getting soft with too much money, too many automobiles. I know now the best thing I ever did for myself and the children was to begin life over again like any average person.

The one outstanding lesson I have learned and the one Father always taught me was, "Think of the other fellow first." Human nature is such a wonderful thing; people are so fine and real when you least expect them to be. You see, I really love people, all people and every class of people. Another thing I was taught is, "Give part of yourself."

Anyone with a little money can write out a check, sit back, and tell someone how to spend it; but the real joy in life is the personal touch — the warm, helping hand held out and the feeling, "She really cares for me and it is not only charity." Many examples of this come to mind. For instance, if, in a movie house, I see a man or woman who seems worried, or if one of the patient ushers or doormen who are so kind and considerate seems sick or discouraged, I always manage to get into conversation with them and often I am able to help in some little way. I have followed a poor mother out of a movie when her baby was yelling, and sat with the child and sent the mother back to finish the show, knowing full well she had had to bring the child, or not get the simple fun and rest for the afternoon if she did not bring it, because she had no one at home to leave it with.

I have my own little secret about the blue Hope diamond, of which so much has been written. It is not the lovely blue stone I wonder about; but I have great respect for and a great deal of curiosity about the thought concentrated on it. Perhaps when people do think about it, their first thought is, "It is evil"; and with a stone so well known, and with so many people keeping that thought in their minds, that might be the reason for its power and the cause of so much unhappiness always following the stone. I had it blessed myself and I am sitting back on the side lines letting the curse and the blessing fight it out together. Personally, I have so much faith in goodness and right working out in the end that it never worries me.

I have never done anything in my life without putting hard, personal work into the little I have accomplished. With my babies, I walked the floor night after night when often I was so weak and sick I could hardly stand; and there was always a trained nurse in the house. I have tried never to pass a worried or sick person anywhere at a time when there was the smallest chance of helping them.

Money is lovely to have and I have loved having it, but it does not really bring the big things of life — friends, health, respect — and it is so apt to make one soft and selfish. If I had only had the courage to lead my own life years ago I might by now have helped so many poor souls, and might have done infinitely more good.

The real things, I have found out, are quiet and peace in your own soul, love and thought for the people around you, and, above all, the care and devotion you give to your children.

It does not matter how other people treat you. That is their lookout. The only real thing is how you treat them. Give love out, but do not worry and expect any in return, and you will be happy and contented.

In returning these proofs to my publishers, I feel that I must add a word of appreciation and gratitude for the many heartening letters which I have received as a result of the serial publication in the *Saturday Evening Post*, and for the true friends which I am making through my story.

It is a great happiness to me to think that the book may serve a useful purpose.

EVALYN WALSH MCLEAN

Friendship
January, 1936

CONTENTS

ILLUSTRATIONS

FATHER STRUCK IT RICH

CHAPTER I

I Tell My Right Age

W<small>HEN</small> I had my hair dyed because streaks of white were showing in the blackness of it, I went right to the telephone and one after another called my friends and so-called friends — especially those I knew would spread the news fast.

"Darling," I began with each one, "I have become a blonde —"

My habit is to tell things first in preference to letting the gossips make exciting discoveries. I have been doing this for years. Long ago, as a Washington hostess and as the wife of a newspaper proprietor, I learned it is next to impossible to cover up anything, no matter how much you might like to keep a few secrets. In this book I am going to tell all my remaining ones, and some others. That is why I begin by telling my right age, adding three years to what heretofore it has been the polite thing to believe. I uttered my first cry at half-past four in the afternoon of August 1, 1886, in Denver, Colorado. It was a Sunday. That, I can tell you right now, is a fact entirely without significance in my life — Sunday, I mean.

A nurse was hired to attend Mother and me during the hours Father had to be away from the house. When the nurse was there I slept quietly enough, but each day soon after her departure I would begin to fret and then to cry as one bewitched. The crying would continue until the nurse returned the next day. She could soothe me. Mother had lost her first baby, born five or six years before, and she and Father were terror-stricken by the thought that I was going to follow my little sister into oblivion. Mother was so ill that she sent for her mother, my Grandmother Reed.

How beautiful is the word "Grandmother." Mine was truly a grand old woman! Virile and self-willed, she took charge at once, and within a day discovered that the monster of a nurse had been feeding me morphine in a soothing syrup. My appetite had been destroyed by the drug, and even when I did take milk it would not stay down. Father drove the nurse out of the house and tried to have her prosecuted. Grandmother Reed, for weeks thereafter, carried me around on a pillow — a puny, bluish little creature that almost no one expected to live. All that did keep life in me was the tenderness, the care, and the mother-shrewdness of Grandmother Reed. To the last minute of her life there was a strong bond of sympathy and understanding between us.

We lived in so many, many places when I was a little girl that I cannot possibly fix upon the exact succession of our homes, but it does not matter; except when we visited elsewhere we were always in the mountains of Colorado. The first memory of my life that I can bring into focus is of the half-dark interior of a two-room log cabin. It was comfortable and warm. Snow was thick against the outside of our small window except for a frosted corner through which, when the sun was shining, came a tinsel glitter.

I was crying bitterly. My small brother Vinson, one year and eight months younger than 1, was crying and sniffling. This was our protest against being taken into the knife-edged cold of the outdoors. Hands, my mother's hands, were pushing my arms and legs into thick garments. A scratchy woolen fascinator was draped firmly over my head to cover my ears and then crossed below my chin, the ends being tucked far back under my arms. Mittened and mummified, I was stood to one side while Vinson's wrappings were completed; that meant I was ready, so I began to yell with ferocity, stamping my feet for additional emphasis. Then Vinson was ready, and as Mother rose with him on her arm his yells were intensified. Then Mother opened the door and plucked me, with a thickly gloved hand, after her into the cold.

It is my understanding that we were then wintering high up in a mining camp near Leadville, and the cold I am talking about was an arctic cold. As the latch of the heavy door clicked behind us I walked, clutching my mother's glove, up a flight of treacherous and glassy steps that had been chopped (probably by my father) in the ice on the slope of the hill into which the cabin was imbedded. When our feet had crunched to the top step we turned into a pathway of black and icy footprints in the snow at the level of our cabin's roof.

Several cabin-roofs along that pathway was another and bigger cabin, that stood higher on the slope. This one sheltered the mining-camp boardinghouse where we took our meals. There is a fault in the vein of my memory after that. I must have been about four years old.

The next thing I remember is an occurrence in Denver. There were streetcar tracks in front of the small and ugly house. One side of our backyard was bordered by a weatherblackened fence that enclosed the yard of our next-door neighbors. They kept a dog there. Vin and I often heard him, and we had been told we must not climb the fence because the dog would bite us. Whenever we hit the fence with a stick he would bark and his chain would rattle. One day Mother put us into the back yard and told us not to go out of it; she was going downtown. In a little while Vin and I were bored. What was it we were forbidden to do? Climb the fence. Climb the fence—just that quickly it became an impulse on which I acted. Poor little Vin, who so many times was led into trouble by his Sis, climbed with me. It could not have been a very high fence; it only seems so in my memory. We dropped into the neighbor's yard. Everything there looked inviting. There was grass, and in one far corner a doghouse. But the dog was not chained in his house. I heard the animal growling before I saw him, heard his claws clicking on a brick pavement, and then he scampered around a corner of the house and came for us at a dead run —a white bull terrier.

Ourselves two frightened little animals, Vin and I scuttled to the fence and began to climb. I felt as if I were half-petrified, but I got over and dropped into our yard.

Poor brother! Slower and smaller, he was astride the fence as the dog ended his charge with a leap. Vin screamed piercingly.

What I remember next is the vibrations of heavy footsteps that told me of the arrival of the doctor. From my hiding place under the bed in the front room, I could hear water running in the kitchen, could see a long black satchel on the floor and now and then a hairy hand that reached down into it. There was dust in my nostrils and grief and regret in all my fibers. At intervals there were more screams from Vinson. The doctor was working some fresh kind of torture on the dreadful scarlet rags of flesh on my brother's leg. They did not find me until after the doctor had gone.

The shock had caused Mother to have one of her headaches; a wet towel was bandaged at her forehead and her swollen eyelids were red and tearstained. Father had come home. He was getting his gun. Afterward I became well acquainted with that old forty-one caliber revolver that had been with Father through all his years in the Black Hills and around Leadville. But this time it was just another awful item in the list of things my wrongdoing had brought to the surface of our lives.

"Where you going, Tom?" Mother's voice was shrill with fresh alarm.

"To kill that damned dog." I saw him go out the door, vest unbuttoned, his head cocked a little to one side, three fingers of his right hand held as delicately away from the butt of the erect revolver as if they were the fingers of a too-elegant lady balancing a fork. My father was ready to "throw down" on that beast that had torn the leg of his precious boy; Vin was his idol. I felt that there were ultimate horrors ahead for all of us, and dived back under the bed. I have no recollection of any shot, nor do I remember anything else about that affair. Vinson thereafter had deep and shiny scars on the calf of his leg, scars that I saw with feelings of guilt.

We moved away from the ugly little house, but where we went is not clear to me. Sometimes we lived in deep bowl-like valleys where I would have to tilt my head way back to see the sky roof above the mountain walls. With the swiftness of a stage effect, day would change to night and then come again in the same way. Sometimes we would be living in an unpainted board house so far up on a mountain that, almost any time I wished, on a wet day I could suck a wisp of cloud fleece right into my mouth or swing my arms to and fro and make a piece of cloud flow and eddy along the ground as if it were smoke from my father's cigar. Generally we were in the mountains in summer, and Father would come and go on the back of a horse. These animals were changed even more frequently than our houses, because they were hired animals. When cold weather came we usually retreated to Denver; mining-camp winters were deemed too severe for Vinson and Mother and me. There was one time, though, that we certainly were living in a mining town in the winter. The place was Leadville. One man was distinguished from all others in Leadville by a black patch over an empty eye-socket. He was John Campion, owner of the Little Johnny, and a shrewd and hearty friend of my father.

I always pleaded with Father to let me go with him on his trips, and one day at Leadville when he was going on farther up into the mountains on a sled he consented to take me. He frequently did when it was possible. This time he was going to see a man about a mine. That is about as much as I remember of his errand; probably it is as much as I knew.

The sled seat was close to the ground. When Father had tucked the grizzly-bear robe tightly around my legs to shut out the cold, and when I had nestled myself close beside him, I was lower than the horse's body. I could look between its hind legs and see its thickly coated brown hide as if it were a bloated ceiling. I kept my eyes there, because the bright sunlight on the snow brought tears. Oh, it was a thrilling day! The sled runners sang on the ice of the road, and my papa and I smiled, feeling ourselves sliding so smoothly. Here the roads were wider than in most of the mountain regions I knew. The trot, trot, trot and clinking of steel on ice lulled me. I slept part of the way. When I woke up, we were riding in a gray mist. Flakes of snow were catching on my eyelashes, and the sun was hidden. I no longer had to keep my eyes fixed on the dark body of the horse. The road was steep, and now and again the horse was permitted to stop.

Then we came to a cabin and Father called out, "Hello." As we got off the sled, the horse's nostrils were flaring so as to reveal the red lining. Its exhalations were smoky as a dragon's breath. Father covered the tired beast with the bearskin and then we hustled into the cabin, the door of which was opened for us. A prospector lived there.

We ate lunch and then, when Father had finished his business with this man and several gunny sacks lumpy with rock specimens had been thrown with a clatter into a corner, I was helped into my coat. The prospector, a man with a drooping mustache like Father's, urged us to stay. He called my father "Tommy."

Father's eyes left the man's to rest significantly on me.

"My wife would be worried," he said. "I can get back all right."

It was snowing very hard as Father covered me to the neck. The bearskin now was moistly warm, and smelled strongly of horse and of something else that may well have been the odor of itself, of bear.

The prospector was regretful, because of the lonesomeness that would descend on him when we vanished; but, little as I was, I could realize also that there was genuine concern in his eyes looking at me under his shantied brows that had gone thickly white with the falling snow.

He spoke again —"Better stay."

There was a slap of the stiffened lines against the brown rump that swelled above me. We began to move as Father said, "We'll get home all right."

Then the house was gone from sight, and the sled was slithering to the lower side of the road so that Father had to drive very slowly until we got down the steep onto a more level stretch. In a little while I was aware that there was no longer any sound from the sled runners; nor did the horse's shoes clink against stones. The animal was laboring in deeper snow, lifting each foot with exaggerated strides, but its efforts made no sound that I could hear. I put my mittened hands beneath the bearskin and tried with all my might to hear something anything. The cold was hurting my face and I no longer could pluck my clothing closer, with fingers that had become numb and stiff. The white streaks of the falling snow just beyond the horse's bobbing head became solid white through which I could not force my vision, strive as I might. Neither seeing nor hearing, I became frightened and started to cry.

Father began speaking to me with affected cheerfulness.

I interrupted him to ask if we were lost.

"No," he said, but made no effort to prove that we were not. We lapsed again into a feathered silence that was terrifying. I whimpered, and Father said I was a big girl. I said I was cold. Then he spoke to the horse, stopping it. To dislodge a clot of snow between its ears the animal shook its head, causing the rings of its bit to rattle, and I was glad of the sound.

Father stood up in the sled and I saw that the cold had made his face blue. Mine hurt. He took the bearskin that in the morning had kept us so snugly warm and wrapped me in it. Then he placed me at his feet in the bottom of the sled. I still was cold; he bit the ends of his mustache when he saw me shiver. In the bottom of the sled I ceased to feel or think.

The next thing I knew we were in the kitchen of a farmhouse and a woman and a man were rubbing snow on my hands, which felt as if they were on fire. I cried out protests and squirmed to evade them. My father had me on his lap, and in his hand he held a cup from which he wanted me to drink. He was insistent. My hands hurt as if they were being pierced over and over with hundreds of needles. The flat tongue of yellow flame in a coal-oil lamp on the brown oilcloth of the kitchen table was a comfort to me. I began to like the endearments of the woman, even though the snow she applied to my hands continued to burn. She was telling me why it would be necessary to keep me from getting closer to the glow of the stove on the other side of the room. My hands had been frozen, and for weeks were the chief objects of concern in the lives of my mother and father. There was some dreadful possibility that made them keep questioning me, with the utmost tenderness, as to how my hands felt. For a while they were not sure (I learned this when I was older) that amputation could be avoided. During that time Father could not walk and frequently he swore to ease his pain. I heard him tell Mother that in the blizzard, when we were lost, he no longer had any power in his clublike arms to hold the reins and guide the horse; that he had been in every way exhausted and hopeless when he saw the faint gleam of yellow light from the farmhouse window.

One day when I was skipping in bright sunlight on a path behind some houses, thinking about my black pigtails bouncing on my neck, I was overwhelmed by a drenching of warm, greasy water. A young woman cried out an unfamiliar exclamation of vexation and engulfed me in tender arms. Then she all but smothered me as she strove to towel from me the worst evidence of her carelessness, all the time berating herself in what I afterward learned was a Scotch brogue. What she had thrown from a back door, without looking, was the gray fluid of a clothes boiler. That was my first meeting with blue-eyed Annie McDonald, who soon thereafter became our first hired girl and the protector and companion of Vinson and me.

Annie was there to comfort me when I broke Aunt Lucy, my doll. Aunt Lucy was a lady doll with long dresses humped over a bustle, and with brown curls arranged in a cluster at the back of her bisque head. I had named her for my mother's sister, the prettiest woman I had ever seen. One day Mother took us all into a store, and there I tripped and fell, crushing Aunt Lucy's head. I cried until they had to put me to bed. Mother had the doll's head cemented together, and though she was no longer beautiful I kept her for years. Always the network of cracks in her face had the power to make me see visions of places in Denver.

Somehow we had become better off. We had Annie and we moved into a little frame house in Vine Street that seemed lovely to us. It was in a much nicer part of Denver than I previously had known, and I had a room of my own with a bay window where I kept my dolls and played house. Across the street lived a little girl about my own age, and we became chums. Sometimes Grandfather Reed came to sit there with me and try to join in my pretense that I was the mother of a lot of children and had many servants. Over the top of his gold-headed cane he would clasp hands with ridged fingernails. (I still have the cane as my only memento of him.) His checks were bearded, there was a tuft of white beard on his chin; his hair was white. He was gentle and dignified.

That was the year, 1892, that my school life began. When Mother asked me what I wanted for my birthday, I said I wanted the biggest slate she could find. I watched her walk down to the car tracks. When she came back, she gave me a double slate that opened like a book. It had four black surfaces fixed in creamy wooden frames bordered with red felt. Black cord was laced around and around that red felt. Some time after I began carrying that possession under my arm as I walked to school, I was required to memorize a verse about a lily. My starched white dress stuck out in front, because I was shaped like a small keg. I was given a calla lily as I started for the platform. Grown-ups sat there, among them my father. I made a bow -and that very action erased from my mind every word of the verse. Suddenly I burst out crying and ran to my father. He hugged me tightly and I was mad at everyone else because they all laughed.

Every spring and fall a spinster, Miss Ewing, came to the Vine Street house to make dresses. The living room became the sewing room and Vinson and I had fun teasing Miss Ewing. Cautioned to leave her alone, we turned stealthy. She discovered that her sewing machine would not operate. I had put chewing gum in the works.

My mother said, "To-morrow, Evalyn Walsh, at twelve o'clock I am going to give you a good spanking."

There was blackness on the face of the earth. I had never been whipped. I tried to play. I went across the street and sought forgetfulness with my chum. I had no

MRS. LEE (AUNT LUCY)

*Sister of Evalyn McLeans Mother
and Mother of Monroe Lee*

appetite for supper, and when Annie put me to bed I remained for a long time miserably wide-awake. The next morning Mother went about the house as usual and I began to have hope that she had forgotten, but when twelve o'clock struck she sent me into the basement and then appeared with a black buggy whip. She ordered me to take off my flannel petticoat. I howled for mercy, but I was appealing to a cold, aloof stranger. I think that was the only punishment of the sort ever administered to me. Thereafter Miss Ewing was left in peace. She made me a canary-colored silk guimpe dress that was the glory of my life. It was something to be worn only on Sundays, when I went to a church where I sang "Onward, Christian Soldiers" at the top of my voice. This must have been galling to the kinsfolk of my father. Tom Walsh had got so far away from the Roman Catholic faith that he had become a Mason. Grandfather Reed was a Mason. I can't say now where I heard it, whether in the rarely visited house of Uncle Mike Walsh or in the seldom seen home of Aunt Maria Lafferty, but someone once spoke in my hearing against the sin of it: a Walsh child a Protestant!

Well, if I was not a Catholic, at least, Aunt Maria, I was never a very good Protestant.

CHAPTER II

An Immigrant Lad from Ireland - and a Church Organist

SOME months before I began this book, at a time when I was wretched in my mind, I went to the enormous, million-dollar house that my father had built at 2020 Massachusetts Avenue in Washington. There are many other great houses in the Capital which, by sad changes, have been resolved into dust-stained mysteries. I have been in all of them: when they were alive, gay with music, laughter, champagne — when they were bright with jewels, fine fabrics, and lustrous eyes. As I rolled under the porte-cochere in my green Dusenberg a few passers-by gathered on the sidewalk. One of the great plates of glass in the outer wall of that carriage shelter had been broken, possibly by a thrown rock. My instructions had been obeyed: the doors were open; an electrician had thrown the electric switches, breaking the current of the burglar alarm wires that made the place into a great trap. As I mounted the stone steps I shivered. A stream of air was pouring out of all the reaches of the house. It was so cold, so much colder than the outdoors winter that it was almost visible, and it flowed swiftly. The house was as a cavern, a subterranean place in my past, and its deepest chill was lodged in my heart. This place had been my home.

From a basement room that had served as his office I resurrected all my father's old papers, cardboard letter files, canvas, covered account books, and other memorabilia of his existence in those years when I took everything for granted. In upstairs rooms I dislodged from closets and desks old scrapbooks, photograph albums, boxes of letters. I found some souvenirs of my honeymoon, of my darling baby Vinson, but I shed never a tear that anyone could see. It had become my intention to weave into the strand of my memories all that this material might reveal. By doing this, I had become convinced that where my own recollections were faulty or dim I could bring my reveries into focus with reality. On each floor, shrouded into whalelike shapes by paper wrappings, were great quantities of furniture. In a fine cabinet containing mineral specimens I saw actual lumps of gold; but the richer values that I wanted were more likely to be found in the receipted bills of a multimillionaire. The values I wanted were emotional ones. I wished, intensely, to rediscover in my own heart how devotedly we Walshes loved one another.

Father was a comparatively rich man when he met and married my mother in Leadville during the boom. He was rich and poor by turns several times, but it was not of such things that he talked when we sat close to the stove as a mountain wind howled around our house at Silverton or Ouray. Often I would be on his lap, one arm thrust behind him in what was half a caress and half an impulse to play with the little metal buckle that dangled on the back of his vest; my other hand played with the points of his pencils where these protruded from his pocket, and where my ear was pressed I could feel the beating of his heart. When he told about blizzards or Indians or bad men my own heart thumped. Of course, those things were not the beginning of his story.

Tom Walsh was a farmer's boy, born at Clonmel in Tipperary on April 2, 1850. I know little of his life as a boy except that his father, my grandfather, was a favorite in the community because he had a violin and could play on it. As a lad of twelve my father was apprenticed to a millwright, and when he had served his apprenticeship and could do anything that a carpenter could, and a great deal besides, he came to America. His brother Michael had come here in 1865, had enlisted in the army, and had been sent West to fight Indians. With his father and his sister Maria, Tom Walsh came over in 1869. For a while he worked at his trade in Worcester, Massachusetts. Then, when he was nearing twenty-one, he and his sister went West. Golden was the town where he went to work, building bridges for the Colorado Central Railroad. Two years of that; then, naturally enough, the mining fever got hold of him. That was what he called it: "the mining fever." Never to the end of his life did he get it out of his blood, and he never wanted to; it was grand fun for him always, although sometimes heartbreaking.

By the time I was ten, old enough really to understand what he was looking for, he had been possessed by that fever for twenty years. He was then forty-six. His health had been undermined by worry, disappointing business affairs, the stresses of rude climate, mining-camp food, and other hardships. In 1896 a doctor warned him that if he wanted to live he would have to take the utmost care of himself. When you think what he had been through in the preceding quarter of a century, that was a comical thing to tell Tom Walsh! To "take the utmost care of himself"!

Why, for years he had been inured to sleeping on the ground, often under canvas in winter blizzards, exposed to all manner of hazards.

In 1873 Father had been caught by the excitement of fresh gold strikes far southwest of Denver, near the border of Arizona. He joined the rush, but spent most of the winter working in Del Norte; since he was still green as to mining I suppose he worked at his trade around the mines. In the spring of 1874, he went back to Denver and then went a few miles westward to Central City; he was there when all the men were made frantic by news that there had been rich gold discoveries to the north, in the Black Hills of South Dakota. Father went as a member of a wagon-train party that included some of the most experienced mine operators of Gilpin County. The country they passed through was Indian territory. The unwary were apt to be scalped, and some were unwary. Father was in and around Custer for nearly a year and then, in 1876, he went over to Deadwood.

Deadwood! Probably a good deal of the frail illusion that its muddy thoroughfare was lined by two-story buildings was actually the handiwork of Tom Walsh: all the stores, barrooms and gambling houses had false façades that rose above the actual roofs. Somewhere along that street of deep, ungraded mud he had a shop. Right in the street near his door was a placer mine with a wooden trough. Literally, there was gold in the street. Thousands of booted and seldom washed, rarely shaved gold-seekers were clustered in and around Deadwood. Many were men who short years before had been fighting each other in uniforms of blue or gray. There were gentlemen in Deadwood, and thieves; there were heroes and homicidal maniacs; there were nice women and prostitutes; there were many Chinese, and some Indians. Calamity Jane sometimes strode along the street in the buckskin clothing and black slouch hat of a plainsman. Her rifle had a skeleton stock, her eyes a hard glitter. She called my father by his first name. Swill Barrel Jimmy and Antelope Frank were among those who came rushing into sight when loud shrill yipping and the sounds of galloping horses in harness announced the approach of the stagecoach. So many times have I heard my father describe that exciting moment of a Deadwood day that it seems as if my own eyes actually had seen it: the wheels throwing mud clots as the coach rolled up the gulch, the octagonal barrels of buffalo guns resting on the forearms of the guards on top, the dirty canvas window curtains flapping and the coach careening each time a wheel found a deep place in the soft mud. Of course, I never did see that stage; but as a girl I heard my father talk with lean and gray-eyed Seth Bullock, the sheriff.

In Washington I was in a hotel corridor one time when Father came together with long-haired Captain Jack Crawford, the poet scout.

"Say, are you the Tom Walsh who struck it?"

"They say I did strike it."

They peered at each other closely, grins beginning to crease deep wrinkles in their weathered faces.

"Why, ain't you the Walsh that rode with the Black Hill volunteers who went after those redskin murderers of Preacher Smith in seventy-six?"

"That's who I am: that same Walsh."

They grasped each other by the hands and then they talked of the Custer "massacree", of the Homestake mine and Smoky Jones.

One day in the spring of 1876 there had come into Father's little shop in Deadwood a stranger, ragged and filthy from a long stay in the hills. Something lovable and charming shone in the eyes that peered out from a frazzled, uncombed mat of hair and long beard. Exposure to the sooty breath of his campfire had given to this prospector the dubious complexion of a slab of bacon, and with merciless accuracy Deadwood had fixed upon him the name "Smoky" Jones.

Smoky had asked Father to do some trifling job for him. It was about lunchtime, and Father had asked him to come and eat with him. The obviously hungry man declined shyly, but it was wholly characteristic of Tom Walsh that he should insist. As they ate they became friends and when they parted Father told Smoky Jones never to come into Deadwood without visiting him. After that, Smoky came often and Father always saw to it that the prospector had a good meal inside him before he hit the trail back into the hills. Somewhere out there, Smoky Jones had a prospect in which he had great faith. He showed specimens of rock to Father and talked with enthusiasm about his strike. Then, one day, he proposed that Father become his partner and help him develop his mine.

Father protested that he knew nothing of mining: he was a builder, a millwright. Smoky urged, and Father decided to consult some of his Colorado mining friends — men with whom he had come from Gilpin County into the Black Hills. They were Mining men with "learning." So Tom Walsh told these oracles of Smoky's offer.

"Have nothing to do with it," they said dogmatically. "It's a slate formation and even if there is a little gold there it is only a freak. No mine can be worth fooling with that is not a true fissure vein in granite." (I have this in Father's handwriting.)

Father was keenly disappointed, but he was convinced. He told Smoky Jones that he was going to abide by the advice of his Colorado friends, and declined the offer of a partnership. Precisely what he declined, in his ignorance, was a half-interest in the Homestake, one of the world's greatest gold mines. From it came the vast fortunes of United States Senator George Hearst, the father of William Randolph Hearst; and in nearly sixty years the Homestake mine, still a producer, has given up more than $266,000,000.

When my father talked of the incident in after years, it was always with a rare kind of Irish pride at the size of his blunder.

But where another man might have gone on being foolish, my father buckled down to learn all he could of mining — of Nature's customs, of her whims, in depositing precious minerals in the earth. He learned from experience, out of the minds of other men and even out of books. To the last year of his life he was ready to point out with grim satisfaction that, while those dogmatic Colorado mining friends had been among the first in the Black Hills rush, not one of them had acquired any of the great properties of that region. What had cheated them, he used to say, was not a matter of luck but their own technical prejudices. As for Tom Walsh, ten thousand times in his succeeding years he stooped to pick a bit of float or to chip a specimen from an outcrop that another mining man would have passed by without pause. If it had not been for that habit he might have died poor. Indeed, but for that habit there might have been little out of the ordinary for me to tell.

Some time in 1877 Father left Deadwood and returned to Colorado. To show for his hardships, hazards and labor in the Black Hills he had between $75,000 and $100,000. Whether he made any part of it trading in claims or mines I do not know; it is reasonable to suppose he made most of the money as a builder, since his sort of skill would have been at a premium when Deadwood was becoming a town. At any rate in 1878 he was attracted to another boom camp, Leadville.

Nearly eighteen years before my father arrived swarms of placer miners had cleaned up about $5,000,000 in gold dust by washing the sand and gravel of the stream bed in California Gulch. All that remained of that activity in the

14

succeeding years was a village of about five hundred persons. It was called Oroville. Then some man, more observant, more curious, more thorough than all the others who had passed that way, made an exciting discovery about the black and water-worn boulders of the stream bed. The earlier fortune-seekers had levered some of these out of the pathways of their sluices. This man found that the boulders were masses of silver-lead carbonates. The place was renamed Leadville and for a few years thereafter—to all America and beyond—stood as the one spot where a man or a woman might hope to win a fortune overnight. Tom Walsh arrived in 1878, soon enough to see the arrival of most of the thirty thousand who came. In that halfmad maelstrom of humanity my father and my mother were to find each other.

For a single night my father owned a third-interest in a saloon in Leadville. "The next morning," he said, "I took my share of the whiskey and poured it into the gutter."

I am inclined to believe that must have been an incident in the history of the Grand Hotel. Tom Walsh, aged twenty-five, had the status of a capitalist when he reached Leadville, and, soon after, he bought—with Jerry Daly and Felix Leavick—the old City Hotel, which they enlarged and renamed. It stood near the west end of Chestnut Street, a three-story building with a half-dozen dormer windows along the front of its mansard roof and several more on either side. The second-floor windows on the front opened onto a balustraded gallery that formed a shelter over the wooden sidewalk.

The Grand Hotel really was grand! The sheets were not always clean, but the guests were not particular; they were glad of a chance to sleep turn-about in three eight-hour shifts, at a time when most of Leadville's inhabitants were living in tents or even less adequate shelters. Soon all those thousands were trapped there in the mountains by severe winter conditions. An appalling number died from exposure and pneumonia. Then the surrounding forests were cut down. Bricks were made. Leadville had little order, but increasing comfort. In 1879 Tom Walsh became the sole owner of the hotel.

The other large hotel there was the Clarendon. In his book, "Here They Dug the Gold", George Findlay Willison wrote: —

The Grand, built over and around the old City Hotel on Chestnut, attracts the more sober and respectable. It is kept by Thomas F. Walsh and his wife, a rather refined lady who claps the name of St. Keven's upon well-known Sowbelly Gulch when her husband happens to make a small strike there. Although the Walshes do well enough from roomers and boarders they do not attain bonanza rank during this boom.

I am grateful to Mr. Willison for his research, but as an authority on Mrs. Thomas F. Walsh I can assure him that he was excessively cautious when he wrote "rather refined." Why, Mother was the *most* refined woman I ever knew; and she was not an isolated case even in the wildest days of Leadville. My grandmother,

Mrs. Anna Reed, had taken her there in response to camp publicity about the need for schoolteachers. It is lodged in my memory that the family, a short while before, had left the home village of Darlington, Wisconsin, and stayed a while in Birmingham, Alabama, where Grandfather's brother, was a florist and Mother played the organ in church. Then, because of Grandfather Reed's lungs, they went on to Denver. There was a second daughter, Lucy, and a hell-raising, ne'erdo-well son, Steve. My grandfather, Stephen Reed, was a sweet old dear who probably hovered around while Grandmother made plans and carried them out. It was Grandmother who determined to place her eldest, Carrie Bell, in a schoolteacher's post in Leadville.

Carrie Bell, my mother, had a figure that men turned to stare at; she was nearly as pretty as Grandmother and she sang beautifully. While she was growing she had been required to walk around the house for hours balancing a glass of water on her head. Because of these exercises, with her feet— even her toes— concealed under a wealth of petticoats she could, with the utmost elegance, glide so as to appear to be rolling on casters. And it was this tempting creature that reckless, determined Grandmother Reed took to Leadville. They made the journey in a stagecoach over a terror-inspiring trail that followed the edge of a succession of precipices. On that highway there was an unforgettable cavalcade: mule teams dragging canvas covered wagons with screeching axles, men and women afoot, with packs on their backs, bull teams, horsemen, laden burros.

On that road to Leadville there were other unseen chasms besides those that created such giddiness in any who let their eyes stray outside the windows of the stagecoach. Indeed, a young and handsome girl did well to keep her eyes cast down when there were so many on the road who were quick to read a challenge in an honest glance. There were professional gamblers, gunmen, crooks, riding on to Leadville. There were veterans of other camps, hard-featured women whose entire baggage consisted of their evil intentions. There were traders in all manner of things that a mining camp's population might require.

There were criminals there soon after the rush began. Father used to tell me that Jesse James was working in a near-by gulch, partner in a claim with two men named Ford. (Bob Ford later shot Jesse James in the back.) But at Leadville, as anywhere, there were more decent men than crooks: swarms of hard-working fellows, pick and shovel laborers, teamsters, carpenters and miners— and they all wanted fortunes quickly, just as my father did.

There were numerous churches in Leadville, and Mrs. Reed and Miss Reed promptly associated themselves with one of these. I cannot identify it further than to say that it was one of the Protestant churches. What really puzzles me is how Tom Walsh, an apostate Catholic, ever happened to stray inside. He did though, and heard my mother singing; he was entranced. I have his word for it that then and there he said, "That is the girl I am going to marry."

They were happy! They were married on July 11, 1879, and on the first

MRS. THOMAS F. WALSH

Mother of Mrs. McLean

anniversary of their wedding, Father handed to her the sweetest gift he could have devised—four verses at the top of which he had written: "To my devoted, true and loving wife Carrie B. Walsh, these humble lines are dedicated." If they were better verses I might think some out-of-luck poet had written them to work out a board bill at the Grand Hotel; seeing what they are, I dare to submit a sample and ask if such words possibly could come from other than the one who felt

> Ah, well I know what priceless luck was mine,
> That brought the day, the hour, when you became my bride.
> Heaven, indeed, could give no choicer, rarer gift
> Than you have been to me, my dear and precious pride,
> My more than life, my darling Carrie Bell.

The eructative name of Sowbelly Gulch tempts me to believe it was the scene of my mother's first housekeeping experience in the mountains. I know that about a year after their marriage they left the hotel and went out to live at a mine father was preparing to operate. I can well believe she renamed it "St. Keven's", because she did many things to transform the place. There was no suitable cabin, so Father had a boxcar (one of the first to arrive on the new railroad) taken from its trucks and placed on a foundation of logs. For steps there was a short flight of half-logs imbedded in a ramp of earth. There was a stove inside, a table, and a bed. Father fashioned some windows; Mother made curtains of checked gingham, and in the window boxes she planted flowers less hardy than the native, wild ones. She had great trouble saving them from the sharp frosts. Whenever she told me about that first little home her face showed a little quirk of smile. She was better off than most women who followed gold- and silver-seeking husbands into the mountains. What the average camp cabin was like I know from my father's story of one of his adventures in gold-seeking. It was in 1880, and he had gone for a few days' stay at a mine in which he was interested, in the Frying Pan district west of Leadville. It was a prospecting trip, and he started out one morning burdened with a gun and a prospector's pick, to look over a near-by hill. After several hours of tramping and sampling he decided to have a smoke. Close by, against the hillside, was an abandoned log cabin. Obviously it had been the shelter of some miners who had lost faith in the prospect. The roof was formed of poles covered with earth and rocks. Father put the butt of his gun on the ground and tilted the barrel into a slot formed by uneven ends of the poles supporting the low roof. Then he lit his cigar, and as he did so his eyes were caught by the gleam of quartz particles in the stuff piled thickly on the roof. It was likely vein matter. He tried to find the vein, but saw no trace of it. Not far off he discovered the shaft which the vanished miners had sunk in the hill. The hole was in decomposed granite, absolutely barren. He investigated a rubbish pit beside the cabin, clearly the place from which had been taken most of the earth piled on the roof: beneath its debris there was no quartz or other indications of minerals. Finally he went inside. There he noticed that the earthen floor was made uneven by chunks of partially exposed rock. With his short-handled pick he broke off corners of the rock. It proved to be nice-looking quartz. In a flash he saw what had happened. The men who made the location unwittingly had built their cabin squarely on the apex of a vein, covered the roof with dirt and rock from that vein, and then had gone fifty feet away to sink their shaft—into barren granite. He sampled the roof and when the samples had been assayed the returns indicated a hundred ounces of silver to the ton.

Father hunted up the owners and paid them their price, which was not much. Then he put two men to work and within several weeks a fine vein was uncovered. In two months the claim netted him over $75,000, and years after he had sold it —indeed, more than a quarter of a century after his discovery—it was still a large producer.

A little girl was born to my parents, and died. The price of silver was declining from year to year. One or the other of these things caused them to leave Leadville and go to Denver where Father invested in real estate. They were "comfortable", except for the fact that Father was not well. I was born in 1886, and on April 9, 1888, my brother Vinson was born. Mother's younger sister, my beautiful Aunt Lucy, was living in Denver with her husband, Samuel N. Lee. Uncle Sam and Father went into business with a Chicago man named David S. Wegg, who it seems owned the rights to exploit in Colorado what was known as the "Austin smelting process," a means of extracting values from low-grade ores. An old account book of Father's reveals that by a series of assessments during 1892 the newly formed Summit Mining & Smelting Company received from Mr. Wegg, $25,172.22; from Uncle Sam and Father, each, $12,586.11. Uncle Sam was president, Father was treasurer and the secretary was a fourth participant, Amos Henderson, who put in $4,195.37. That enterprise explains for me some of the moving we did: to Kokomo where a smelter was built; then to Silverton where another was established. Some English capital was invested in the Silverton smelter. Uncle Sam and Aunt Lucy had moved to Kansas City.

Grandmother Reed—"Nannie" to all of us—was still living in Denver. One visit to her was made unforgettable by what happened to a white fox terrier. Her son, Uncle Steve, was there and this is my only recollection of my mother's brother. He was drunk and cursing terribly because Nannie would not concede something he wanted, probably money. Suddenly he bent down, grabbed the squalling fox terrier by its hind legs and threw the poor little animal at Nannie.

I learned afterward that even as a boy Uncle Steve had been a dark-eyed fiend. He was frequently in trouble and his sister had lived in terror of him. Yet the family blamed, always, not Steve but "the drink." In a letter Mother wrote to Father while I was quite small and he was trying to mend his health in the East, she reminded him that he had said he would be willing to pay Steve's keep in some liquor cure. Then she added that Nannie now knew where her son Steve was.

However, just to balance the matter I want to state that at Pueblo, Colorado, Nannie's brother was a prominent citizen, State Senator Elton T. Beckwith.

CHAPTER III

"Daughter, I've Struck It Rich!"

I WAS nine when Father came home to our Vine Street house one day and announced, "We are going to live in Ouray."

Ouray was wonderful. A child first glimpsing that valley from the mountain trail scratched in the rocks high above it could look down upon a toy town the few streets of which were cross-hatched as if a giant had chalked on the basin's floor the patterns for a couple of games of ticktacktoe. Most of the mountains roundabout were crested and streaked with snow and were lavender where rocks showed through the white. Half a mountain had collapsed into one end of the valley, after ages to become a pleasant island hill of green, part pasture, part woodland. From our house we could look across the valley at the mountain from which that enticing debris apparently had fallen in the geologic past. There was a perpendicular red rock-wound so stratified that to my fancy it seemed a rich and tempting many-layered devil's food cake—that is, until my father made it even more tempting. From our front porch one day he directed my gaze to that red-brown escarpment and explained that there I saw plainly what his eyes tried to divine when he went prospecting: the very heart of a mountain.

Little Annie was with us as our hired girl at Ouray. She cooked and scrubbed and did her best to keep Vinson and me out of trouble. Each morning she stood beside me as a monitor until I had put on the red flannel union suit I so loathed. Each Saturday night she put me into a tub and gave me a bath with so much soapsuds and vigor that I went through the entire process with my eyes screwed tight and my nose wrinkled in the most hateful expression my imagination could devise. We had a " front" room at Ouray, an extra chamber in which a guest might be sheltered for the night. Sometimes we had as a guest an old prospector who was doing some work for my father. When he came to see us his hair was slicked down with water and he wore a coat that was green at the seams. Red underwear showed below his cuffs. There were great calluses on his hands and a thick tuft of hair sprouted from the depths of each ear. He was Andy Richardson. Father called him "Andy"; he called Father "Mr. Walsh."

One time Annie, Andy (he was in love with Annie), Vinson, and I went for a walk in the woods. We sat down to rest on a log. Some chipmunks that had scampered from sight would come back, Andy told us, if we were real still. Vinson and I sat breathless until we saw one of the little ground squirrels running along a near-by log. It sat up, bright-eyed, to watch us. Suddenly Andy threw a stick and stunned it. He put the little creature into his pocket. When we got back to the house it was as lively as ever. We fed it and gentled it until it became so tame I had it with me all the time.

When cold weather set in Mother's neuralgic headaches were so bad Father sent us all to Kansas City to stay with Aunt Lucy, Uncle Sam, and their little boy Monroe. There was a golden oak folding bed there for me. It had a mirror in the top that was supposed to make a secret of its character when it was folded against a wall. There were heavy springs to help draw it up past what Uncle Sam called its "dead center."

My little squirrel slept with me and by day rode around on my shoulder or cuddled against my neck. I had grown to love it as I never loved any of my dolls. One morning I could not find my little pet. I looked and called all that day. Some of the family said it was like all wild creatures, it could not really be tamed and probably had got out of doors. I did not believe them. At last it was time to go to bed. As Mother lifted the pillow I saw something that made me scream with horror. My squirrel had been there all the time under the pillow; now it was stretched flat on its back, its mouth open, dead.

We went back to Ouray in June of 1896, and Mother and Father had a new brass bed that I thought the most elegant piece of furniture any family could possess. I had a collie dog named Prince. There was a fat little pony in the yard. By that time I was a tomboy. I had always wanted to be an actress, to wear a lot of lacy things, smell of perfume, and paint my cheeks and lips; but I was made to wear red flannel union suits, so I became tough. I wore boy's pants, flannel shirt and sweater. Vinson and I had a gang of boys.

An exciting pastime was to visit the main street and stand in front of the window of the Chinaman. He was a bucktoothed fellow with an extraordinarily saffron complexion. The fore part of his skull was shiny with bluish skin that he kept shaved but on the rear was his astonishing queue. We felt utterly superior to him as we chanted an accusation that he ate rats and engaged in other unpleasant actions. He would take a mouthful of water and spray it on the clothes he was to iron. Often he was so annoyed that he stamped his feet as if he were starting to chase us. We would squeal and run. One day one of us lighted a firecracker the size of a banana and tossed it in. With a cry like the whinny of a horse the Chinaman went berserk. He snatched up a large kitchen knife and rushed after us, gibbering. We were panic-stricken. Fleeing as in a nightmare, with the Chinaman close behind and coming closer if the sound of his felt slippers meant anything, I saw the president of the bank straighten from his lounging position before the Beaumont Hotel, as our little pack of hellions came along. He saw we had goaded the laundryman too far. He stuck out his foot and our pursuer sprawled on the sidewalk. Someone told my parents, and for a while I was forbidden to go to the town.

My father had piercing blue eyes that could be gentle as forget-me-nots or cold as a blizzard wind. I was really scared of his wrath, but his work took him away from home so much I tended to get out of hand. Especially was this true while

Mother was away seeking relief from her headaches, at Kansas City or Excelsior Springs, in the company of Aunt Lucy Lee. At such times I was more than a handful for Annie. But there were certain rules I was expected to obey. Father was going away for four or five days in the company of John Thompson, who was better informed about mining stock than about mines. Mrs. Thompson, a yellow-haired woman of the Lillian Russell type, was a friend of Mother's. They had met four or five years before when the Thompsons and the Walshes were living at the Princeton Hotel in Denver. Little Faith Thompson and I were chums.

When Faith came up to our house she was full of chatter about a dance to be given that night in the hotel dining room. We had no thought of actually attending the dance, but we wanted to observe it and get ideas.

"We can peek through the side windows," said Faith.

In front of our house Andy Richardson was just then engaged in what was, for me, a fascinating activity: he was loading a pack horse and preparing to show off his supreme accomplishment (in my eyes) by "throwing a diamond hitch." Never had I watched his movements so closely. The packsaddle with its double cinch had been adjusted and then Andy proceeded adroitly to weave his pack rope so that a diamondshaped loop took taut form on either side of the load where the bulge was widest. Andy was flattered at my interest; but what I was really thinking about was the dance.

If Father and Mr. Thompson were going away, I wouldn't have to be home for supper. Soon afterward Faith and I skipped down the slope into the town, and for the rest of the day played at Faith's house. I ate my supper there, wishing all the while I was not forbidden to spend the night away from home. I was not allowed to do this, even with people we knew as intimately as the Thompsons. By the time Faith and I reached a side window of the hotel, the dance was in full swing. There was not an evening dress on the floor; but we were impressed by the formality with which rather ordinary men jerked themselves forward into a bow when they asked a lady for a dance. We saw with sympathetic dread the forced animation of the wallflowers. An hour passed and then another before I permitted myself to think how late it had become.

"I think I'll stay with you, Faith." I knew that if I went home I'd be lectured and scolded but if I stayed all night little Annie would be too scared to tell Father. I wasn't being very logical, but I went to sleep soon after Faith and I got into bed.

Next thing I knew there was a terrific pounding on the door of the bedroom and I recognized, with terror, my father's voice.

"Get up and dress yourself this instant," he commanded me.

I began shivering, and the hands with which I buttoned and hooked and gartered myself into my clothing were wet with perspiration. I knew Fate had played me a dirty trick: Father was supposed to be twelve or fifteen miles away sleeping beside Mr. Thompson under a tent. I dressed with a haste I hoped would gain a little mercy, and soon appeared. Father's red mustache was bristling like the hackles on my collie's back. The nostrils of his finely chiseled nose flared with each breath,

EVALYN WALSH
AT FOUR

THE WALSH HOME IN OURAY

Before the discovery of gold at the Camp Bird Mine

but he spoke no word until we were out of the Thompsons' house.

"Now!" he said fiercely. "You have disobeyed me: you know it's against the rules to spend the night with anyone. Anyone!"

I reached for his hand as was our custom when we walked together. He pulled away and directed me to walk behind him. I followed as if I were a dog and each of his quick strides seemed to hit my heart. I was entirely miserable. When we reached home all he said was, "Go to bed. At once!"

Poor Father! He had enough troubles without having to fret over my misbehavior. The year had begun badly for us. We had a dull Christmas and New Year's owing to Mother's illness. Father himself was far from well, and spent much of his energy in sleepless nights. A whole series of ventures had gone wrong through no fault of his. A drop in the price of silver had turned a profitable smelter at Kokomo into a liability. Real estate that he had bought in Birmingham, Alabama, had become unmarketable. A corner he owned in Denver at Champa and 22d streets had ceased to bring him any revenue; possibly it had been mortgaged. He had another piece on Arapahoe Street, near the post office, between Sixteenth and Seventeenth.

These and other investments had become unprofitable or else had been mortgaged or sold to provide him with funds to engage in some further mining enterprises. The depression of 1893 had contributed to his worries, of course. For one thing it had deprived him of the support of his partner in Chicago; they were separating after some years of association. Night after night when the rest of us had gone to bed Father was sitting up writing to David Wegg.

The struggle my father was having in 1895 and 1896 to keep our little family from want is revealed poignantly in those letters.

Now, Dave, [he wrote] don't think that I have my Irish up or that I have any grievance against you. Heaven will bear me witness that I have no feelings but those of a brother towards you or ever will have. I am utterly unable to go on with the leases I have on hand. I was disappointed on Black Hawk [at Rico, Colorado] and Mt. Queen. Since my last I have been a week on the Black Hawk. We worked a chute of ore 200 feet wide down to a point where the value gave out; but the vein continued. We shall try to sink on this chute in hopes that the values will come in again. At present 5 men are employed, mostly all working in upper workings on small stringers trying to make expenses and if possible get a little ahead so as to prospect the bottom of the main chute. It is difficult to hazard an opinion as to the result. The giving out of the values was like a thunder-clap in a clear sky.

The Mountain Queen pay streak does not hold its value going down. For 600 feet on the surface it averages 100 ozs. Four feet down it falls to 30. On account of snow I have been unable to work the Vermillion yet. The Black Girl ran behind $200 last month but we are doing a good deal of dead work. The Hawkeye paid $150 more than expenses. The Neodeshaw was a dead loss and I quit it. I have made no tests on the Mt. Queen as a concentrating proposition as I have had no means. I paid in the early Spring an assessment of $250 on [Ben] Butler. We are getting some good ore from this mine but expect it to play out any day. You can form your own opinion of a country that will play out in 20 feet with such surface showings as you saw on Butler. . . .

24

I will give up about the 10th. I have no money, myself nor family beyond our support. I will quit clean-handed anyway. What I shall do I have not decided. Some friends may and may not help me. I exhausted the little reserve I had in paying incidentals like taxes, Ben Butler, &c. Hence when I needed it I did not have any strength. Within myself I feel—even though no one else agrees with me — that I recovered victory from defeat at Silverton [smeltor], made what was a lost investment worth something. Kokomo was ruined by a drop in silver. Under the circumstances I don't know how we struggled along so well but now I am disheartened and sad, tired of making rosy promises and giving blue results. I have no money, nor no bank credit [the bank was pressing him to reduce a $5,000 note] so there seems to be nothing left for me to do only to shut down. I wish you would advise me for I am in need of calm advice now if I ever was. To add to my troubles my wife had to go to her sister's three weeks ago because of continual headaches here.

I am very poor, I have nothing to look forward to. In regard to Black Hawk and San Bernardo I gave checks amounting to $675, dated March the 31st on the 1st National [of Denver]. When my other checks out come in there will be only $50 balance to meet this $675. 1 am trying to get some parties here interested in the leases. My position is desperate and I must do something to protect my name. I had to send those checks.

I seem to see him again as he was at that time. He would suddenly put down his knife and fork at table and begin to figure with a pencil on the back of an envelope. Probably it was from some of those calculations that he gained the courage revealed in his postscript: —

P.S. Of course if there is any way for me to keep on and hold on to our leases I will do it. I do not know just how I will carry Black Hawk & San Bernardo. I may get the men to wait [for their wages]. From hints you dropped I gathered that you would like to get completely out of mining interests.

Father did hold on somehow. His imagination was bewitched. He felt there were richer deposits of minerals in the earth than ever had been found. I am sure if he were alive he would say as much right now about what is in the earth. He was constantly exercising perceptions that transcended ordinary human sight in his efforts to discover what was within the mass of each of those steep mountains over which he rode and walked and climbed and crawled, always sampling. I was with him on some of his trips that summer. I was ten and my legs were long enough to straddle a mountain horse named Dewdrop. Father's horse was Nig.

In the Imogene Basin, nine miles from Ouray, was an area that particularly held his interest. The mountains there contained known veins that my father was trying to get possession of as part of a plan to develop a profitable smelting plant. Along in the eighties, millions of dollars had been expended there in the development of silver-lead veins and in the erection of mills. On our rides we often visited one or another of those abandoned and dismantled sights and camps. Small animals sometimes scuttled from view when we came among the low-roofed log buildings, giving me the feeling that I was being watched by eyes that should not be there. A silent movement in a tree usually would reveal itself as the action of something having the small and friendly form of a camp bird whose first chirp would be like a greeting.

"What do you see over there across the gulch, Daughter?" Father once asked me.

"You mean that black hole, Papa?"

"Yes."

"Well, that's what I do see; just an old mine. Maybe a bear uses it for a cave now."

"Maybe," he said. "But look with your intelligence, too, Daughter. Look below surfaces. Feel with your mind as well as your fingers. Think of all the holes like that one which we have seen around here. There are miles of drift tunnels and many mine shafts hidden from your eyes: see them with your mind."

There were crow feet wrinkles printed at the outer corners of Father's blue eyes. We were eating our sandwiches. I could hear the incessant sound of little roots tearing as the horses cropped grass behind the rock where we sat. Father told me that veins of silver-lead ore reached up inside the walls of the basin where he was spending most of his time that summer. But he wanted copper. There were only a half-dozen known bodies of copper in the region. If he could find a copper mine or an iron mine or both ' he could bring success to the pyritic smelter he was trying to develop at Ouray. He told me that the Una and the Gertrude claims had been staked here years before I was born — 'way back about the time he was getting ready to leave the Black Hills.

"It was the time of the big Leadville excitement. After three-four years of hard work and spending there was failure. The camps around here were dismantled and everybody left."

As he talked I could almost hear the racket of hoisting machinery, the grinding pulsations of big concentrating plants; yes, even the clink of shovels and picks of the men who once had dug inside the hills that threw their cool shadows over us as we rested. I knew Father's plan because he had discussed it a hundred times. He felt that if he could get possession of the abandoned properties and make a large output the Austin smelting process could make the low-grade mines pay.

I knew that already he had acquired a large number of abandoned mines, mill sites, and undeveloped claims. In most cases the scattered owners were eager to close at any figure. The earlier failure bad put a blight of human disapproval on the section. Only one man had kept his faith alive in the Imogene Basin — Andy Richardson. When not in Ouray be lived in a tent on a claim he called the Ptarmigan. Once, holding tightly to Andy's dry and horny hand, I walked into a drift tunnel, each of us keeping a candle high to light the way. When we were a hundred feet in the hillside, so that when we blew out the candles, the entrance was merely a disk of light, Andy asked me with his deep, deep voice how I "would like to work here with a pick and shovel."

I shook my head and then, realizing Andy could not see me, I released a "no" that came forth a booming, echoing sound in that subterranean place. There were a few other men working individually on claims in the surrounding hills, but Andy had been there from the beginning. He told me that he was the first white man to cross the range from Red Mountain to prospect the Imogene Basin. There was pride in his voice, and his hand slapping against the wall of the tunnel had in it something of the feeling with which one pats a beloved horse. Andy loved the place, and because Father believed in it Andy loved Father.

All our journeys were to prospects or mines with fascinating names. As we rode, single file, along the narrow, rocky mountain trails Father would toss over his shoulder an identifying word or two. "Yonder," he'd say with a lift of his hand, "is the Ivanhoe." Then I, too, would see in the rocky mass he indicated the faint suggestion of a crenelated castle wall that had inspired the vanished fortune-seeker who had named the place. Ah, but there were more exciting names!

While my father delved and sampled rocks, sometimes for whole half-days I dwelt in reveries. Some subtle feelings that perhaps for years had hovered in the deepest mountain glens now touched my mind. I had wanted to be an actress, and there in the hills I was an actress. Not alone sunburn touched my cheeks, but the paint of my fancy; my hateful red flannel union suit ceased to itch and became all lace and soft linen. By perceptions less than clairvoyant I knew the past. All about me were droppings to tell that the close-cropped grass had nourished wild mountain sheep and goats, but there was more. To some of the broken land lonely men had given names that were as echoes of the purposes that had brought them from far-off places high up into those hills. An escarpment of rock that was iris-blue in the sun surely told me it had been named in memory of haunting eyes,—the Norma. The white and never-melting snow on a rock that cut off half my sky? It was for someone's white-haired mother; that one had been called the Emily. In that richly colored world of rocks there were positive clues to explain that Gertrude had red hair and that Una, too, was blonde. Men who once had staked their claims and hopes in this basin had shaped themselves, for me, in such fine names as Canuck and Yellow Dorg and White Swede. I thrilled when I heard my elders speak of Hidden Treasure, Talisman, Oro Cache and Argosy. But it would be Father himself who would reveal what secret loyalties to past experiences had fixed upon his newly staked claims such names as Tipperary, Old Ireland, and Deadwood. The Boxer was for Vinson, and Tam o' Shanter—why, that was the kind of hat I wore when I rode beside him.

Mother was often invited, but rarely went. Father said she brought him luck; he would remind her of a time when they had been riding in a buggy. He had stopped the horse, stepped down into the road and picked up a piece of rock. When this sample, which had a matrix in the near-by earth, was assayed it showed rich values—as easily as that he had discovered a mine that he afterward developed and then sold for a nice profit.

In June, 1896, father was lobster-red from sunburn when he returned from five or six days of riding across the mountains to Silverton and back. "There is lots of snow yet," he said to explain his burn, and gave the tired pack mare a kindly slap that sent her trotting into our yard.

It seems to me it was only a few days later that the telegram came telling of the death of Grandfather Reed in Denver. When we returned from the funeral Father resumed his prospecting trips, but Mother, blue and troubled incessantly with neuralgia, spent much of her time in a dark room. Once that summer, though, they did canter out toward the toll road. With them rode Mr. Thompson, floridly handsome, and Mrs. Thompson, her big soft hips spreading wide above the cantle, so that Father, as they started forth, had half his red mustache lifted in a grin the others could not see. That time I cried with vexation because I had been denied permission to go along. But I was along on the most important day of all.

Father had been offered another claim that was 'way up near the summit of the range. He had been over the ground with Andy Richardson and for some reason was eager to get back a second time. So we rode forth one morning, following the familiar, dizzy road that was cut into the canyon wall so high above the feathery waters at the bottom of the gorge. Father was tired before we started; his skin was touched with an unhealthy yellow. Never before, though, had he taken me quite so high. On the steeps the horses bobbed their heads and breathed noisily. The wind was cold, for at that altitude there were never-melting glacial snows lodged in deep fissures in the crags. Bare black rocks were underfoot. Similar reddish rocks reared themselves steeply above us, cutting a jagged line into the turquoise of the sky. On foot we climbed higher and higher, Father carrying his canvas saddlebags and his prospecting pick. He would talk to me as if I were grown-up, and a man to boot.

"I like the looks of this ground, Evalyn."

"But wouldn't all the other prospectors that have been up here—the thousands who have passed along the trail—"

"They were looking for silver," he said, and squatted on top of a rock slide. "Besides, there are lots of poor prospectors who might have been rich if—"

That was a favorite theme of his: the careless prospectors who ceased to be careful and methodical in their search; who were always ready to assume that the first prospectors to look at any piece of ground had been thorough.

"In the mining game gold is just where you happen to find it. And you never know what's under your feet."

Each time the shining, bluish white point of his pick broke off a sample Father would wet the bit of rock with his tongue to make its metal shine. Near the ground he sampled that day was another claim that he owned. Buried under a snow slide was a tunnel and other workings we could not see. Father pointed out to me the outline of the dump. About the middle of the afternoon we mounted the horses and started back; that high road was not pleasant traveling after dark.

Father had to go to bed soon after that trip. He had developed a case of jaundice; his skin and the whites of his eyes became the yellow of gold. As soon as he was permitted out of bed, he was ordered by the doctor to go to Excelsior Springs. Before he would consent to go, he insisted on seeing Andy Richardson. There in our house he gave him instructions to go up on the Gertrude and drive a tunnel

The Walsh Family In 1897

through the snow until he could get into the workings.

"Sample the tunnel." Father spoke with such intensity as to seem almost irritable, which ordinarily he was not. Of course, he had been quite ill. "Have 'em for me when I get back."

In a few weeks he came home from the Springs and, in his own phrase, he was still as "green as leaves." He had come back to Ouray against the orders of the doctor. He was mysterious with Mother—with all of us. There was something he had to " 'tend to." He was obviously weak, and so thin the bones of his shoulders made pathetic ridges on the back of his coat. Nevertheless, he saddled Nig in the morning and set out to see Andy Richardson at the cabin over in the basin.

Mother had bad news that day from Denver; Grandmother Reed was ill and needed her there. She would not make the decision to go until Father returned, and when darkness had filled our valley he still had not come. It was unusually late when Prince began to whine and scratch at the front door. Somehow he could distinguish the beat of Nig's hoofs among those of all the horses that moved around Ouray. Vinson let the dog out and stood waiting on the porch. Then Father came, almost exhausted, and grunting a little from the weight of his saddlebags. He never left those in the barn when he had been out sampling; he always put them under his bed. That night his eyes were so bright that Mother was convinced he had a temperature.

Next morning he had vanished with his saddlebags before I was dressed. Then he had to go back to bed; the doctor insisted, or else he would not be responsible. However, Grandmother Reed's condition made it necessary for Mother to set out for Denver, and once more Vin and I were in the care of Annie. A few days later Annie told me Father wanted me in the bedroom.

"Daughter, close the door."

I did and then rested my chin on the cold, shining footboard of the big brass bed.

"You must keep a secret I am going to tell you. Promise?"

"Yes Papa."

"Remember the trip we made up near the Gertrude? I found some gold in those samples I made that day. It ran about two dollars a ton. Now I have had reports on samples I took this last trip."

He hesitated; after all, I was only ten. If mother had been there I am sure he would have told her instead. Feeling as badly as he did, he had to tell someone, someone he could trust. He motioned me to come around to the side of his bed and showed me a piece of grayish quartz; it was not very impressive. He wet it with his tongue and held it near my eyes. Like thread-ends in its texture were glistening circles and specks of black.

"That's gold."

I was ready to whoop with joy, but he sharply interrupted: "Whoa! Remember this is a secret. If you should tell a single person before I say you can, you might ruin our whole future." I have forgotten most of his words, of course, but I remember their import: the report he had received on his samples was better than his wildest dreams.

In the intervening years I have thought often about that action of my father. Why did he tell me, a ten-year-old child? He dared not tell a soul outside the family until he had completed all his pending deals for the claims and prospects and mines in that long deserted region. He had no partners; it was all his own. Yet he was a sick man who knew his clutch on life was none too firm. If he died his secret would die with him, and we who were so deeply loved by him, for whom be bad scaled mountains and dug and worried — we should be left in want. He had to tell. Mother was in Denver, Vin was a little too young, but I was ten and I knew where the gold was. So he told me and the secret was kept as securely as if we had been a family of mountaineer Corsicans. Almost the whole of his message was imparted with a single spoken sentence. He did not have to write anything that a prying eye might see. Even if he died he knew that some day I would grow up and sensibly interpret what he meant when he whispered, —

"Daughter, I've struck it rich."

CHAPTER IV

The Camp Bird Mine

WITHIN a few weeks there was no secret to keep because it no longer was important to maintain secrecy. Around Ouray everybody knew that Tom Walsh had made a gold strike, and in a silver region that was news. As bigger and bigger orders for mining machinery began to go out by telegraph the news spread, first throughout Colorado and then in the big city newspapers. I have no recollection of any immediate change in our way of living; indeed, I am pretty sure that for a while there was no change. What I remember best is the thrill the family all had each late afternoon when the jack train came down from the mine into Ouray: each jack was bestridden by an enormous pair of saddlebags and on each of those bulging canvas receptacles was lettered in black paint "CAMP BIRD MINE."

A few friends were close enough, trusted enough, to learn the whole story from Father; and often the tale was told at our fireside in Ouray—how he had found gold nine miles from where we lived:—

When Father returned from Excelsior Springs against the doctor's advice, it was because of his eagerness to see the samples from that mine tunnel that was covered with snow. But when Andy Richardson handed him the sacks full of samples some voice in Father's deep self prompted him to go and take his own samples. After all, Andy had been in the basin for eighteen years and never had found gold. So Father threw aside those sacks and despite the kindly remonstrances of the old prospector he insisted on making the long, hard trip up the mountain. He reached the mine after an exhausting effort and found there a dump of very showy ore having zinc, lead, and some copper pyrites. He went into the tunnel, and found an eighteen-inch streak of the same kind of ore that was on the dump. Then he saw something that made his heart pound.

Between that streak of obvious ore and the hanging wall was a three-foot vein of quartz. There was no shining mineral in it, and most miners accustomed to silver-lead carbonates would have regarded it as worthless; but Father, with a richer experience, knew it for what it was—gold in a tellurium form. His illness was completely forgotten. For twenty years he had been searching for what he saw there; and it already belonged to him when he found it. He took so long to sample that grayish quartz that Andy became uneasy and entered the mine.

"There's the pay streak, Mr. Walsh." With a finger Andy traced the narrow vein of less important galena zinc ore.

"Never mind. I see it; but I always assay everything."

Out on the dump Father found tons of "waste" that when assayed showed values of $3,000 a ton. Indeed, it was from the dump of that abandoned mine that he got some of the first of the extraordinary riches of the Camp Bird. Why (he once said), with no better tool than an ice pick a man could have knocked off a comfortable living for a family.

Meanwhile I was still a tomboy and nothing could be done about it, although Mother tried hard enough. Brother and I were the chieftains of a pretty rough gang for which our yard was a rallying place.

I'll never forget the day we all decided to play firemen. Among the cluster of typical outhouses in our back yard was a shed with a gable roof above its cramped second story. It was agreed that Vinson and I were to rescue the others from a burning building. So we herded them up a ladderlike staircase into the top chamber of the shed, closed its trap door, and set fire to the place as calmly as you please, in our enthusiasm using entirely too much old paper. Before we quite knew what had happened the structure was a roaring furnace, but making considerably less noise than our slowly roasting friends. Vin and I were so frightened we could not move; we had planned a gentle little fire that we would put out with the garden hose as soon as we had made use of the ladder on which the whole scheme was based. Luckily, Father was at home. He went into action with the hose, rescued the other youngsters, and cussed Vin and me—all, as it were, with one breath.

As fast as we got out of one scrape we got into another. Vin had been given one of the Camp Bird burros for a pet—a strong-willed, hard-mouthed little beast. Right after he mounted it in the yard one day it trotted under a clothesline that was tight against Vin's throat before he could say "whoa." He was jerked from the donkey's back, landing on his head. He lay unconscious; he had a nasty concussion that made the doctor stick out his lower lip in silent concern. Mother was away and Father was at the mine. Annie and I were scared as we could be that Brother would die. However, he recovered and we soon got ourselves into other difficulties.

The Camp Bird had become a place of the most fascinating activities. I do not think any mine of like magnitude had ever been developed so swiftly.

During the first year Father worked as hard as ever he had worked in his life. He took charge of the development work; no one was so well fitted by experience to make that development work pay for itself. There was no selling of stock, no borrowing. Some Ouray men with picks, shovels, drills and dynamite extended the original tunnel farther and farther into the mountain, almost directly under the jutting cliffs that form the side of the Basin. That which had been the core of the tunnel became, almost overnight, the pay of the miners; and a growing excess was steadily transformed into modern mining machinery. Happily for Father's peace of mind, fingers of the veins were found close to the surface.

"Sugar quartz" was what they called the stuff packed down from the mine on the backs of the burros. The ore was practically free milling gold. That was the grand phrase we heard often at our supper table in those days: "free gold"! No wonder Father was too excited at times to sit through a meal. The West always had been exciting to him; that one of its potentials which now had become real had kept a spell on him through all the years that he had been prospecting in the mountains. Yet even while his bonanza was igniting the imaginations of those who mined in basins and valleys adjacent to Ouray, on some of the other crazily tilted surfaces of Colorado's gorgeous scenery, Father himself was fretting. Doctors had told him he must, he absolutely must, stop subjecting his body, his heart, and his mind to the strains of mountain climbing, exposure and worry; but he no longer had time to talk with doctors. That was because he was a mining man to the core. If he had inherited that red mustache of his from ancient Britons, then why not also some of that British instinct for finding metals that long years ago brought Phoenicians coasting up from Tyre to trade their purple fabrics?

It was that same instinct, ripened by his years of experience, that kept him fretting. Too many times for ease of mind he had been compelled to face the heartbreaking consequences of having a rich vein pinch out, leaving him confronting debts and sterile rock. Up there on his mountaintop, so high that sometimes the nearest clouds were a half-mile down, he could see on near-by slopes, as grim reminders of the wreckage of other miners' hopes, black holes that were deserted tunnels, low log structures that were dismantled mills, neglected graves of the forgotten. There was in the mine itself a cure for the forebodings of such dismal things: touching the ore of his mine with his hands was a healing action as soothing to his mind as a dose of some narcotic. This was why he was reluctant to desert the mine.

No man can dwell in those majestic mountains without reverence for the creative force that shaped them so magnificently. During the year my father was unlocking the treasures of his mine there was fixed in him a firm belief that a Supreme Intelligence had guided him to the bonanza that other men had blindly failed to see. He believed there was a nice balance in the world by which men's acts automatically measured out to them all that they received of justice or misfortune. Because of that belief he was unfailingly kind and generous; and then, just at the end of his year of development work, he had in his nostrils the ugly smell of death.

It seems to me now that things were always happening to the Walshes; but this particular experience happened after a late summer outing in Denver. Why we had gone there, I do not now remember. The Thompsons, with their little girl, Faith, were along; also Father, Mother, Brother, little Annie and I. Annie and I were in one lower berth together. Outside our car window the night was by turns dark from the narrowness of the gorge through which we traveled and acrid with the breath of the railroad tunnels. The curving pathway of our green-curtained bed had made us dizzy and glad to sleep.

I think I had been asleep for hours when I was pitched with terrifying violence into a chasm I could not measure. The blindness of my plight caused me to shriek, but the sound echoed only in my mind—because the world had become a place of grinding, splintering clamor, smelling of stale dust, and I could not breathe. I

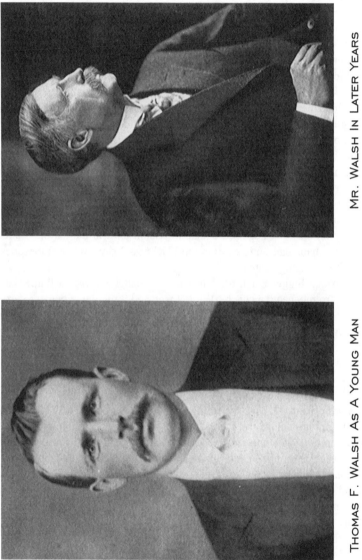

THOMAS F. WALSH AS A YOUNG MAN

MR. WALSH IN LATER YEARS

knew I was choking even as I heard the moment of silence that succeeded the final smash and rain of breaking windows. I was head downward as in a strait jacket of harsh Pullman cushions and bedclothes. I heard dear, faithful Annie half-scream an injunction for me not to be frightened. I kicked and writhed until my mouth was free, but before I could yell there came the voice of my father—

"Evalyn?"

There was entreaty in that cry, addressed to something higher in the scheme than me. He was calling frantically to each of us in turn—to Mother, to Vinson and to me. I managed a whimper, and in a few seconds felt his strong hands clutch one of my kicking legs. He plucked me upward as from a barrel, and when my arms were locked in terror about his neck he kissed me. I could feel him thrusting upward into the darkness so that his chest expanded joltingly against my cheek. Glass showered on us and he crouched over me. He was in frantic haste to get me through one of those car windows that had become our tilted ceiling. Up through the opening he had made he pushed me, and bade me scramble to the ground. Because my nightgown was up around my armpits as I slid over the rough surface of the car roof I scratched and cut myself a little. For a time on the ground I was too close-fenced by darkness to move. Under my bare feet I could feel cold, sharp stones and cinders. Probably I was worse confused because of the bumping I had received, but slowly I acquired a shaping vision until in the darkness ahead and behind the chaos had outlines. On the blackness I saw amber arabesques being written by swinging lanterns.

There was a bigger patch of light some car-lengths away; a flame that jetted furiously from beneath a coach. While I watched it the flame began to grow long tongues. There were awful sounds: cries of pain, moaning, screams, and the bellowing of cattle. I must have walked a short distance, because soon I saw near me a man who, as I watched, gave up in despair his futile effort to drag himself along the ground. His head with rather long hair dropped a few inches to the dirt and then the advancing fire drove the shadows from his face and body. His legs in torn trousers were drenched with dark fluid and he reached a hand toward me.

I sat beside him. He was speaking far back in his throat, and trying to lift his head. In mining camps even the children are aware of the obligation to succor injured persons. In a situation in which a city child might have determined that the case was one for a policeman or an ambulance surgeon, I, as a matter of course, pulled that poor man's head into my lap and patted his cheek. He was speaking over and over the same two words: "Wife, babies."

I have no recollection of a reunion with my mother. The events of that dreadful night are a jumble. But I know that as I held the man's head Mother was close enough for me to see hair braids hanging against the whiteness of her torn gown.

Brass buttons glinted on the open vest of a bareheaded man who trotted toward us. He was wheezing for lack of breath when Mother stepped into his path. When he stopped, his lantern was close beside my head. There was a faint hiss as a dark bubble formed on the hot globe in its protection of wires. I saw that blood was streaming down the hairy back of the railroad man's hand from some dreadful source hidden by his darkened sleeve. I saw my mother grab with her hands this man's other arm, and I heard her imploring and then commanding him to go back to flag any other train that otherwise might swoop unwarned around the curve into our part of the gorge.

By then the fire seemed to fill the cut in which most of the cars were piled. The man whose head I held stopped moaning. My legs had become numb and gone to sleep. Something bad happened to the man. Perhaps he had fainted. As I stood up on legs that were wobbly and without feeling, I saw Annie appear through the side of the Pullman. Then a hand thrust her away from the opening and the head of bulky-bosomed Mrs. Thompson rose into view. Father was doing that. I saw his head once and his eyeballs reflected the near-by flames. One end of the car was blazing before be himself finally crawled out, still in his nightgown with its red featherstitching at the neckband. Blood dripped from cuts on his hands and arms. Ever thereafter they bore white scars.

There was a nauseating stench in the air. We knew that not everyone had got out of the blazing cars. Suddenly something about that figure on the ground, the relaxed mouth below a wet mustache, frightened me. I lost my head completely and began to run down an embankment. I cut my feet on a barbed-wire fence. For weeks afterward I could not walk, so badly bad I torn my feet.

We learned that our train, westbound, had crashed head on into an eastbound cattle train.

Thirteen bodies were recovered before the train was consumed by fire but it never was determined how many persons actually were lost in that wreck. For a while thereafter I was afraid to fall asleep in the dark. Once I woke up screaming because of my latent fright that was renewed by the sound of breaking glass. Annie came rushing to comfort me. With tender ridicule she showed me a smoke-blackened lamp chimney. It had been left too near a mirror on the dresser. From my bed I could see the fragments of broken mirror—but even with Annie's arms around me I could see, also, that horrible scene that still shapes itself out of a speck of memory through the simple exercise of trying to index some almost forgotten contents of my mind.

The railroad wreck was all the excuse the Walshes should have required, I think, to decide to leave the mountains, to enjoy Father's find by translating the gold into happiness. In Mother's opinion, the decision could be made none too soon. It would be bitter tragedy, she felt, to labor all those years walled off from the world and then through some rude trick of fate to miss the well-earned fun. But there were, Father objected, so many things to be done.

Up at the mine Father's right-hand man was John Benson; he wore a fierce mustache that spread beyond his cheeks and had the form of the downward-curving horns of a range bull. When he came to our house at Ouray his hair would be waterslicked so as to become, along the rim of his forehead, a stiffly fixed wave. Mr. Benson had a voice that indoors could be safely employed only as a whisper;

nature had designed him to be a full-throated mine boss. He was one of the kindest of men, and had helped Father operate the Deer Horn mine at Cripple Creek and the Black Hawk group at Rico. They had profound faith in each other. They had been together at the scenes of fresh strikes of gold and silver. They had seen bloody labor wars where men fought each other with heavy caliber revolvers, with repeating rifles and dynamite bombs. They wanted no labor troubles at the Camp Bird. That payroll—which, inside of a year, had grown to more than one hundred names—was expected to increase eight or nine fold. Tom Walsh planned to make those men more comfortable than any other group of miners in the West.

Aunt Lucy had come to Ouray to visit us, to visit the mine and make us all less impatient for the outside world. She brought her son Monroe, then a lad of six or seven, and he became the very shadow of Vinson. Every night there were talks by the sisters, designed to woo Father from his cherished mine. Not all they said was said to him; but most of it he was supposed to hear. His blue eyes were kindly, sympathetic; but the thrust of his jaw showed that he was not softly made. He did not want to go before the mill was built; everything seemed to turn on the mill.

We were taken to see the parts of the mill machinery when the first big pieces arrived on flat cars, but Aunt Lucy roguishly kept talking about Eastern fashions, fine horses, parties. Then, one day, little Monroe became ill. He had such a severe diarrhea that Mother in great fear sent a messenger up to the mine for Father. Several hours later, as it was turning dark, we heard Nig's hoofs in the familiar canter that always made Prince bark joyfully.

Monroe was lying in Aunt Lucy's lap, too weak to open his eyes, and his long lashes were as dark smudges. He was shuddering in a violent chill. Father took one long look at him and vanished into his bedroom, excitedly saying, "Bring the child to me." He stripped off his own clothing, got into bed, and took the little boy into his arms; in the meantime, Annie, Mother, Aunt Lucy were carrying out his orders for hot-water bottles, for hot flatirons, and other utensils. I saw Annie fill a pie pan with brandy, and touch a match to it. When the blue flames were rising from a boiling fluid, she smothered them with another pan. Soaking a strip of red flannel in the bubbling, aromatic liquor, she wrapped it about Monroe's stomach to ease his cramps.

When the child ceased to shiver and quake Father told us of a dreadful experience he had had while riding fast down the trail from the mine. It happened where the river chasm was deepest.

Nig, ordinarily a sedate horse, shied violently as they came around a bend in the canyon wall. Speaking reassuringly to the animal, Father caught one glimpse of a flapping, grotesque object, and then felt his horse's hind legs slipping over the edge. He threw himself forward on the animal's neck to keep his own balance, and dared not turn around. Looking down along his thigh he could see that Nig's hind hoof was engaged with a revetment of logs that supported the road on the curve. Saying "Whoa Nig, whoa Nig, whoa Nig," over and over, Father managed to keep the creature from struggling farther while he climbed toward the beast's head until he could step to earth- then he encouraged the horse to climb back on the trail. Father was horribly shaken by the experience.

"What a slight thing!" he kept saying as he marveled. Some workman who had been repairing the road at that point had left a spade stuck in the earth and hung his coat on it. The wind, setting the sleeves of the garment in motion, gave Nig his fright; but Father thought too much of Nig to blame him. "He thought it was a bear," he said.

Nevertheless, that incident, coming so soon after the dreadful wreck, determined the next step in our life. The Walshes, Father announced, were going East— to live in Washington, D. C.

CHAPTER V

The Walshes Meet the McLeans

I NEVER have forgotten the excitement of our first winter in Washington. Every single thing we did was an adventure that gave us some fresh revelation of the meaning of the Camp Bird Mine.

We were living in a pretty suite of rooms at the old Cochran Hotel. There, one night, Mother timidly tried on her first evening gown. She shuddered at the mirrored reflection of the creamy nakedness of her own shoulders. With cheeks flushed rosy from her embarrassment, she vowed she'd never step outside her room in such a state.

One of the beauties of Washington was our guest that night: Marian Cockrell, the daughter of Senator Cockrell of Missouri. This charming girl whom we called "Mary" was our first friend in Washington. Her manners had been polished in a Paris convent, and our faith in her counsels was complete and deserved.

"Why," she exclaimed, to overcome Mother's timidity, "see how large and lustrous your dark eyes appear. Your slenderness is so shapely. Come on!"

She seized Mother by the hands and led her into the corridor and downstairs. For Mother, it was an experience almost as overwhelming as if she had been taken direct from that cabin of my first remembrance into a glittering ballroom in Washington.

Mother really was timid, and never made advances; Father was as friendly as could be and everybody liked him. The Walshes made many friends that winter, and learned a lot.

We children had been entered in good schools. Vinson, a skinny little fellow who read "Beautiful Joe", "Black Beauty", and other animal narratives, wanted to be a great athlete. He was attending the Friends Select School for Boys. I wanted to be an actress and was under orders to become a lady. I was attending Miss Somers' school, the Mount Vernon Seminary. I was taken there every morning by little Annie; we either walked or rode on a streetcar. Some of the other girls came in rather smart turnouts. My chum there was Elizabeth Eddy who wore a big bow of ribbon on her taffy-colored hair. She was Miss Somers' niece.

Among the important persons Father and Mother had met in Washington were Mr. and Mrs. John R. McLean. Mrs. McLean was sponsoring a dancing class for children; the instruction was to be given in the drawing-room of her house in I Street. I think it was as a preliminary to my attendance there that I was invited to dinner at the McLeans'. My hair was in two braids down my back with a ribbon bow behind each ear, my dress stopped at my knees; as I walked into a room filled with chattering people I felt as if I had been impaled on a pin and held under a bright light. I had a bewildering impression of older young people, especially of girls somewhat older than I—haughty girls who did not speak to me.

Mrs. McLean introduced me to some and then she brought her son to me. She called him "Neddie." We were both eleven but he was a gawky creature so extraordinarily tall he seemed more like fourteen. He bent his neck and stole sulky looks at anything that won his interest. His mother enjoined him to take me in to dinner, and to my surprise he obeyed her. I really was in terror, because I had been cautioned against a myriad of blunders I might make. There was a confusing array of silver on each side of my plate. Somebody spoke to me in raillery and I burst into tears.

Next to me sat a man who, just as if my behavior was the usual thing at dinner, said, "Now, now, you'll get used to this. This is your first dinner; wait till you've been to as many as I."

Edward Beale McLean, that gawky youth, never opened his mouth to me that I remember; he had plenty of shyness of his own to deal with. His mother and father, however, were as sweet to me as they could be. It was at dancing school that I first found out how frightfully they were spoiling their son.

Mrs. McLean, a marvelous hostess, was trying to instill self-confidence into Ned. Some of the boys at dancing school used to boast that when they played parchesi or crokinole or even baseball she would bribe them to let her son win. For ten cents, or fifteen, most of them were delighted to be bought and maybe were not greatly harmed; but Ned was being utterly spoiled.

My parents were honestly concerned to keep Vinson and me from being spoiled. Mother was determined that I should become a lady—but then, practically all mothers in the nineties had similar expectations for their daughters. I do not now recall just when the thought began to churn in my mind that we were rich, because there never was much talk of money. I do know that we returned to Colorado in the summer of 1897, and that there was a noisy Fourth of July celebration, including a parade. My pony cart sprouted plumes of red, white, and blue tissue-paper under Father's hand, and I drove this vehicle just behind Vinson, who wore a plumed hat and, a grand marshal's sash, and bestrode his new pet, Daisy. She was full of the devil, and when a string of firecrackers exploded on one side of the street Daisy backed to the other and put her haunches through the plate-glass window of the drugstore. Vinson was not hurt but Mother shrieked and for the rest of the day was all a-tremble.

The point is, we really were not rich. Thirty, forty, or fifty thousand dollars was recovered from the Camp Bird cleanups every month, but most of the money was put right back into the mine. More than a million dollars was scheduled to be spent in that way, and at home we continued to think in terms of "Can we afford it?" Just a week or so after the Fourth of July parade, I wrote to "My Darling Papa" at Ouray to ask him to be sure to bring the Kodak, because "at Glenwood Springs there is a dark room and you can develope your pictures for nothing. The instruments and stuff goes with the room so you can develope for nothing."

Nevertheless, we soon began to pass out of that stage where the cost of things ruled decisions.

By the time we were back in Washington, I had become aware that if Mother so much as breathed a wish for anything,—even a set of $1,800 furs from Gunther's, —she got it, overnight at the latest. Probably that is how I got my idea that walking to school was a little trying for my dignity. At any rate, I went to Father's room and found him standing before a small round mirror, his face covered with lather. I was forbidden to touch the razor or to talk with him when it was actually in contact with his face. So it was while he turned with the utmost care and concentration to slide it back and forth over the glossy surface of his strop that I put him to a test like the one to which Aladdin subjected the slave of his lamp.

"Papa, do you think you could afford to hire a horse and carriage for me to ride to school in sometimes?"

"Rent a horse and carriage, hey?"

I saw creases forming in the mask of white soap under his nose and around his mouth, and he began to laugh heartily. He laughed so much I was chagrined; then he sobered and began stropping his razor once more.

"Darling, I guess I can manage to rent you a horse and carriage."

One afternoon soon afterward he called me to the street, and there at the curb in front of the hotel was a blue victoria with the top down. Harnessed to it was a pair of sorrels so sleek that their hides were iridescent in the sunlight. Their silver bits were frothy, and both animals pranced as if to prove their fine ancestry, but they quieted when addressed by a deep bass voice that came from the throat of a colored coachman who sat on the box. His name was Terrill; he wore a silk hat and gloves. For a moment I was speechless, then jumped into Father's arms and hugged him.

The next day I deliberately made myself almost late for school so that all the girls were clustered in the yard ready to enter when I was driven up. That was my first full realization of what had happened to us, and I should be a liar if I tried to say I did not enjoy right down to the bottom of my soul the "ohs" and "ahs" that came from the other girls.

Drink has been an evil influence in my life—drink and drugs. There was a liquor closet in the fine house Father had bought for us, but nothing that closet contained was half so intoxicating as the sheer delight of being a part of that household. On the street corner stood a lamppost, a fluted iron column that supported a U. S. Mail box at the level of my head and, on its top, above a short crossbar,—an easy climb, an inverted pyramid of glass through which the gas jet was visible. Just above the line of glass appeared the names of the streets of this intersection, LeRoy Place and Phelps Place. We called the house, always, "the LeRoy and Phelps Place", picking out of the confusion of Washington an identity for ourselves. In Ouray I would have hung by my knees, first thing, from the crossbar on the lamppost, but in Washington the magnificence of the carriage neighborhood was strong enough to

MRS. JOHN R. McLEAN

Mother of Edward Beale McLean

MRS. WASHINGTON McLEAN

keep me on the ground. The house was a three-story yellow brick with a tile roof, and there was no ugliness either outside of it or in it. It had been the home of Mr. and Mrs. Conrad Jenness Miller; Conrad was a minor celebrity in Washington, a widely traveled lecturer. Father bought the place "complete"; so that we emerged from our hotel chrysalis to become full-winged Washington householders as we stepped over the threshold. We were now possessors of all manner of "things": books, ornaments, rugs, curtains, towels, and other intimate appurtenances of the cultured. It was like magic. (An old account book of Thomas Walsh reveals that in 1899 such magic could be worked for $58,129.91, cash.)

A canopy of blue satin over my bed filled me each time I awakened with the realization that life had changed for Evalyn Walsh. The figured blue satin that covered the walls did not lull me; it was as a signal for me to get up quickly, to put on one of my new frocks, to live. I went through the house as a squirrel goes through a forest. One of its most fascinating recesses was the liquor closet.

With the attitude of a chemist striving empirically to find an effective catalyst, I went from bottle to bottle. That way I came upon the crème de menthe. In it I found complete satisfaction. Of course, we children had been forbidden so much as to open the door of that closet; but I was crafty, as children usually are when there are forbidden things around. I would wait my chance. When mother had gone out and the servants were rattling dishes and chattering over their food, I would step into the closet, fill a glass with fluid emerald and scamper up to my room. A piano that had been thrust upon me made a first-rate hiding place until I was ready for my drink. That would be at the minute before I was ready to go downstairs to be driven in the blue victoria to the dancing class at the McLean house. Then I would toss off my drink and leave home feeling elegant.

Father began to complain about the rapidity with which his crème de menthe evaporated; finally, he said flatly that somebody was stealing it. I think he suspected one or another of the servant girls. I kept my eyes focused on my plate during his complaints; but I kept my habit of drinking. One day a maid observed some sticky circles on top of my piano and mentioned them to little Annie. Smart as the dickens was Annie McDonald. She loved me as a sister, and knew me better than she knew herself. She knew she'd have to catch me dead to rights, so she hid in my clothes closet. I had my head tilted as she bounced out and with a leveled forefinger indicted me as a thief of crème de menthe.

"I'll tell your father," said Annie, and wilted me completely. "You've got a taste for the stuff. Think of what drink did to your Uncle Steve!"

"If you tell Papa—" I was outraged.

"All right. I won't tell him—if you stop your drinking."

I cut down a bit, for I didn't want to hurt Father. There was usually some around even when we traveled, although Mother never drank and Father less than he would have liked—whiskey upset his stomach. Nevertheless, he kept it around because he wanted his friends merry.

There were constant excuses for merrymaking in the beginning of 1899. Some of Father's Colorado friends were urging him to run for Congress, but he refused the nomination. His friend Charles Spaulding Thomas had been elected governor of Colorado. We were all Republicans. We were "for" McKinley in 1896; and in 1899 Vin and I were permitted, after washing our hands, to hold and examine something the postman delivered, a rectangle of cardboard, stiff, gold-edged, and bearing a gold shield. It was from the Executive Mansion—an invitation to Mr. and Mrs. Thomas Walsh to attend a reception at the White House. It had come from the President and Mrs. McKinley. But that event became as nothing when other things began to happen.

On February 20, 1899, Vin and I flopped down on the floor to enjoy to the full the sensation of reading that President McKinley had appointed Thomas Walsh of Colorado and Washington a Commissioner to the Paris Exposition. We were going to Europe!

A month or so later, Father unrolled before our fascinated eyes a parchment scroll that had come from Denver. With that document Governor Thomas had made my papa a colonel and an aide-de-camp in the service of the State of Colorado.

Late in May, Washington celebrated the National Peace Jubilee—which had, I suppose, something to do with the end of the War with Spain. There was a parade in which were many floats: stages mounted on horse-drawn wagons, set with such tableaux as the Landing of Columbus, the Birth of Our Flag, Washington Crossing the Delaware, and so on, and there was an enthroned white-robed female figure representing Peace, with white doves supported not by their outspread wings but by quite visible wires. We had good seats for the parade, as we did for most affairs in that time. Father had a gilt badge which identified him as a member of the Finance Committee. I suppose he had made a contribution. It was pretty generally known by that time that Tom Walsh was a man with money. A short while before he had bought the Oxford Hotel, paying $125,000; there was an $85,000 mortgage on it. He was rather constantly going about looking at real estate, and most of his callers were men who wanted to sell him something or, as they would say, "interest him" in some project. In the course of a few months he bought four hundred $1,000 registered United States Government threes, paying $433,850, and one hundred registered United States twos at a cost of $102,937.50. Tom Walsh was nobody's fool, even if he did have, in the phrase current in Washington, money to burn.

A few days after the close of the Jubilee we sailed on the White Star liner Majestic. In the party were Father, Mother, Vinson, Aunt Lucy, her son Monroe, and I. Oh, yes—and Annie McDonald. It was something less than a vacation for Annie, because she had her hands full with me.

This is not going to be a travel story if I can help it, but that trip was important to me because during it something occurred that lodged, I think, in the depths of my mind, to remain there as a troubling, foreboding thing, subtly influencing my behavior.

We toured England, France, Switzerland, Austria, and Bavaria, and it was all fun; but for Father the great, heartswelling days were those we spent in Ireland. For him, the whole of our journey was simply part of a pilgrimage to Tipperary. Some others had joined us by the time we reached Ireland, a fascinating Irishman whose identity has eluded me and a woman I shall not identify. She was beautiful, and sweet, too—normally. In her jewels and furs she was as understanding as anyone when we all stood in the courtyard of the whitewashed, thatch-roofed farmhouse at Clonmel. The chickens pecking in the mud were not merely chickens to my father; they were creatures in a chain of life that had touched his long before. He picked up the threads of many old friendships, and his hand was in and out of his pockets throughout the days; he made no show of his giving, not ever. He went to see the grave of his mother, who had died while he was a baby. There was a stone cross that he had paid for with Black Hills gold.

We were on our way to Queenstown when what I speak of happened. In the twilight of our train compartment I became aware that this lovely woman was drunk. There was something else wrong, but I did not know quite how to define the trouble. Father, I could see plainly, was provoked. Then we reached our station. I remember that in the darkness I felt with my foot for the platform and started into the station where we were to get something to eat. Just then I whirled around. Father, swearing, was bending over. The woman had fallen flat. A misty or a foggy night will evoke that scene in my mind as long as I live. They got some black coffee for her in the station and she began talking. Father had made her wrathful by a rebuke and by this time she was not in the least beautiful: disordered hair made her haglike.

"Tom Walsh! " She spoke his name with sober fury. "I want to tell you something." Her eyes roved from one face to another until she fixed her gaze on me, clinging tightly to my father's hand. "Tom Walsh, I curse Evalyn. I want you before you're dead to see her in the gutter, to see her worse from drink than I am." It was all said quietly, and no other person spoke.

An Irish curse on me! My mother had her hand clasped to her mouth. Father, keeping hold of my hand, walked out to the platform; its boards were soft under our feet from the dampness. He said nothing, but just kept walking back and forth. I looked up at him as we passed into the yellow glow of the station lamp. His face was wet with tears. The night was full of evil. Heavy fog that billowed visibly wherever there was a bit of light seemed charged with menace. Of course I was just a child, and this should have touched me no more than a bad dream; perhaps it did no more—and yet I wish, because of the Irish in me, that curse had never been spoken.

Probably I did something on the ship, and Vinson, too; I have forgotten what but I remember that when we landed in New York Mother's mind was fixed on one thing: she was going to hire a French governess. I was fat, thick-waisted, graceless and harsh-voiced as a peafowl. It had been agreed in a family council that the work of transforming me into a decorous lady should proceed with a hurry like that which so quickly brought the Camp Bird into big production. They were going to work on me in two shifts: school all day, and a governess morning, noon, and night. Against this scheme I was an outspoken rebel; but I was taken along to the agency when Mother went to interview candidates for the position of making my life miserable.

Mam'selle was French, of course; she had snapping black eyes, a suggestion of gelatin at the hips as she walked on her high heels, a strong "zese" and "zose" accent. I hated her at sight, but Mother hired her, although I never could understand why. (Certainly that French flirt was not a sensible bit of baggage to take to a mining camp.) Mother asked where we could drop her and after a flustered protest Mam'selle gave an address that proved to be a fine brownstone home just off Fifth Avenue. She was slowly mounting the steps as we drove off, but when I took a peek through the glass at the rear of our hired carriage she was hustling down the steps again. I saw her turn toward the river. (God knows where the woman really lived.) I told Mother, but she said it did not matter. She never had a trace of suspicion about anybody; indeed, she was interested in New Thought and deliberately sought to keep out of her mind all but generous, kindly emotions.

Father and Mother were bent on enjoying their money to the fullest extent, but both of them had discovered rich satisfaction in doing for others. They seemed to be agreed that if they could translate most of the gold of the Camp Bird into kindnesses great good would result. I remember one incident on our way back to Colorado.

As we pulled out of some station I was rocking on my elbows in the open, unscreened window of the Pullman. Beside our car in semidarkness a man, bent low, was trotting on the black cinders. I looked down upon the X of his suspenders against his rain-faded blue turtleneck sweater. Once he turned his head for a stealthy look behind, and I saw that his face was as black with soot as the mask of a minstrel. Then, as our train picked up speed, I saw with shrill horror that the man had vanished right beneath me. I was sure the wheels were grinding him up and I let out a shriek for "Papa."

Father came running to hear my bleat that there was a man under the wheels of the train. He, in turn, roared for the conductor, and the train was stopped. Trainmen with lanterns ran along the right-of-way, and each pause they made filled me with something like nausea. They started back and, surprisingly, halted in an angry cluster just under the place I had regained in the car window. The man in the blue sweater was dragged out from his perch on the rods. The station agent came running up and as he was trying to catch a full breath the conductor was giving him orders to take the young tramp off to jail.

"Not a bit of it," said Father in a tone that made everybody listen. "This boy's got a ticket. I'm buying it."

On the train, Father helped the young man get cleaned up. I saw how thin his sweater was and that he shivered, possibly from excitement. He went with Father to eat in the diner, and then I saw his face, wistful and half-dazed, vanish behind the green curtains of the lower berth Father had, bought for him. There was money in his pocket, too. I could almost feel his gratitude as I began to doze. Ten years later, that boy wrote to Father to express gratitude and to say that he was settled in a big Western city, making good.

I'm sure a thousand tales like that could be told of Tom Walsh.

CHAPTER VI

The Walsh Gold Engine

THE great gold engine my father had brought into existence high up in the mountains was making its loudest, grinding clamor as we returned to it. It was still twilight when I began to hear the voice of the mill. Sometimes as the road passed around a slope the voice died away only to return abruptly as an overtone to the constant sound of the heavy stage wheels and the cropping of twenty-four hoofs on the road metal. I could tell when Father's ears caught the sound, because then I no longer heard the twanging burr of his pleasant voice. He became quite silent — which was not strange, since the sounds were the echoes of instruments that had been shaped first in his mind and only after that con-ception had received a synthesis in what is called reality.

Each time our six-horse stage rounded another curve notched into a precipice, I had a breath-taking instant. The vehicle became a top-heavy thing of which I was the quivering apex. It was better, I found, to keep my eyes fixed on the horses' backs, watching the patterns of their jouncing harness worked out in sweat marks on their hides. They were blacks and bays except the off leader; he was a dappled gray. Without fear I had ridden this road on a horse's back, and would again, but the seat -of the stage was a dizzy perch from which to go tumbling in my fancy to the bottom of the chasm. That terror was blotted out as the canyon filled with darkness. The mill noise had become incessant. The horses began picking up their legs faster and faster until the driver, uncomfortably aware of his lady passengers, spoke to his animals crossly, "Haw, you; haw, haw!" The leaders' ears I could no longer see, but the wheelers held theirs cocked stiffly forward. Whatever the Camp Bird mill might mean to the half-score of us in the stage, to the horses it meant oats, stable warmth, and the deep crisp straw of their stalls. Then the driver pulled them to a walk as his hand became dramatically whiter and the metal of the harness shone in a strange brilliance that we had entered.

We had reached the Potosi Basin, and our end of it was bright with the bluish effulgence of a monstrous electric arclight; its globe was suspended more than a hundred and fifty feet above the ground. Papa identified the masses of shadowmaking structures for me. A big one was the mill itself, doubled in our absence to contain forty of the thumping, big, eight-hundred-and-fifty-pound stamps. Even the buildings he saw for the first time had a matrix in his mind: the General Manager's headquarters, the cottages of the officials, the storeroom, retort chamber, and assay office. The big light, he showed me, made a ring of brightness beyond all the buildings, to give the watchmen the jump on robbers.

His eyes went back to the harsh brilliance in the arc-lamp. It was the pivot of his world.

Our French governess tried to take charge of us at the new cottage and, with the aid of Vin, I made a scene. Why, I had been up here when there was no mill or mine; just a snowclogged tunnel that only my papa and I knew was rich with gold. In the morning I dressed early, in a sweater and a pair of pants, and walked to breakfast with my thumbs hooked behind my suspenders, defiant of Mam'selle.

Higher up in the adjacent Basin was the mine itself, and there they had built the boarding house. I heard my papa say it was the finest money could buy. Now I saw it: a great barracks three stories high and more than two hundred feet long, designed to keep its numerous, restless tenants comfortable in all the extremes of mountain cold and heat. Its walls and ceiling were tongued and grooved woodwork, glossy with varnish. The floors were of hardwood, kept waxed and polished. In the wide corridors that were furnished with chairs, tables, books, magazines, and pictures, there was marble wainscoting higher than my head. There was marble in the lavatories, and the bathtubs were of porcelain, as fine as any I had ever seen. At a touch the taps provided hot and cold water. Against the walls were platoons of brackets supporting the shining reflectors of oil lamps, but over every table there dangled an electric light bulb— ugly, but impressive in 1899.

From a staunch timber platform high up on the mill wall, Vin and I were helped by John Benson into the iron howdah of an elephantine mechanism called a "tram." Its cable sinews were stretched on skeletal towers to become threadlike and then vanish before they crossed nearly two miles of valley bowl and reached up the mountain to the rim; up there was the mine. Our car was suspended by a heavy steel arm from tandem trolley wheels slotted, one set above a second, to a pair of the heavy cables. We swung out on a fantastic journey, our course following the rough contours of the terrain and only our heads above the thick steel side of the car. Ahead I saw a chasm and then, too swiftly for comfort, the earth dropped away, taking to the rocky bottom of a canyon all my daring. I fixed the fingers of one band tightly to the big shoe of John Benson and tried to trace with my eyes the least detail of blemish inside the car; to look out and down was to fall through the limitless space of my imagination. Yet I had to look, and Vin did too. Trolleying downward from the mine on the cables strung on the opposite side of the towers that supported our flight came a tram loaded with the gray-white heart of the mountain that was the essence of our new life. Vin and I rode repeatedly in tramcars until the belly-chilling power of the adventure was gone.

Vin wanted to be a fighter, he wanted to be able to knock down anybody, to run faster and jump farther. I think I sometimes got my ambitions mixed with his. Most of the time I wanted to be an actress and have all the men clamoring after me. I wanted to excel somehow— even, I may say, anyhow. Maybe that's why Vin and I induced a foolish, easily cajoled foreman to let us go to the bottom of the shaft in the cage the miners used and then start upward on the vertical ladders kept there for emergencies.

No one dreamed in that time of such giant structures as rise from our cities now and yet in every extensive mine the subterranean excavations commonly were of such proportions as to dwarf the biggest skyscrapers men have dared to build. From the spire of the Woolworth Building to the ground is not so far as from the top of the Camp Bird to its bottom level. I know we did not climb so far, but in my dreams sometimes, when I am very tired, I am back again in the blackness of that shaft. My legs and arms are weary. My brother's thin legs are above my head, the foreman's head below my feet. The ladder rungs are wet and slippery. My hands ache and threaten not to keep fast hold. The flickering carbide lamp on the front of my hat touches with yellow light the failing fingers in my dream, and I know I am approaching the crisis of that foolish adventure. Somehow Vinson stepped free and up just as the rung from which he reared gave way. I thought I'd fall just from fright, and I could not cross the interval. How long I balked I cannot say; but the miner would not let me retreat. It was nearer to the top, he said, and with a mighty hand boosted me from below until I grasped a higher rung. Water dripped on me; I was saturated. I began to slip more often, and Vin was going slower and slower. I must have whimpered, because the foreman was half beside himself and tried to keep one hand locked about my ankle. When we did get to the top, my hands were raw with broken blisters.

John Benson growled into his red mustache that the foreman would die when he got his hands on him. Father said the man would have to leave the mine. Vin and I were scolded and made ashamed, but we shed real tears and roared loud protests to save our friend. We made such a fuss we got him off; but we ourselves were thereafter kept closely under the thumb of the governess. We had become just a pair of nuisances to her.

There was an assistant manager of the mill or mine who would have taken any lady's eye. I was jealous as the devil, and when I saw she was interested in this man I writhed inside. When we were supposed to be asleep our Mam'selle would slip out of the cottage and stealthily enter the tiny house of this official. I said nothing about that to anyone, but I scowled whenever she proceeded with our lessons or in other ways exercised her authority.

Uncle Sam Lee had arrived to see the Camp Bird. He and Father yarned with John Benson night after night. Their talk always was exciting and if Vin and I kept out of sight until they had taken a drink or two they would rehearse old times without regard for our young ears.

Often I heard Father tell about the time his partner, with whom he lodged in a cabin shelter at Deadwood, went mad — whether from loneliness, or drink, or what, I can't remember. This man was going to kill Father. Snarling oaths, he plunged into the cabin — to emerge a second later with a big revolver, held, barrel up, at the level of his ear. In the West, bullets were started on their killing pathways as if they were stones thrown from the fists of those who fired them. Father had a narrow choice: he jumped barehanded at his berserk friend and caught his wrist. This incident was the basis of his oft-repeated motto, the sense of which was to meet trouble face to face.

Uncle Sam had a bullet hole right through his thigh from side to side, just below the hip. Monroe and Vin had been allowed to see that old wound, even to explore it with their fingers; I heard its history often and always with my spine prickly with sympathetic fear. After he abandoned mining Uncle Sam became a railroad contractor. He built sections of the Sante Fé, recruiting his workmen in the lodging houses of South State Street in Chicago. Armed guards held as prisoners all who had accepted passage; otherwise the train would have arrived at the construction camp empty. This human freight was difficult to handle. Gamblers, prostitutes, every kind of fiend and harpy showed up at the camps for payday. With one of these men there was trouble. Uncle Sam took up a whiffletree and clubbed his opponent until the man's face was a mask of blood. Only this saved my uncle from being shot by this man's big six-shooter. Then Uncle Sam set out to run and hide, and the staggering victim pursued. Darting around a corner, Uncle Sam slipped into an open doorway and took refuge in the dark beneath a bed. For a moment he thought he had eluded his pursuer. Then he heard boots on the doorsill. From his hiding place he could see the man wipe his eyes free of blood and take a quick look; then another wipe. Then their eyes met.

"Now you—" Uncle Sam never left out a word of what had been said to him as he lay under the bed expecting to die. He took us half-instant by half-instant through his moments of dread. He watched the man stoop and extend a left arm so that its wrist became a rest for the long pistol barrel. He saw him squint, and himself writhed closer to the wall. Then the gun roared and the whole world seemed to explode into fire. The killer strode off after a minute of satisfied cursing, believing the limp form beneath the bed was simply the body of a dead man. However, —and this was the happy ending, —the bullet had only torn a hole through the right leg and cut a deep notch into the rear of its mate. So Uncle Sam lived to tell us.

There were other stories of the days when the Leadville Camp was full of hell and my Aunt Maria's husband, Arthur Lafferty, was a two-gun police sergeant. The most grisly yarn of all concerned a man who was respected by my kin. In one of those Western towns where law was beginning to interfere with natural practices, he had been forced to kill a man. He had reason to fear the man's associates. His pressing problem was the body on the floor of his kitchen. Afar off he heard sounds; wild hog invaders were grunting and quarreling for a share of the swill of his tame ones lodged in a pasture pen. He shouldered the body and went out toward the pasture, dropping his burden into the darkness on the other side of a rail fence. In the morning when he went to the pasture there was nothing there to cause him embarrassment. The domestic hogs were stretched out enjoying the sun and took no interest in the pail of swill he emptied into their trough. The wild hogs had gone.

CAMP BIRD MINE

THE MILL AT CAMP BIRD MINE

The strongbox of the Camp Bird was sheltered in a frame building called the retort room. Twice a day at the mill a greasy accumulation of amalgam was cleaned from the rectangular plates where it had collected as repulsive slime. This was carried to the retort room and there, after careful washings, was poured into a crucible that from its shape alone could be known the monstrous heart of our engine. When this retort was closed Mr. Coates, the mill boss, would turn a valve wheel that released into it an unseen fury in the shape of a steam of quicksilver. Twice a day I would be on hand to see the crucible opened to watch the yellow stuff 900 fine, now cooled and strangely heavy, lifted out and packed for shipment to the Denver mint.

Rarely was there less than eighty pounds of amalgam; often there was much, much more. In addition, there came out of the mill each day a carload of riches in a less dramatic form, called it "concentrates." This was worth $150 a ton, but to Vin and me the impressive return was the fresh pot-shaped ingot that twice a day was laid before our bulging eyes. We had been told the worth of those rare solids. The Camp Bird was producing $5,000 a day. Each morning we Walshes arose richer than we had gone to bed. Mine and mill ran night and day.

An iron chest was lifted to the oak flooring of the stage, and into that the gold was locked for the guarded trip to Ouray. A wrinkled boot of grease-black leather would be lifted from the brake as the driver gathered his six horses. Then two guards with rifles held like precious toys across their breasts would climb up with him. Whiffletrees would lift from hocks to midlevel of the straining haunches and another load of our treasure was started off to become distantly, mysteriously, somehow more definitely, ours.

There were persons in the mountains covetous of the gold; we knew that. A man was dismissed from the mill because he was constantly smoothing his thick hair with fingers greasy with the amalgam slime. Others were sent away because high grade ore had been found in their clothing. Oh, a hundred tricks, I think, were penetrated before most of the leaks were stopped; even then the tempting power of the stuff continued to itch too many minds.

One day when Vin and I, after the departure of the stage, had started for the cottage we heard a shot, which was not unusual. Then there were six or eight in quick succession, followed by as many as if someone had fired off a pack of giant crackers. In response to some further alarm the mill men came running into the open. All carried rifles. The stage had been held up. The driver and guards had been killed and the chest of gold carried off into the mountains. The robbers were never caught.

After that there were four guards with the stage and they rode horseback. The treasure chest was bolted solidly to the floor of the heavy vehicle.

Everything that happened, each fresh excitement, seemed to make me less tolerant of the supervision of the governess. On top of this, I found myself growing furious with jealousy every time I looked at her. Vinson and I agreed to get rid of her if we could.

One of the places where visitors to Ouray always were taken was Box Canyon. Rocky cliffs were so close together that I think a goat could have jumped from wall to wall. At the bottom of the gorge a mountain stream cascaded white as milk down a succession of falls. A footbridge spanned the walls of this canyon at the dizzy top; on lower ledges where no sunlight ever fell there were railed wooden walks. Far down in the chasm an electric arc light had been suspended so that the beauties of the place could be observed by night. The lowest walk of all was at the level of the light and this cavernous, damp perch, always echoing the roaring of the waterfalls, could be reached only by descending a ladder. Vinson and I had it all planned out. We persuaded the governess to go with us to the lowest level. She was last as we started up again. Then, by design, I dropped my pocketbook and squealed so much she backed down the ladder to pick it up. As she stooped over Vin and I, already at the ledge above, hauled up the ladder. She was trapped at the bottom of the canyon.

At the house we were asked about Mam'selle. We shrugged—an appropriately French form of lying. She had gone shopping, we said. That was true as far as it went. It grew dark and we had supper. Father returned from somewhere and his inquiries about the French girl were more stern. We confessed. A group of men set off with lanterns to find her. When they came back the governess was moaning hysterically. In her fright she had torn her clothing, her waist was in ribbons and mudstained; she had tried to climb out in high-heeled shoes. A doctor was called. She did not get pneumonia, happily, and the next day she was driven to the train. She had a ticket to New York and a gift from Father that made her eyes sparkle. We were punished, but I am afraid not severely enough.

By that time both Vin and I had decided that nobody should be allowed to teach us anything. Vin, I think, was not so sure we were acting right; I was. I was not going to be a lady, not if I could help it.

CHAPTER VII

We Meet a King

MY father's charm was strong enough to win the lasting friendship of a king. You can bet that made me proud when I was just a girl. But there was more to it, more that makes me stop to wonder how many, many of the things that I'd call chance could be unraveled from my life and traced back, through endless patterns, to those days when we were learning how kings spend money, and what for.

What I remember best, of course, are trivial things; an adventure on the Ferris wheel; walking up and down the Eiffel Tower, thereby having stiff legs for nearly a week; my greedy interest in the naughtiness of the streets of Paris I was not allowed to see; the convent where I was for a while immured. But for my boldness there, I guess I should not have met Leopold, King of the Belgians, on that trip.

You see, my father's power to grant my wishes had grown as great as if he had become a magician; but sometimes when a wish had been granted there were quick and mischievous complications. This was so the time I said I wished I could learn French. That wish just happened to coincide with the fact that I had been making a fourteen-year-old nuisance of myself.

While Father was officially representing his Government in Paris we occupied nearly the whole second floor of the Élysée Palace Hotel. The banquets my father was giving there and at the Ritz had made him the talk of Paris. In our party we had Marian Cockrell, Alice Rochester, and the daughter of the Secretary of Agriculture, Florence Wilson, whom we called Flora. With Father, Mother, Vin and me, and little Annie, that made eight. It was Annie who took me around at first, and what I thought I ought to see in Paris made her blush.

When I wanted to be in the streets of Paris, seeing for myself the Coney Island stuff that made my elders whisper and giggle, Annie —homesick, probably —would have me standing, tired and bored, in the Exposition building on the Champ-de-Mars called "the Palace of Mines and Metallurgy." John F. Campion's Leadville mine had an exhibit there of leaf and crystallized native gold, and right beside it was the exhibit of the Camp Bird mine—which was producing, so the gilded legend told, $5,000 a day.

On the boulevards I saw the streetwalkers, whole platoons of them, and if I said they shocked me I should lie; to a child they did not seem to lead so bad a life. My mind was not equipped to think of all they had to do to live, nor could I wrestle with the reasons why: they were human beings, girls, engaged in a strangely exciting occupation. If I lacked understanding, at least my mind was powered with curiosity stronger than the actuating current of our mountain mill.

Annie burst out at me as the sunlight beat upon us when we left our hotel one day.

"Why, Evalyn," she whispered in shocked fright, "you've got a face as red as Bordeaux claret."

I minced my steps to a half-stride and said, "I licked the covers of a hotel book and got the paint off on my tongue."

"You little hussy! If your father sees you now—"

She only made me mad with that old threat, which she so rarely carried out. We walked a bit while Annie pondered, and then she spoke with downright rage.

"You did . . . You did! I saw you!"

Well, I had. With fine mimicry I had looked a challenge at a man who passed, and had rolled my greenish eyes. He turned his head and, with a smirk, lifted in a mock salute of gallantry his glossy black taper-crowned silk hat. I was fairly snatched back to the hotel for that imprudence; and at one in the morning, when we had been long abed, Annie still was fishing deep in her Scotch vocabulary for words to berate the thing I had done. "Malapert" and "brazen" were not strong enough, but dear Annie could not say to me the awful word that was hot upon her tongue. It was not until the morning that she whispered to my mother how I had acted on the boulevard. "Just like a French—" Annie pursed her lips and substituted "bad woman." Mother sent for Father, who was still in bed.

"It's proof," he said at once, "of the poor child's innocence"; but more than that I was not supposed to hear, and so the door was closed upon their conference.

In a witless moment later in that probationary day I said, aloud, "I think I should learn to speak in French."

"So you shall," my papa said. "We'll begin at once."

I suppose it all had been arranged. They sent me in Annie's charge to a convent at 35, rue de Picpus—the Convent du Sacré Cœur. We were admitted through a gate in its high wall by a porter so feebly old he must have been alive when the ancient place was built. No man, except in priestly robes, ever got inside. It was lovely there, I know; old nuns and young had dedicated their lives unselfishly to God and fixed their minds on prayer and future glory. For me, accustomed to the wild, free mountain air of Colorado, it was full of stench compounded half from lack of plumbing and half from fetid airs that seemed to come from somewhere underground. Moldering in the convent cemetery under richly nourished grass were the severed heads and bodies of a thousand aristocrats. Through a little grated door I saw that green graveyard, and clutched Annie more tightly as an old nun spoke of the blood that ran from the guillotine.

Both Annie and I wore white dresses by command. In chapel a white veil was scratchy against my neck and ears and my hands looked thick in white cotton gloves. We did have a nice room, but its high door could not be locked, and it opened into a black corridor that was drafty as a cave. In the nighttime, while I lay close beside unhappy, Protestant Annie, the soft footfalls I occasionally heard outside seemed to be not those of nuns. My fancy was alive with ghosts, come, I thought, from the mysterious crypts below to make me take the veil for life.

I knew the names of some—I had read them on their tombs: De Boiseliu, De Rochefort and La Rochefoucauld. That made them so real my convent nights were loud with horrors. A romance of mice squeaking just beneath my bed became racktorture cries from specter lungs. My common sense today tells me that nuns, like all old women, have need to leave their beds at intervals, but in that black-dark place the softest shuffling steps could only come, I knew with shudders, from the movements of things that never should have moved.

In the convent a bath was something a girl could not take at will—it must be arranged for, and not too often; but I got one that was not scheduled. After a few days of boredom I frizzed my hair until I had a mass of curls and then I licked another book that had red covers, putting bold disks of hollyberry shade upon my cheeks and a deeper tint like a monsignor's bib upon my lips. I was playing actress to relieve my boredom and sulky Annie said no word to keep me from this sin. Then, before class, I went with Annie into the green freshness of the garden. There were cypress trees growing high above the walls, and the morning air was fragrant with shrubs. I was in a mood to like the place for the first time since my arrival.

I saw Annie's mouth turn down at the corners and looked where she did—to see a tremendous human figure rolling toward us in a wheel chair. A nun with lowered head was pushing an enormous female. We started off, but this vast woman called out sternly, "Stop, child! Stop! " I swear she weighed four hundred pounds at least and much of it was uncorseted belly tightly swollen against black bombazine.

"What are you doing with your features painted? And your hair . . . !" Deep disgust had shaped each word, but she spoke in the best English I had heard inside the walls.

I was scared, but I did not have the least notion who she was. I asked her to tell me and she said, "I am the Mother Superior." You can bet I listened then, with downcast head. I was really afraid of her mighty powers over all who came inside the convent.

"You are very wicked. God will not protect you when you offend him!"
I was petrified.

"Sister!" She spoke then with the voice of a general, and a somber creature who had been walking a few paces behind her came up to stand beside me. The Mother Superior, in a cascade of French, gave further commands; and soon I found myself being held by the hand as I was walked into the dormitory. A drenching pitcher of water took the friz out of my hair. Strong brown soap cleansed my cheeks and lips of all their paint, and there was a final indignity; a soapy rag was rubbed inside my mouth.

When I was dressed again I was told that I must put on my white gloves and veil, and go to the gallery of the chapel and pray for two hours. Annie was forbidden to accompany me.

But I did not pray. I spent the whole of my two angry hours scheming how I might get out and back to the arms of my darling father.

When I rejoined Annie I told her my plan and she was halfready to endorse it. I wrote a letter and put it in an envelope that I addressed to Mother. That was the gimmick, if you know what I mean, of my trick. They had supper there quite early, so it was early evening when Annie and I, without our hats or coats, approached the door. I held my letter conspicuously in my hand. There was only a young girl there, a lay sister. I put the letter before her face and in English said I wanted to go out to mail it. She shook her forefinger from side to side in a gesture to forbid our passage while she went to ask about the matter.

The instant she disappeared I seized the heavy latch and lifted it. Annie and I ran as hard as we could go. We turned corners to the left, ran another block, then right again. We were breathless and had no money. I had not the faintest idea where we were and Annie was, already, full of regret and wanting to return. Then I saw a heaven-sent *voiture*.

The horse was white, and its drooping lip hung almost at the level of its broken knees. The vehicle was an old victoria, cracked of leather and odorous of stable and the cheap perfumes of curbstone blondes; but the driver was as friendly as Santa Claus. He was very fat and laughing all over. He had a high hat that was fashioned out of some kind of white oilcloth and on his green old coat, lying in echelon, were three capes, the shortest at the level of his shoulders, the longest reaching to his elbows.

"Élysée Palace Hotel," I said to him as we climbed in and sat close to one another on the musty cushions. I had to repeat the address two or three times before he caught my meaning, uttered a loud "Bon," and with a high gesture of his arms slapped the reins against the drooping horse.

At the hotel I rushed upstairs so fast that for a minute I was breathless and could not tell my mother what was in my mind. She had turned from her dresser in her white underthings, her dark eyes showing white circles of astonishment.

"They have been cruel to me," I gasped and believed what I said.

Mother called out, "Tom!"

Father appeared in stiff white shirt and vest, his hands working as he struggled to form a string of tie into a white butterfly against his throat.

I spoke of cruelty again and told about the bath. Father burst out laughing and I knew I was all right. (Mother just once, in my whole life, that I remember, lost her temper, and then she only slammed a door.)

"We've missed you so," Father said, "I'm glad to have you back. Now we'll get you a governess—one that you will like."

So, next day, I was in the custody of a Frenchwoman who was sweet as she could be, but stern when I needed stern treatment. Her name was, in our household, Miss Haye. With her to keep me straight I saw a lot of the Exposition. Mrs. Potter Palmer was one of the twenty American commissioners, and she had become a family friend. She came to our hotel early one evening when Father and Mother were giving a banquet for three or four hundred people. She came, she told me, just so I could see her emeralds that I had asked about.

I thought she was old because her hair, in a pompadour arrangement, was snowy white; but she was only fifty-one and with such a flawless complexion that she was completely lovely. She let me finger to my heart's content her necklace of emeralds and diamonds, and seemed to understand the passion in my eyes as I looked at them. She loved jewels. Strand upon strand of pearls had been fashioned into a dog collar for her throat, to cover up the wrinkles that come there first of all. I was allowed to touch her stomacher and exclaimed aloud when I saw into the green of the emerald drop that was suspended there as a kind of jewel climax to all she wore.

"You know, Evalyn," she told me, "I'm devoted to your father."

Then I walked downstairs with her, holding her hand, feeling her large diamonds set in rings sharp against my fingers, catching the glitter of her bracelets in my eyes. There were a hundred small tables in the dining room, and at each lady's place the waiters were putting an orchid corsage. A man more grandly uniformed than ever I had seen was helping with the place cards. A thick *fourragère* of gold was knotted at his shoulder, made ponderous by the golden fringe of his epaulette. A helmet with a golden chin-strap chain and a white horsehair plume dressed straight back so as not to hide the golden U. S. eagle shield in front—all that was carried on his arm. This man, then a colonel, was the military aide of our ambassador to France, General Porter. He bowed as low to me as to Mrs. Potter Palmer and so, throughout my adult life, there has been always in my heart a glow of friendship for General T. Bentley Mott.

The three of us walked along by the windows opening on the Champs Elysées, and set in each was a full-sized cake of ice with candlelight to make it glitter as it shed cool air into the banquet room. That was an extravagance, Mrs. Palmer said, quite new to Paris. Bentley Mott lifted from Mrs. Palmer's creamy shoulders her cape of sables and then my part of the night was over and I had to scamper upstairs to bed. But I got up and sneaked back to a gallery where French musicians with their fiddles and brass horns were tuning up. That was the way I generally got to our parties in those days.

That, I think, was the night Mary Garden sang for the Walshes' guests and moved in a cloud of perfume as alluring as a garden of camellias. I wished and wished I had her looks and voice.

In the morning Father was beside himself: Mrs. Potter Palmer's emerald drop was gone!

He was simply wretched with embarrassment over the missing jewel, and wanted Mrs. Palmer to permit him to replace it; this she would not listen to, and hushed him up when he kept saying he felt responsible. They searched the hotel inside and out, but never found a trace of the big emerald.

Our friendship with Mrs. Potter Palmer lasted. She was a fixed star in society, and deserved her place. She told us once that Potter Palmer was more than twice her age when they were married in 1871; she was twenty-two. Four years before that time, possessing a fortune, he had retired from a lucrative partnership in Chicago with Marshall Field and Levi Leiter. After rest and travel he had gone back to Chicago, putting his money into real estate until there were thirty-two big buildings returning rents to him besides the income from the Palmer House, then new. This was his position when she married him. In that same year the Chicago fire made him almost poor. That was when her mettle helped. She was a partner as wise as Field or Leiter. They built another Palmer House on the warm ashes of the first and when that was losing money she knew what to do. She told me this: she walked into the hotel dining room, and with a pencil marked new prices on the menu, an extra nickel here, a quarter there—until once more the place returned a profit. I thought she was grand then, and I still do. I sometimes wonder if from my strong admiration for the sure social grace and beauty of that great lady I did not catch an infection that has made me, like her, the slave of jewels.

With me to instruct and to handle, poor dear Miss Haye earned her money. I made an aeronaut of her within a week. At the Exposition there was a captive balloon, a monstrous spherical gas bag jerking at its fastenings, that fascinated me. The passengers were helped up a small ladder into a wicker basket; four already were aboard when by a miracle of persuasion I convinced my governess that this was, positively, the most instructive experience a girl could have. The wicker basket squeaked and metal rings clinked together musically as the attendants cast off the lines. At first it was no more stomachfretting than a swift rise in an elevator, but then the free wind above Paris began to play with our strange vehicle up there in the sky. The captive's cable tether made things worse, of course, and all the others were sick as if the roughness had been caused by visible sea waves. I never have been seasick in my life, and was less timid than on my first ride in the Camp Bird's tram. I saw the curving leaden pathway of the Seine and was completely thrilled to have all of Paris swelling under me as a living map. We got down safe, to Miss Haye's surprise, but next day all her dire feelings were justified. The rope broke, the balloon sailed off, to come to earth, as I recall it, in Switzerland. I regretted that we had not waited a day; but Father gave Miss Haye strict instructions to avoid rides that were dangerous. In spite of that precaution she and I vanished.

I had convinced her the Ferris wheel was sedate and entirely safe, and she followed me aboard one of its first-class cars swung from an axle on its outside rim. We traveled upward and had creaked half around the orbit of its many cars when —there we stopped, precisely at the top. The thing was broken.

The wind shook and swung our private car of boards in an arc so wide that poor Miss Haye turned green again; she retched and moaned and prayed. Far down on the ground I could see a crescent of upturned faces of people marveling at our plight.

I had a gorgeous time; but Miss Haye, when she saw the sun go down and purple hazes at the horizon turning into darkness, quit sending prayers aloft and directed a scream or two at earth. A workman who wore a sloppy cap of tweed began to clamber up the framework; when he was close enough to touch our car I saw that his baggy corduroys were belted with a beetcolored sash. Miss Haye heard only a little of his explanation of the causes of our fix, before she broke in to say, *"Vite, vite, vite!"* But they were not quick, and another workman clambered up to bring us food. I ate it all; Miss Haye still was sick. Then, when it was quite black up there above the golden powder that was made of Paris lights, we swung noisily backward to earth. At the hotel my father had been so full of fears for me that he had brought police officials there, had telephoned hospitals, and had sent messengers wherever any helpful friend suggested I might be — but not one had thought to send to the top of the Ferris wheel.

My father had become the friend of M. Georges Nagelmackers, president of the Compagnie Wagon-Lits, and together they decided on a trip to Belgium. It was in a special train, made up as if for royalty with what were truly palace cars, as wide as rooms in houses, with costly paintings, fine Oriental rugs, and a swarm of liveried servants who seemed to spend two thirds of their time serving foods and wines.

We stayed a few days at the Chateau d'Ardennes and explored its forest. Long years after, I found among my things a picture postcard of the place, which Flora Wilson had written on and then forgot to mail. On the picture side there was a message for "Dear Father" but on the address side it simply said: The Secretary of Agriculture, 1022 Vermont Avenue, Washington, D. C., U. S. A. Almost everybody called her father "Uncle Jimmy." We were practicing formality then, I guess, for we were soon to meet King Leopold.

Leopold was living in the Chalet du Roi, at Ostend. That was where my father met him. Except that he wore an enormous beard, was very tall, and limped, I saw at first nothing to set him apart from other men; but that very fact, I suppose, was what could turn a person's head. He took a quick fancy to my father, because he himself was a first-rate business man and had heard about the Camp Bird mine. After we returned to Paris, Father went a second time to Belgium just to visit with the King; and when Leopold came to Paris to see the Exposition he lived at the Élysée Palace Hotel in what we considered a modest apartment.

The climax of our trip, I imagine, was not the night Tom Walsh gave the grandest of his banquets; rather, it was the day he had as his dinner guest King Leopold. It makes me happy to remember now that, after years and years of hard knocks and worry, my daddy was so quickly recognized, when he had riches, as more than just a man with gold.

Throughout the King's stay in Paris, Father saw him often. They stood together, once, before the gold exhibit from America in the Palace of Mines and Metallurgy. A piece of Camp Bird ore was hefted by the King and when they walked on, my father said, the King had one hand on his arm. Oh, they were friends, there is no doubt of that. The King, my father told us, wanted him to go into the Congo and be his partner in the mines to be developed there.

I know that Mary Garden sang at the party Father and Mother gave on the day before we sailed for home. She was then singing regularly at the Opéra Comique. Frederick Townsend Martin had become our friend, as had the Countess Spottswood Mackin and a host of others. The papers said the whole American colony had attended the reception. On a platform under palms that touched the ceiling an orchestra of Hawaiians played guitars held flat on their thighs. Mother was receiving in a gown of Irish lace over silk and mull with insertions of fine black French lace.

Sailing homeward on the steamship *St. Paul* I sometimes saw that Father, pondering, had his lower lip stuck out beyond his thick mustache. The house at LeRoy and Phelps Place in Washington, he had decided, was too small. He planned a bigger place to cost, maybe, a million dollars. Not much was said to Vin or me about the price of things, and that was startling. It was an exciting thought and in our stateroom Brother and I talked it over. There was to be, Vin said, a suite of rooms in it just for the King. We argued late over that, but Vin was right.

It was so rough that night we could not sleep and from his upper berth Vin chattered on. All of a sudden there was an awful crash. The boat shook, then quivered, and my feet were jammed against the end of the bed. In my fright I took fast hold and squealed, "What was that?" Brother, who was brave as anything said, "Oh, it's nothing. I guess a whale just got caught in our propellers." That seemed all right to me, so I went to sleep; but in the morning the *St. Paul's* decks were slanting alarmingly. Some thick rod of steel in the engine had broken and been driven through the vessel's hull and we were shipping water. We were four days late getting in to New York; since there was no wireless, it had been feared that we were lost.

The day we landed I left the Waldorf to go shopping with my mother. She got new furs at Gunther's, a pair of monster vases at Tiffany's. We left nearly a thousand dollars owing when we walked out of Altman's, and half as much at Stern Brothers' and Wanamaker's. Father grinned and said he was glad to see that she no longer suffered—and then he grinned again—from *mal de mer*.

I should have been Aunt Lucy's daughter, for she was the complete opposite of my quiet, even-tempered, book-reading mother. It was Lucy who had extravagant enthusiasms for clothes, jewelry, and fine show horses, whose ears were attuned for compliments. She was vividly colored and alluringly shaped, and had almost liquid brown eyes. When I heard people say she ought to be on the stage, why, then I knew again just why I wanted to be an actress: I'd be like my Aunt Lucy.

I tried to fix my hair so people could see how much I looked the actress. Edna May caught my fancy about that time; my hair was frizzed and parted in the

63

middle, then dressed low to hide my ears completely—a hairdresser fixed it so. Knowing I never could restore the mold, I left it that way day on day, my ears unwashed and turning yellow for want of sunlight. Written complaints from Miss Somers' school were supplemented by my mother's bleats until at last my father spoke to me.

"Listen, the thing you want more than all else in the world, I think, is a diamond ring. I'm right?"

"You surely are, my daddy!" I was flip when I was going on fifteen.

"Well then, if you will wear your hair back off your ears as other nice girls do, I'll give you such a diamond ring as will make you quite the envy of all your friends."

I thought he had the ring in his pocket then, but he shook his head and said, "First fix your hair."

It was an awful pull for me to give up what I truly thought was my personality, but I did it and that was how I got the first of all my jewels.

My first proposal came soon after that—brought on, I now suspect, because I kept that ring in sight and quite a mystery. My papa's gift? How quite absurd I made those dancing school companions seem who suggested such a thing. I sneaked out of the class to ride with gawky Ned McLean in his back-firing motorcar. Not many boys had automobiles then, nor old folks either, but his parents gave him anything he wanted. We rolled along, and crossed a bridge and came at last to a farmhouse where Ned thought we might get strawberries and cream. We did, too. A baby with an old tin spoon was digging in the dirt right near the porch where we sat eating.

I saw Ned watching me and I observed the black down on his upper lip that could soon become a mustache. Just then he pulled my dish of strawberries out of my greedy reach and blurted out, "I think you ought to marry me."

Well, I didn't know just what to say. I felt a swelling in my mind that was a sense of triumph. After this, I knew, I could not fail; without half-trying I had caught a man. So naturally I did not say no to him, but neither did I say yes; and if my daughter were to ask me now I think I'd tell her that was just the thing to do in such a situation. Hell! The cards are stacked against us women in any other field we tackle.

That must have been about the time my brother Vinson ran away. In my room I found his note that read:—

Dear Sis:

I have decided to become a man and seek adventure. I don't know when if ever you will see me again. All my love,

BROTHER

My screams could have been heard a block away from LeRoy and Phelps Place that night. I really made a racket as I took the news to my parents. Mother took

MOUNTAIN ROAD LEADING TO THE CAMP BIRD MINE

fire from my excitement, but Father had spent too many nights with just a blanket between him and the outer edges of the universe to worry over Vin's exposure. He took it calmly; but when two days later Vin came home, and entered by the kitchen door, my father met him; he was grimly angry because the boy had carried, on that escapade, one of Tom Walsh's six-shooters—the type called a "hog leg", loaded. He took my brother down from man size to a proper twelve-year-old with a leather slipper used effectively for just about five minutes. The licking was administered, of all places, in our drawing-room bay window. For two days Vin stayed in his room. I think that was his only licking, and I cried more than he did.

That spring I had my first deep heart affair. Elizabeth Eddy and I went to the theater and saw, as Sherlock Holmes, the grandest actor I had ever seen—William Gillette. We both fell madly in love with his exaggerated profile, but whether we called a truce or meant to share him half-and-half I can't remember. We pooled our money and bought some letter paper that was stiff and grand. Each day we banded a half-dozen notes to Annie, who had access to the stamp supply. I used to lie awake at night and wonder what I should do if he answered. But he never did, and when my sanity returned Annie gave me a proper scolding; then she saved my pride by telling me she had burned the notes.

We went West that summer because we wanted to see the Camp Bird, and Father was wishing he could find another mine. It was not money that made him feel that way. It was a kind of game he had been playing all those years before he made his richest strike, and so he really yearned for the inner thrill of finding hidden treasure. He knew quite well he had much more than he could ever spend even with all of us to help him. What he wanted all the time was more and more excitement. I loved it, too.

We used to love to jump aboard a train just when it was pulling out. On that very trip we did that several times and once, at some station, I got back aboard but Father had not come when the train began to move. I was frantic! My darling father had been left. The train was racing when I made up my mind: I reached up and yanked the cord that only the conductor was supposed to touch. The train stopped so quickly I nearly turned a cartwheel in the aisle. The conductor rushed up to me, raving.

"You go back and get my father," I said, half-crying.

He swore. "I don't care," I said, "you let me off or back the train."

He glared for six or seven seconds.

"You know what this is going to cost your father?"

"I don't care," I said.

Back we started, and then to my great relief I saw my father running down the track. I think he settled the case for three or five hundred dollars, but when we were alone together he grinned at me and tweaked my hair.

CHAPTER VIII

"Don't Sell the Camp Bird Mine!"

THAT was a summer to remember. My mother's dear sister Lucy came to Colorado and brought Monroe, then ten or eleven years old. Aunt Lucy wore the things my mother had brought to her from Paris and she chattered of the handsome show ring saddle horse she had, a gift from my father. Another visitor who had exciting tales to tell was John Hays Hammond. He had brought along his boy, Jack, then thirteen, which was Vinson's age. They made a pair for mischief; and with Monroe and me to aid them, got into plenty.

Mr. Hammond was trying to persuade my father to sell the Camp Bird mine to a London syndicate which he represented, but Father only laughed whenever he brought the subject up and Mother, too, would sniff at such a foolish notion. Only a few years before in the Transvaal, after the Jameson Raid, Mr. Hammond had been sentenced to death for that attempted coup d'état—which was not at all, he said, his fault. Then he had been told his sentence was changed to fifteen years, and that was almost worse than death. He told us how he felt the day he was taken out of jail and given freedom upon payment of a fine of $125,000.

Up at the mine we gave him a scare. He was supposed to be in charge of us that day, but Jack and Vin and I climbed on our horses and galloped off onto the canyon wall, at breakneck speed. He heard the hoofbeats, saw our cloud of dust, and yelled at us to stop. But he never caught us, because I knew the road and I was riding poor Dewdrop, who, after two years, remembered to push my shoulder with his nose when he wanted sugar.

Mr. Hammond was far behind when we pulled up just out of Ouray. Dewdrop's head was low, his mouth wide open. I had not realized the poor thing was old. I saw his knees bend until his muzzle pushed into the dust of the road. I was no tomboy then, when Dewdrop rolled over on his side and died. My thoughtlessness had killed him. I cried and cried, and when Father came and looked at me with scorn I cried some more. For years Tom Walsh had not hunted game, and continually he preached to us a creed of being kind to animals. That spoiled, of course, the fun I had thought would come from scaring Mr. Hammond. He said— and he was angry—that at every bend he had expected to see our mangled bodies far below him on the canyon floor.

In July we went to Glenwood Springs to celebrate the Fourth. Mr. Hammond had gone East and left young Jack in our care. In Washington, Vin had taken lessons from a stage magician and whenever he received a trifle of encouragement he would give a show. This Fourth, however, it was Jack who gave the show. Our shooting crackers had been shipped from China—pimento-colored cylinders that, Mother warned us, were full of death. Each one had two uncertain fuses. We would light them both from a piece of punk and then just before the fuses sputtered out of sight we would hurl them in the air. Jack Hammond held one too long. It went off in his hand. His thumb hung loose and blood poured out. Though he tried to keep his lips tight, he was pretty shrill before the doctor sewed that limp thumb back to the hand where it belonged. (I have often thought of that when I have read of some astonishing new invention fashioned by that same hand: a thing to explode torpedoes far out at sea, and many other war machines that I can't understand.)

The White House débutante that winter was my mother's guest sometimes. The first occasion I remember was the night Madame Lillian Nordica sang at a Walsh musicale. I still wore a pigtail down my back, a thing that seemed to pull my ego out of shape as I looked at other girls whose hair was Up. That night, what I wanted most of all to see was Alice. I tried hiding under Mother's bed but there was not enough concealment, so I got inside her closet and peeped out from behind an ambush of velvet frocks, furs, and satin. Hearing Nordica was not half so exciting as seeing Miss Roosevelt put powder on her face and offer (actually) a cigarette to that brunette of mystery, Countess Cassini, the Russian Ambassador's daughter. That night the talked-about countess wore against her lovely throat a gigantic bow of chiffon. What people said behind her back about her birth was not too nice, and it was gossiped later that the President had told his daughter (with a show of teeth) that she was forbidden to accept the Russians' invitations. When the musicale was over I went into our guest's bedroom to see Nordica helped out of her clothes and eyed her as she rubbed the red corrugations left on her hips by corsets. She rarely wore them, so she said.

"Why, Evalyn," she said to me in answering some one of my thousand questions, "I have not had a bath in thirty years."

I envied her and asked another question.

"My maid," she said, "always sponges me. I don't believe that bathing in a tub is healthy. Those sort of baths take strength a singer needs."

I do not agree with that and yet I really mean it when I say I learned most of what has been helpful from such conversations—from peeking or from bolder observations, rather than from any of the schools to which I was sent. After the Mount Vernon Seminary, I was enrolled at the Holton Arms—very small, very select. That's where I met Katherine Elkins.

Out at Ouray, my father had some plan afoot to deal with the Belgians' king. Yet what now comes to light, by turning over yellow papers and other souvenirs, was for long years simply a mystery to my mother. The Camp Bird mine, she would insist, should not be sold. She said she had a premonition. I suppose I heard a thousand mild arguments about the presence at our mine of John Hays Hammond, a wily fellow representing London clients.

"Don't sell it, Tom. What can you buy that's half so safe as a six-mile vein of gold right through your own land?"

"But, Carrie Bell," my father would reply, "how could you keep it going if I were gone? A regiment of mining men are not so easily handled. Who is to make decisions when I am not around? Whom can you trust?"

"Don't sell it, Tom," was her whole argument. This is a kind of force that women have to help them get their way. Men call it "nagging", even when it's partnership. In Father's case there was a need of freedom; he lived, more than we realized, by struggle. He wanted something more than ease, something that his womenfolk knew not how to measure. King Leopold had given him the vision of a partnership. In the Congo forest there were copper, gold, and God knows what else to tempt a miner. My father had engineers' reports to show those jungle mines could be made into quick producers that would dwarf what we were getting from the Camp Bird, provided he applied to them the same hustling effort he had used in Colorado.

"Why, Tom," my mother asked him once, "how do you know this whole mad scheme is not a trick of that old king to buy the Camp Bird cheap?"

My father laughed and went ahead with Hammond. They made a deal for cash, plus ore, plus stock. It was fair enough, no doubt; but my mother continued, always, to believe it quite foolish. As for me, I sometimes entertained another notion; I halfway felt we had angered fate or God or something not to be expressed in words.

Why, as I recall it, almost in the hour that the deal became a verbal promise we got the telegram about Aunt Lucy. In her shiny black victoria she and Monroe had been driving in Kansas City. The top was down so that she could see and be seen. The coachman had to get down to fasten a strap. She stood, to hold the reins he tried to pass to her, when suddenly the horses were frightened beyond control. Standing up, she thought first of the little boy behind her; she pitched him out so shrewdly that he landed on a patch of grass unhurt but dazed from the suddenness of their plight. Then she jumped, her long skirts tangling about her feet, and fell backward to the street. Aunt Lucy was wearing a jeweled comb which was driven deep into her skull. The message told us she was dead.

In that same year my father gave a library to the people of Ouray. To David Wegg, his former partner, he had passed along about a hundred thousand dollars for some project; but just to show it was no money-making enterprise, for him, he wrote it down as "profit & loss." In other days Mr. Wegg had done as much for him. Old scores were being settled.

To the day she died my mother insisted that Father had been hypnotized by John Hays Hammond. Of course, that was just her way of expressing something she could not fathom with her mind. I know the price paid to my father and I know the buyers got back eightfold what they paid. The price was $3,100,000 and it was paid at noon, May 1, 1902, in the offices of Guggenheimer, Untermyer and Marshall, at 30 Broad Street, New York City. Beyond that sum he got a paper obligating the Camp Bird Mining Company, Limited, to give him one-fourth of all the net proceeds of its ore until he had, in cash, $2,000,000 more. Another sentence in the printed bargain that now lies before me gave him $100,000 worth of stock. He got it all—$5,200,000—to add to the two or three or four other millions he already had gouged out of his fantastic mountain. He had that other money salted down, to use his phrase, in real estate and bonds. But that was not all he had: right near the Camp Bird vein there were other claims, old mines and prospects, that he called the Hidden Treasure Group. The London crowd that had its offices in 43 Threadneedle Street took option on that stuff, too, but that part of the deal fell through. For years and years I've paid the taxes and had assessment work performed. What I have out there in Colorado, so I think, really is a hidden treasure that my sons can go and find some day just as their grandfather did.

Charlie Thomas, my father's dear friend, was named in the agreement, to represent him in any disputes, and John Hays Hammond had a similar obligation for his foreign clients. There were no disputes. Indeed, when it was discovered that the deed did not include twenty miles of water pipe line and other water power rights, my father simply told them all to fix it up, for he had meant to sell the stuff. Tom Walsh was never one to play smart tricks with ink. His word was his bond. I have no notion here of "fixing blame" on anyone. I wish he had not sold, and so did Mother, but the deal was made and it was legal.

When the ex-owner of the Camp Bird mine had planted his too fluid capital in more real estate and bonds, he took us all to Europe. There was something on his mind. He had plans he never did confide to us; but in September we knew that he was considering a business proposition made by King Leopold. I only know what happened in my presence.

The King was staying at a place called Bagnères-de-Luchon, in the Pyrenees.

"Would you like to go to see the King?"

Anybody knowing me knows what I said.

We traveled all night, and late the next day we came into a place all rocky, purple steeps like the Colorado mountains that were home to us. The King himself met us at the train. He was incognito when he lived there. We dined that night with Leopold in an apartment that was not so grand. What caught my eye was the way he ate, pushing food into the red mouth that gaped under an enormous nose in his vast white fabric of beard.

Some birds were served. I think that in my memory they have changed their mold. I remember them as quail, and I know I could not eat mine with half a dozen bites; possibly they were only larks. Anyway I saw the King impale one on his fork. He caught my eyes—and there is no doubt that I was rudely staring. His monocle was tucked against his eye behind the projection of his cheek and skull and through its convex glass one half his gaze was magnified—and while I watched he popped a whole bird into his mouth. I could not take my eyes away. He never chewed; he just swallowed once and passed a napkin before his face.

Then he chuckled and spoke again to Father, whom he called "Tommy." (Father called him "Sir.")

There was a young aide-de-camp around, Lieutenant Binje, who tried to be polite to me. There was not much I could do, except to giggle.

I studied Leopold covertly. His big nose seemed to have a mulberry tinge—from drinking, I suppose. But there was something else that kept me watching: the stiffness of his pose. I had a notion the King wore corsets.

My father and he talked throughout the evening while I was left to look at some old book of scenic pictures. Leopold was urging Father to do something, and since they were talking of business I hardly listened. The next day we went for a drive and I sat beside the King in an open carriage while Father faced us. I was puzzled about the King's fixed shape, and so when we trotted toward a curve I leaned out a little as if to see ahead. Then I let the turning seem to throw me off my balance. I fell against the King so that my elbow poked him. I did not touch his ribs! He was encased in something hard as iron. It was no ordinary corset that he wore, but probably a special bullet-proof garment.

The King gave Father his entire attention for three days. Once when we were alone my father was in a rage.

"The way they handle things down there in the Congo—" he said. "I wouldn't touch it!"

Another day we drove over a historic road up the Valle de la Pique, with the King acting as guide. He told how Romans then Moors, had used this same road to carry out their schemes of conquest. Once he pointed to some projecting rocks far overhead where no carriage could hope to go and said that he had gone up there on foot clear from Luchon just a week or so before. Father whistled his astonishment—"I hope when I am sixty-seven I can do as good!"

When we got back from that trip Luchon was clothed with flags and bunting—red, black, and yellow—in honor of the King. French military bands were there, and I was excited because then the King would have to rig himself in all his glory; but, worse luck, we had to hustle to catch the boat for home. Those two shook hands as cronies, but I knew something the King did not suspect: my father's mind was firmly set against the Congo; and yet he liked the King and in his mind there lingered a hope that they would get together, some way, in a deal or two. More important, though, was the promise made by Leopold to come to see us in America.

"Nineteen-three, sir?" Father said, and Leopold answered, "Right."

Officially the King was to come to see the St. Louis Exposition; but actually he wanted with his own eyes to see Americans making money. I think, too, he had a notion that by being nice and friendly he could start a stream of capital flowing into his domain in Africa. My papa was not putting any in; he told me that on the train by saying, "I'll keep my money home where I can see it. Of course, I don't mind little flyers."

Nevertheless, he spent plenty building "2020." We've always called it simply that, as if to compensate for its regal size and splendor; and yet some of the neighbors' houses in Massachusetts Avenue and some in other streets in Washington were just as big and cost, I suppose, as much. Indeed, a few had what ours did not—porticoes with great stone columns supporting pediments as heavy as the one that overhangs the front porch of the White House.

Sixty rooms are chambered in our Massachusetts Avenue house between the roof and ground, and on the third floor (my father spent $5,075 for elevators) there really was, and is, an apartment for a king. The architect was Henry Anderson, well known in 1902, and he was told by Father just what was wanted. They selected curly birch for the trimming, and it was done in Empire style. But, hell, I can't see anything more elegant there than in the balance of the house. I won't deny it: I love the place; for me, it really is a palace that expresses dreams my father and mother had when they were poor in Colorado. This should not give rise to any notion they were sadly "nouveau", as that term is used to label people outside of society trying to get in. We were in; make no mistake about it. Everywhere, thanks to Father's charm and Mother's modesty, they passed the tests; at Palm Beach and up at Newport, in New York and Washington, there were no barriers to make them fret. We found people really sweet and kind. I think the reason is that the Walshes never tried to hide their simple start. No matter how many, many years I live I'm not the kind ever to forget that as a child I was kept warm in red flannel underdrawers. But that's no reason for wearing them now. Why, the sheets I sleep on are pink satin soft as something for a fairy princess and the lace around their edges is woven out of (I fancy) spider frowns. I paid four thousand dollars for them and got a bargain because, as any woman knows, forgetful, restful sleep will take out wrinkles.

Green veins show in the smooth, round marble columns that define the doorways of 2020. Inside, the great reception hall has no roof until you lift your eyes four full stories to a richly colored surface of stained glass. Why, that alone was grand enough for me to feel, at sixteen, a prideful swelling in my throat. A wide staircase, which led to a landing holding two marble statues in dancing poses, divided as a Y so that two staircases rose to the first of a series of promenade galleries. The first-floor library was so rich with books that my book-loving mother was appalled, knowing she never would be able to read a tenth of them even if she did nothing else. The furniture was dazzling, but it was appropriate. The point is that Tom Walsh and Carrie Bell were smart enough to know their limitations, which is something people long possessed of wealth sometimes forget. My father had hired Mrs. Anna Jenness Miller to scout around and help my mother buy just what was needed for that house; it was a job that lasted several years. She worked with mother and was so often in New York to deal with decorators, art dealers, rug merchants and furniture makers that she had an artist's studio as an office there. She even went abroad to get some choicer paintings and the bric-a-brac we needed. Rugs from Persia, pictures and aquarelles from dealers in the Boulevard Poissonniére in Paris, from the Avenue Louise in Brussels; sometimes her shipments came from Montreux, Switzerland. How the money went!

Ah, but you should have seen my suite of rooms the day I first walked in and saw the perfectly beautiful, pink satin walls; a huge sitting room, a bedroom, and a bathroom that I still think enormous. And yet, the things we had been doing, our travels, the houses of our friends, the rich hotels and other contacts had done something. My perceptions of luxury were no longer, at the start of 1903, the same quick avenues to my emotions. Why, at the first sight of the canopy above my bed in LeRoy and Phelps Place I had fairly screamed with ecstasy; but when I saw my suite at 2020, 1 was sure it was nice but I was not excited. I had everything I wanted almost as I wanted it, so that getting new things was less and less exciting. Still, I really loved the feel of fitting myself into the house. There was my dresser, and on it a set of toilet things - mirror, brush and comb, glass jars, buttonhook, scissors, file; all heavy with gold tops or gold handles. There was also a jewel box. In those rooms—against the walls, on my big Steinway, and on any other furniture that would hold them—were photographs of Father, Mother, Vinson and some others we all loved.

Vinson was the center of things. Almost anything he wanted he could have, and this is what he had in his room: —

1 red rug, 2 small ones.
1 heavy, carved bed couch, 5 red pillows.
1 cabinet with mirror.
1 book and gun case combined.
1 large center table with Navajo blanket cover.
1 Turkish cozy corner, 8 pillows.
1 bookcase full of books
(I remember "Harry Castleman", "Henty" and, what was surely excess baggage in that room, the works of Horatio Alger).

1 sterling silver ship.
1 alligator, stuffed.
1 anchor clock.
1 Hindu bust.
1 Indian head.
1 Madonna and child.
2 sets of armor.
1 shield.
7 pieces of old armor on the wall.
1 silver man-on-horseback.
1 carved bellows.
1 bronze horse.
1 ivory elephant.

However, lots of Vinson's most treasured things were in the top of the house. Of course, the very top was a roof garden; but on the fourth floor, besides the ballroom, there was a theater where Brother could have his shows. By this time he could do all kinds of tricks to fool an audience. With Monroe Lee (who lived with us) to serve as his stooge and helper, Vinson would escape, just like Houdini, from a chained-up sack; and then, when the screen was pulled aside, some chosen spectators would be permitted to open a padlocked trunk - and inside, snug but almost breathless from his hurry, would be my brother. Dear Vinson had bought that trick, and others, complete with all the gadgets from some queer dealer in such things. You should have heard the loud clapping of Tom Walsh's hands whenever Vinson did a card trick or lifted a live and squirming rabbit from a hat. He loved that boy beyond my powers of expression.

A note on stiff White House stationery, through the unimportance of its message, brings alive now some of the feeling with which my father was regarded in Washington. A hansom cab driver, guiding tourists along Massachusetts Avenue, when opposite the scaffolded house at 2020 is said to have lifted the trap door in the cab roof to say (first shifting his brown quid from tongue to cheek), "five million dollar home of the Colorado Monte Cristo; the fellow that's a friend of kings." Well, cab drivers are not the only ones who exaggerate fivefold when money is referred to; actually that house, complete, cost $835,000. But the legend of Father's wealth and power grew.

What President Theodore Roosevelt wrote on October 28, 1902, was this: "When I was riding yesterday in the Park I waved to you."

That letter came within a week of the death of Mother's scapegrace brother, Stephen Reed, in Chicago. (I had forgotten, until I found among my father's papers a receipted bill — for ninety dollars, plus fifteen dollars for a grave in Oakwood — from some West Madison Street undertaker.)

CHAPTER IX

It Is No Fun to Be a Lady

It was about that time that I was shipped away, in Annie's care, to the Misses Masters' School at Dobbs Ferry. The record seems to indicate that I was there until just before the last big party that the Walshes had at LeRoy and Phelps Place. Lovely Marion Cockrell was the guest of honor. She was to be married a few days later, February 14, 1903, to Edson F. Gallaudet, who just before this time had coached a winning crew at Yale. The house at 2020 was not completed, and so after the dinner party there was a musicale at the New Willard Hotel.

But first I ought to tell how I got there, from the Dobbs Ferry School.

I knew what was expected of me there. By some school magic, I was to become a lady; and a lady could do, so I was told, just about nothing that she might want to do except attend all parties. But there was more to make me sad. I really was homesick. We four—Father, Mother, Vin and I—grew faint with something like hunger when we were kept apart.

I cried so much in classes that one or two of the girls usually carried, on my behalf, an extra handkerchief. It may sound silly now, but it was not then. From the day Annie checked me in I was completely wretched. I wrote and wrote, and finally Father came to give me a Saturday of fun in New York. He asked me what I wanted and I said "Jewels."

I suppose he figured I would feel better if -I had something finer than the other girls at school. At any rate he took me into a jewelry store and bought for me a turquoise-and-seed-pearl dog collar. I had it on when I got back to school, and two kinds of paint that I had succeeded in buying on the sly were thick upon my cheeks and lips.

Miss Masters saw me from the porch as I returned late that Saturday. She was stiff with rage as she beckoned me to stand before her. What a talking-to she gave me! I was vulgar, I was common. She ranted on, and I was quite subdued until she made a disparaging remark about the turquoise-and-seed-pearl dog collar that there and then became tight about my swelling neck. My Irish was boiling over.

"My father gave me this," I said; and even now I think that if she had possessed a speck of wit she would have been, just then, a whole lot nicer.

But what she said was, "You disgrace this school."

I called my brother Vinson on the phone and we talked hog Latin. (I never learned the other kind.) We two always spoke in code. I asked him to fix it up with Father to send me permission to see a New York dentist and for Vin to meet me on the following Saturday at the Waldorf.

We met there, and when I got home to Washington I asked little Annie to go to Dobbs Ferry and get my clothes. I broke the news to Father in such a manner as to make him burst out laughing, and so postponed the reckoning. Of course they did not like my leaving school that way, but I never did go back to an American school.

At any rate, I was present at the musicale for Miss Cockrell. That night there was an Army and Navy reception at the White House, from nine to ten-thirty, and Mother's invitations, shrewdly, read "10:30." Consequently her entertainment was thronged with uniforms.

Marian's wedding at the Church of the Covenant was the most brilliant of the winter season. The bridesmaids wore white crepe de Chine tucked and trimmed with medallions of lace over vaguely seen silk slips of green. Their picture hats of white chiffon were shaped to their heads by half-wreaths of green leaves; they carried, quite demurely, shower bouquets of bride roses, leaning forward as they walked because of the corset lacings that had shaped them like creatures of another species. I heard the ohs and ahs at the passage down the aisle of little Anna Ewing Cockrell, 2d, the flower girl, aged three or four.

How unimportant to recall? Not so. The yearnings to be seen and heard, which I felt in my adolescence, were ten times more bedeviling than anything else that gave me irk.

My purpose is to show what made me tick, what made me act so harum-scarum.

Once, in Denver at Elitch's Gardens, I got myself arrested along with Vin and some of the children of Governor Thomas. I have forgotten when, but I was pretty big. We broke some lights and pulled down signs while riding on the roller coaster (I still ride the things, in summers, hour after hour), and I suppose a licking would have been in order. However, an enormous policeman came and grabbed the Thomas boys and Vin. Edith, who had shown no trace of fault, was ashamed and frightened; but I told the policeman who we were.

"You'll be a treat," he said, "for our old lockup."

A crowd had gathered and I begged permission to call up Governor Thomas. (I cannot remember whether he was still in office, but he was certainly an influential citizen.)

"I am sorry," I tactfully began, as Edith whimpered, "but we are all arrested."

What he said was so harsh it made the earpiece vibrate! "I should have known better," he roared, than to let my children go romping with you two wild ones." Then he spoke to the policeman, and we were held in a shamefaced cluster until the Governor appeared and took us home.

My next scrape was not my fault, but rather that of chance—unless it might be blamed upon my fatal addiction to roller coaster rides and other artificial thrills. The French Ambassador and Madame Jusserand, who was by then attached to Mother, had taken a house that summer (1903) at Manchester, Massachusetts. So

Father leased the G. H. Hood estate. . . .

I had forgotten. What brings it back so clearly now is a letter on blue notepaper, written later by a man who worked for us—an Edward Burke. He wrote politely, giving information about some disgruntled servant to Miss Annie Lee McDonald, who had inquired about the matter. He wrote:—

. . . and also I see Eddie get his month's wages at two different times. Once when Mr. Walsh was away Miss Evelyn [sic] paid the three of us she brought the money down just at tea time. Ameal [Indeed, he means Emile] and myself were standing in the dining room and gave Eddie the three envelopes and when Ameal and myself came out he gave us our envelopes. I think Mr. Walsh was in New York that time . . .

Oh, I know it is quite, quite unimportant, and yet that letter written as a kindness is now a potent charm evoking from a pinpoint of my memory whole scenes—a house, an ocean, parts of a summer of my past. I never saw that letter until I began to rummage; but, with a mind-magic I wish I understood, through a forgotten servant's eyes I am enabled to feel, again, myself: Miss Evalyn Walsh, a girl who really had no sorrows, just half-mad yearnings to know the world and all that's in it.

Why, after thirty years and more that dining room is freshly printed in my mind. There was a fourfold Japanese screen with bamboo panels decorated with some Oriental whimsy. There was an oblong, white enamel table with turned and ornamental legs; a bronze gong and hammer; a lantern with assorted colored glasses; eight leather-seated chairs with mahogany and birch frames, and a Smyrna carpet on the floor.

A fine Bokhara made the front hall a soft purple and the parlor floor was covered with a Persian Feraghan. There was a Japanese bronze cylinder vase with a raised design contrived from the writhing struggle of a snake held in the knife-like beak of a big bird. We had a billiard room upstairs. All that household was in the charge of dear Annie, who had become our housekeeper and much more: she dealt with all our household problems. Hers was a post of dignity; she had become "Miss Annie", who traced lost trunks, rebuked the butler, from habit scanned my ears, and daily warned Vin to take it slower in his Winton.

There was a launch that Vinson ran,—here my memory slips a trifle,—and once we started out in the evening to cross some bay to a small amusement park. Nanine Mitchell was with us, and other youngsters. The launch broke down and we were stranded. Our several families, half-crazed by catastrophic visions more vivid than opium nightmares, were gathered on the porch when we came home. As usual, they blamed me.

In the fall we moved into 2020. During the December holidays, the Walshes gave a small ball there in honor of Miss Alice Roosevelt. For many years we have been about together but on that night I was just another Carmen quite willing to pull her hair or fight with other weapons. I was furious because I was not allowed to go to the party. Why? I was too young—seventeen.

Most of the company that night saw for the first time the large Louis XIV salon on the first floor. The dancing began at eleven in the top-floor ballroom, with its walls all yellow with brocade, with yellow hangings and yellow fabrics covering all the benches and chairs around the room. It was one o'clock when the cotillon began, led by Major Charles McCawley, of the Marine Corps, and Alice. Sixty couples passed the tables where favors had been piled: gold pencils for the men, lace and tortoiseshell fans for the ladies.

I got a fan, anyway.

I had forgotten why my family let me go abroad without them until I rummaged in my father's files. (All of us forget much more than we remember, and that's a blessing.) The fact is that we had all expected to go abroad in June, 1904, and then our arrangements were canceled at the last moment because President Theodore Roosevelt made a request of Father—almost a command, it was—to remain and use his influence to settle the disturbed condition of Colorado. (This was the year Roosevelt ran for election to the office he was holding by virtue of McKinley's assassination.)

Thanks to that, we had a summer in a place in Colorado that I described to Dad as "the littlest hole I ever got into in my life; there are a few cows with bells around their necks, a very few old people, and all the rest is mountains." (There is nothing I would add to that now; the description was complete.)

Tom Walsh himself soon hustled out of Colorado. The ex-owner of the Camp Bird mine responded to another gold alarm. With blanket rolls, prospectors' short-handled picks, canvas saddlebags and other apparatus of his early days, he and John Benson joined the rush. The place they went to was Goldfield—and Father almost lost his life.

"I guess I've turned into a tenderfoot," he said when finally he came back to us. The rough camp grub had made him ill, and one ear had lost the power of hearing. An ear specialist stretched him on his side, looked in his ear, then fished around and brought forth a small beetle that had used his ear for a mausoleum. (He had been sleeping on the ground while hunting claims to stake in Nevada.)

"I found worse than beetles," he told us. "While others searched the valleys and stream beds, John Benson and I, remembering the Camp Bird's altitude, went higher and higher. One day we found a tunnel—some abandoned pit mouth of another fellow's hopes. It had been driven into bare rock face above a place all overgrown with mountain laurel, or something very like it, just coming into bloom with little pink-striped flowers. After what I found in an old abandoned tunnel here in Colorado, I couldn't resist what seemed to be another invitation to find a vein of gold. On hands and knees I crept into that hole, which had by fallen rock and rubble been narrowed to little more than twice my size. I pushed ahead of me a stub of lighted candle, kneeling on a slab of rock. I had just room enough in there

2020 Massachusetts Avenue, Washington, D. C.

to swing my little pick, and I was swinging it when I heard a buzz. Under that rock on which I rested was a rattlesnake. I froze, as I have done before when warned by that crisp, scaly flutter. Right then and there, on a level with my ear, I swear a hundred other snakes began to buzz. They were massed in writhing hydra form upon a ledge made by the last blast of giant powder fired in that tunnel long years before. Their roost was not the length of my arm from me. They have a stench, those snakes. I smelled it then, and backed out faster than I usually go forward, and I was sweating as I yelled for John to take care because we were prospecting a den of rattlers. That place into which I'd crawled had become the breeding ground where the young are born and to which the snakes come back year after year, from the valleys where they hunt all summer, to lie dormant through the cold months.

"What did I do? Well, since then I've been having trouble"—he grinned and slapped his stomach—"here."

He grinned, but he was solemn as he promised us, and certain saints, that he would not again go prospecting for gold or any other ore. Throughout the balance of that summer he spent much time in Colorado, taking old friends by their lapels as he talked to them of his friend T.R.

My education was still a pressing problem. Something of the talk and the pressure that was exerted to make me settle down to study comes back to me as I hold a sheet of paper made electric with a charge of love by one for whom I have been lonesome now for thirty years—my brother Vinson. While we were in Colorado he had spent part of the summer in New York getting treatments for some puzzling malady that broke out on his skin. To keep him less homesick Dad fixed it up for him to take some boxing lessons from Tom Sharkey. He had bought some clothes, that sixteen-year-old, from Wetzel's, and then Mother and I had gone with him to Pottstown, where he entered The Hill School. He wrote from there: —

Dear old Sis,

You can't know how fierce it was to let you and Sweetness [that was Mother] go the other day but I suppose it's right that I should be here although it does seem awful hard. I have been feeling too bad to write cheerful news so I haven't written before.

Now, old girl, you are going to have lots of temptations in Paris but you are old enough now [I was eighteen] to know what's right so don't give way to them. Remember, this is your last chance so take it and work like "...." and when I come over we will make the "fur fly." If you are ever in doubt remember that you can always write to me. I don't want you to become a great literary scholar but I do want you to know as much as the people you will have to go with. Well, darling sis, I will say good-night.

Your chum

VIN

My "chance" that Vin wrote about was an agreement reached in our family for me to go to Paris to study—music, French and other parlor tricks of ladies. Flora

Wilson, wanting further training for her voice, was enchanted by the offer of my father to send the two of us abroad. Motherless, she had for eight years held the rank of cabinet lady; and, as she was older, self-governed, and restrained, the family felt she was just the one to be my companion. But that was not the only precaution by any means. We two were to be chaperoned and counseled by Miss Fanny Reed, a notable of Paris. She was the sister of Mrs. Paran Stevens of New York, and she was also the aunt of Lady Paget, King Edward's friend.

What brings that back is a fading London letter to my father from "35 Belgrave Square, S.W.", signed "N. Torlks" — the secretary of Minnie Paget. Something terrible had befallen her; her right kneecap was smashed, her thigh doubly fractured, her ankle broken, besides many cuts and bruises. She had to lie flat on her back, it seems, for three months, in plaster casts; but she had told her secretary to write my father that she had heard there was a chance his daughter would be coming over to stay with Aunt Fanny to learn French; how nice it would be, she much hoped it was true.

But now I've lost track of stating what it was I did that winter, in my concern over that accident to Minnie Paget. The answer is given in another letter, sent by Aunt Fanny Reed from 187, rue de la Pompe, Paris, to my father: —

Your letter of July 20 was received just as I was leaving for Paris as I had been to Carlsbad for a cure — it almost took my breath away to think your dear Evalyn & Miss Wilson were to be here for the winter. I will look about at once for an apartment & if I cannot find something as satisfactory as they wish, perhaps they would come to me. I have in my wing two very good bedrooms, dressing rooms, bath, etc., & I could perhaps find a room for Annie in the house. Of course you have heard of Mrs. Paget's terrible accident, falling down her lift to the basement. I am so sorry for her. Will you please send me by the ladies a box of pecan nuts such as Huyler's prepares — not too salt — I shall be very grateful.

Affec.

FANNY REED

Oh, I did love my father and mother, and never meant to give them the slightest pang of worry on my account. The note I wrote that September night of 1904 as the *S.S. Deutschland* got out to sea is proof of what I say: —

Darling beloved pets,

Here we are safe and sound in our little bed and very comfortable. I have the big lower berth and Flora has the one opposite it. The state rooms are so nice and how can I ever thank you enough for those beautiful flowers!!!

The steward says the fruit is aboard but I haven't seen it yet. Now my own darling pets don't you worry about me at all. I am not going to meet a soul [as I wrote I meant it, positively] and we are going to stay in bed half the day and go to bed early at nights. You were perfect *bricks* tonight and if you hadn't been so perfect I never could have gone. I know now what it means to see two people *absolutely* unselfish. You dear things, if I don't just work hard and repay you both for the brave fight you are making. But don't forget your promise to send for me if you are lonesome at the end of the month. I haven't cried once.

81

Now my darlings goodnight Flora looks so tired and I must put the light out. I won't forget the promise I gave you and Oh! please don't miss me too much. I will send you a telegram Friday with billions of love and kisses from your *very own* loving little girl,

EVALYN

P.S. I can't tell you how much I love you both, but you know! ! !
P.S. Give my love to Nannie and Brother and remember me to dear old Maggie. [That was Maggie Buggy, a servant. At least I have hung on to her.]

My life has been just like that letter; my love something to be freely spent, my feelings sounding off with exclamation points and underscorings.

The *S.S. Deutschland* created in my mind a quite uncomplex notion of the freedom of the seas. For just about the first time in my life I was free to act grown-up. There wasn't anyone around to say "Please don't" or nag me with a plea to "be a lady." Of course, Annie was aboard, but she was such a rotten sailor she stayed in her berth right through to Cherbourg. I had a $10,000 letter of credit, a present from my father, and for the control of my expenditures I had about ten cents' worth of judgment. Flora and I soon knew all the men on the boat and spent most of our time in the smoking room. Two I met that trip were William Gibbs McAdoo and his brother, who was a fascinating devil. That was the year McAdoo had completed the first tunnel under the Hudson River.

At Paris I went straight to Fanny Reed's apartment. Anyone could see that once she had been distractingly beautiful. Then she had become a *grande dame* with snow-white hair, finely sculptured features, and purple eyes.

"Now, Aunt Fanny," I began, "I don't think these two rooms will be enough. If I'm to study I must have space to pace the floor."

Aunt Fanny nodded, and compromised by letting me take an apartment two floors higher in that dwelling at 187 rue de la Pompe.

"I'm going to have the McAdoo brothers for dinner Saturday night, Aunt Fanny," I told her when I was settled.

She blinked, and then she said, "They can come, but I'll be here too."

The next thing I did was to hire an electric brougham, the prettiest I could get; and when I told Aunt Fanny I was taking Mr. McAdoo, the tunnel builder, for a ride in the Bois she smiled and said, "That's right: Mr. McAdoo—and Annie."

Well, it was time for me to take my first singing lesson. Aunt Fanny dressed herself beautifully and we set out for the atelier of some Frenchman who, she carefully warned me, was most particular to teach only students with aptitude. He proved to be porcinely fat, and the dome of his skull shone pinkly as if it had been buffed by an ardent manicurist. He wore a morning coat, striped trousers, and fawn spats. He bowed himself in half, and then took his seat before a piano as he gave me instructions to run a scale or two. I know I have a horrid voice, and singing lessons were not on my secret schedule. I sang the most stridulous *do, re, mi, fa sol, la* that Frenchman ever heard. I know I must have hurt him as a dog is hurt when high notes make it howl. He jumped right off the floor, clicked his heels, and clapped his brow.

"My God," he cried. "My God! Stop!" When I was quiet he addressed himself to Fanny Reed, beginning with restraint but becoming louder and louder, at the same time gesturing me away.

"Precisely what," I asked Aunt Fanny, "does he say?"

She laughed. "He says he would not try to teach you singing for all the gold in America."

"You see, Aunt Fanny, I've got no voice—so that leaves me free today to do a little shopping."

I went to Georges, a hairdresser, but the man, extending his fingers placatively refused to carry out my order.

"Mam'selle," he said, "I can't do theese without a horder from ze papa."

What I wanted him to do was to change my hair from black to red. When he refused I bought, elsewhere, a bottle of hair dye; and that night in my own room I made myself a blonde—probably the most grotesque that was ever seen in Paris. I used too much of the chemical. When I woke up, my hair was red—in places. But it was likewise green and yellow. I went back to Georges, and when I was unswathed from the veils in which Flora and Annie had wrapped me, I said, *"Now* will you fix me up?" He clucked and smote his hands and summoned, one after another, all his assistants.

When I left the place that afternoon I was a coppery redhead. Aunt Fanny howled in despair when she saw me.

The next day I went to Worth's and bought the prettiest clothes that I could buy. I stocked up with black lace underwear, listening stonily while Aunt Fanny Reed tried to explain that the things I wore were much much too— Then she would run out of words and finish up by saying she thought I ought to wear costumes more appropriate for one of my age. Dear Flora was completely horrified at the extravagance of my behavior.

However, one Western girl gone maverick was not too much for Fanny Reed. She understood just why I did the things that were upsetting and tried to guide my taste and keep me in the company of some who might stimulate my ambitions. One of these was Mary Garden. Aunt Fanny had her come one night for dinner; she was there when word was brought that the star who was to sing "Louise" was ill. Mary was the understudy. All of us went to the opera immediately, and I thrilled in sympathy when I saw the whole house rise to its feet to acclaim as a new star artist the American Mary Garden.

I was supposed to spend my days in Paris right under the cultured thumb of Fanny Reed, and so was Flora. Flora took her singing seriously and chattered faithfully in French with those who could improve her accent, but where I improved the most was in my skill at getting Aunt Fanny to go places. (I used to tell her I was getting too much sleep for my own good.) Gradually she began to like the things' I liked. Then Flora proved to be the real chaperone. She was not getting sleep enough, trying to keep a faithful eye on me, and what with this and that she and Fanny sassed each other quite frequently.

T. Bentley Mott came to call, and Annie would not let him past the door. "No men allowed" was her creed where I was concerned. However, I did get out; and naturally I went to places where I encountered plenty of Americans. One I saw was Frank Munsey. He was so anxious to hear whether I was enjoying Paris that I told him just how grand a time I was having. I don't remember when he sailed, but just before Christmas I got a cablegram from Father telling me to come home at once. I cabled back that I was learning so much I did not want to leave until spring. But I had a hunch, and hustled around from shop to shop buying things I thought I'd need: a sable coat, muff, and scarf, some stunning dresses, and other things, until there was very little money left. Father's second cable came just then: "STOPPED YOUR LETTER OF CREDIT SENDING MRS. WICKERSHAM." She was the wife of Father's secretary and she, I knew, was coming for me just like a sheriff.

"Do you," I asked dear Aunt Fanny, "think my family will find me much improved?"

"My dear," she temporized, "I think they'll find you vastly changed. I trust your father is partial to red hair."

I had completely forgotten that, and whistled. However, I cheered myself up by trying on one of my gowns, of yellow velvet, with real lace down the front and diamond stars; it was one of the nicest ones I'd bought. It matched something else I'd bought before Dad clamped down on my credit. That was a yellow Fiat.

Mrs. Wickersham, when she arrived and took me into custody, had arranged that my punishment should begin on the voyage. My good time, she said, was over. Instead of giving me a *de luxe* cabin, my father had engaged for me a tiny stateroom down below. However, it was passage on the *S.S. Deutschland.* I felt powerless, because I had no money and Mrs. Wickersham was as fixed as concrete in her idea that I should travel modestly. She had orders, so she said. Well, who should appear but a smart-looking ship's officer; he said Captain Kemp wished to see me. You should have seen me racing to his quarters.

"Go right to your old room on deck," he said with twinkles in his eyes. "If your father wants to punish you he ought to use a switch and not make all aboard my ship suffer for your sins. Anyway, it's all O.K., because there'll be no extra charge."

Poor Mrs. Wickersham was sick within the hour and did not have the stomach to insist upon the bargain she had made with Father; instead, she went right into Flora's old bed and I proceeded out on deck to show off some of my clothes. A fellow passenger was an old friend, Susan Preston Draper, whose husband, the General, had been Ambassador to Italy. A December passage of the North Atlantic is not the smoothest voyage one can take. Poor Mrs. Wickersham looked like Gorgonzola, and would not even notice when I started out on deck, a redhead in a yellow coat. I was the only woman who was well and I had, be sure of it, the grandest time I'd ever had.

Two men who had been sent by Father came aboard the boat at Quarantine, and one of them handed me a note in which he warned me to declare anything I'd bought abroad. I only had about eight trunks by then. I wrote down some of the things on that confusing declaration, but there were so many good-byes to say, so many addresses to record, that I was not too careful. We were not supposed to dock until morning, but the ship was sheathed in ice and the trip had been so rough that it was decided to let us off at night. There was no one there to meet me. I just left my trunks and went straight off to the Waldorf, and there all of my family who had come to meet me were in bed—Father, Monroe Lee, and Uncle Sam. I woke them up but tried to keep from getting into the light. They kissed me in semidarkness, but Father wanted hungrily to see his daughter. Suddenly he whooped at me: "What's happened to your hair? Great God! It's red!"

I explained just how it happened that I had come home a blonde, and Father scolded - and then he laughed, and then he scolded more. But Uncle Sam, in striped pink pajamas, dropped down on the hotel room floor and shrieked and yelled and laughed just as if he'd been in some old railroad construction camp. I must say I was relieved.

Next day the phone rang. Mr. Thomas Walsh was wanted at the Customhouse. "Are you sure, Evalyn," he said, "that you declared everything?"

"I declared a lot," I said, "considering how little I brought in."

When he had gone I began to feel a foggy scare creeping up from the pit of my stomach, and I told Annie that she and I were going for a long, long drive. We had lunch out in a park somewhere, but in the late afternoon I knew I simply had to go back and face the music. I walked into a room of silent men; not even Uncle Sam was laughing then. Finally Father spoke: —

"I understood you to say you had declared everything. You must have overlooked a few things. I've just had to pay one thousand, four hundred and seventy-four dollars duty for you, young lady. If it had been anybody else I think they would have sent you off to a cell."

"What did you tell 'em, Tom?" asked Uncle Sam.

"I said," replied my father, "that my eldest child, my daughter Evalyn, did not have good sense; that she was just a little—" and then he tapped his head.

Uncle Sam and Monroe had come East to spend Christmas with us. But Mother almost ruined it for me by confiscating all my Paris dresses. They were too old for me, she said, and was not moved by any of my arguments. I cried a lot. Then suddenly I remembered something.

"Papa," I inquired, "why did you cable me when you did, that first time?"

"I'll tell you," he said. "I met Frank Munsey, and he said, 'I see your daughter Evalyn is having a grand time in Paris.' Then I said 'Oh, no, she's not. She is studying French, music—a lot of things.' And he said, 'Whenever I saw her she was riding in a yellow Fiat that only touched the high spots or else I'd meet her roaming around at night with Fanny Reed.'"

CHAPTER X

More about Gold-Seekers

THE Walshes were not entertaining that winter. Our big new house at 2020, staffed with twenty-three servants, could not be used as had been intended, because my father's brother had died in Denver, from dropsy of the liver.

Just see: I had not thought of Uncle Mike in years—yet, if Uncle Mike had not gone West to be an Indian fighter, my father might have stayed in Worcester, or even Ireland, and so might never have met my mother. And now, by dying, Michael was to change further the current of our life.

Just before New Year's, 1905, my father wrote to John Benson:—

We are going back with Evalyn, leaving on the *Deutschland* January 7, via the Mediterranean route. We feel it would cause unfavorable comment if we should entertain this winter and that we cannot be better engaged than looking after Evalyn's education.

That's how it happened that I met the Pope; likewise those two Vinson always called "the Dago princes."

There was (and I should say it here) another reason why my parents wanted me in Europe: they were afraid I'd marry Ned McLean. His mother had been sweet and kind to my mother, and his father was always full of hearty greetings for my dad; but Ned, my family felt, was too completely spoiled to make a husband for their darling. Anything or anyone, that is, was better for me, so my parents thought, than young McLean.

In Rome, that January, T. Bentley Mott showed up; and so did other friends we had made in Paris during the Exposition. And then I met this prince, Altieri. In Rome, indeed all over Europe, I was spoken of habitually as "the Walsh heiress", and on the Continent that is a kind of sugar bound to attract some flies. My father's money was a legend that grew fabulous in repeated telling. He was a liberal spender, and tipped so freely that the frantic service (and servility) of maitre d'hotels was furthering, each day, the opinion that the Walsh millions were unnumbered. However, what Altieri liked about me, so he always told me, was my eyes, my hair, my charm, my verve, my—Oh, you should have heard him, and I admit I liked it.

I remember well the night I met him. We were living in the Palace Hotel, and there was a dance downstairs in the ballroom. I put on a gown of pale blue tulle and then, forbidden to use rouge by Mother, got red for my cheeks and lips by licking the cover of a Baedeker. Foolish? Not a bit! That little trick put armor on my soul, and let me go out to conquer.

I was seated in the lobby, undated, when my father came along bringing with him a small man with patent-leather-black for hair and skin as pale as if he'd been laid out in death. My father introduced us. This gentleman, who spoke beautiful English, was Prince Colonna, grandson of Mrs. John W. Mackay. The Prince's father, Ferdinand, had married the Mackay daughter after she, too, had gone to Europe to spend gold that came from her father's mine. Of course that was a romantic start for an evening—but it was just a start.

I began waltzing with this black-haired prince whose smoldering eyes were barely on a level with my own. A dozen violins, a harp, and cellos were playing "The Beautiful Blue Danube", and as they stopped and we did too a slender, blond man, very tall, approached and spoke a burst of Italian words to Prince Colonna. Scowling just a little, Colonna introduced us. This stranger with the figure and the features of a matinee idol was Prince Altieri, and he quickly asked me for a dance. That was how it all began.

I told him he ought to learn to speak some English. He spoke enough, it turned out, to ask my father if he might call. He called twice before he said he would like to have us meet his mother. She came for luncheon, simply dressed in black with real lace cuffs and collar.

At that time I began each day by opening up an enormous box of fragrant flowers that came from Altieri.

His mother invited us to dinner at their palace. Suite after suite was closed and dusty and other parts of the great structure were rented out; but what the Prince and his mother still inhabited was something to make you gasp with pleasure. There was one intoxicating room with double walls of marble. The whole place was made to glow by hidden lights as soft as if their power plant was made of fireflies. The translucence of that room was as deeply stirring as a moonlight night; its furnishings were old. Right in there, with my parents and his mother looking on, Prince Altieri revealed to me the eight or ten new words of crippled English that he had captured that day.

There were more flowers, and entertainments in my honor until there was not a Roman unaware of Altieri's plan to make me a princess.

One day Prince Altieri led me up to the gates of the Vatican gardens. There could not be many who had keys to open up those gates, but he had one. I was impressed all right, and then as he bowed me in he said, quite prettily, that Eve had now come back to Eden.

But really, Altieri had me miscast; not Eve was with him there in Rome but little Eva, hunting heaven high and low. . . .

And that recalls to me just how I felt the day I met the Pope. Yet what I felt was nothing to compare with the way my apostate father felt. Mother had, by then, moved from New Thought into Christian Science. My father, so I understand, had gone as far as one may go in Freemasonry. I, of course, am just a heathen.

I had been told to dress in black and not show flesh from toe to chin. I wore black gloves, and over my head was thrown a black lace veil. That all was fine, because

I loved black.

I much admired the Swiss guards whose sentry posts we crossed as we walked into the Vatican; but they shrank to nothing when we stood before a certain man who ranked high in the Roman Catholic Church. My recollection is a blend of the man himself and a portrait I once saw of Edwin Booth dressed up in scarlet and ermine as Richelieu; but I am quite certain he was beautiful—glossy black hair and liquid brown eyes. The man was Cardinal Merry del Val. Around his neck was hung a chain of heavy gold, helped by precious stones to support the cross of gold upon his breast. I was absolutely breathless. The voice with which he traded kindly words with Father was richly cultured. I looked at him, and thought to myself it was high time I turned Catholic.

An usher in a sombre suit of plain black satin led us down a long corridor, and presently we were in an ordinary room, where stood a man quite thin and wraithlike. . . . He was as simple as the Cardinal was grand. This was Pope Pius. His robe and cape were white, and his gold cross was rather small, as if he might have had it throughout his priesthood. I knelt as I had been told to do, and tried to kiss the big ring on his finger-but found that it was being made to evade my lips. It was the same with Mother. My father though, was allowed to kiss the ring. Through an interpreter we conversed of our stay in Rome. When we were leaving, the Pope gave his hand to Father, who swiftly dropped to his knees and received a blessing. But Mother and I were not so lucky. The Pope just shook our hands and withheld the gesture that had been such a comfort to my father. (He talked about it afterward, for days. He was tethered to the Church by bonds fixed on him in his childhood.)

I won't pretend I did not like the talk about my supposed romance. There was a fancy dress affair one night at some old palace. Mrs. Craig Biddle of Philadelphia was there, and I found her raillery about the Prince quite satisfying to my ego. She wore her hair back in a great big knot and for all her plumpness she was pretty. Craig Biddle was a man to make one see that all the foreign glitter of an Altieri would surely leave one lonesome and unhappy in the end. Biddle was handsome, and he was American. Two or three things brought me to my senses, but in Rome the case of Altieri and Miss Walsh continued to be meat for gossip.

Waldo Story gave some marvelous parties in a fascinating studio, and pushed against the walls were the stone and plaster heads and bodies that he had sculptured there. He himself was rated "fast" in Rome, but what he said to me was: "Evalyn, don't you be rushed off your feet by titled glamour. You are too damned nice. Think about it twice."

That day a letter had arrived from Brother Vin, addressed to Mother. She read this aloud.

Don't let Sis have anything to do with the prince. I am afraid from your letters that you have been blinded by the thought of a title and are thinking about the high position it would give you rather than of sister's happiness and if you have not yet influenced her one way or the other start right in and get the idea of marrying that dago right out of her head. I am so glad darling papa is getting better and tell him that I am trying every way to build myself into a strong man so I can help him later on.

I told old Waldo Story about Vin's letter and some of my other thoughts upon the subject of international marriage.

"Not for me," I said. "I've seen too many half-frightened women over here who used to be Americans."

"You are right," said Story.

"However," I went on, "I've got a plan to get from Father an automobile that I want right now a lot more than I want any man to be my husband. Actually, I am dying for a Mercedes."

A few nights later Father was giving a great big dinner — and everybody supposed this was to be the occasion of an announcement. The Prince's mother was there, seated at the right of Father. She wore an Altieri heirloom. It was a necklace of diamonds as large as hickory nuts, but those were merely satellites of the orb that hung below the cleft of her bosom. That stone was as large as a golf ball. The jewels needed scrubbing, and thinking how I'd like to wear them, cleaned, I almost wavered. However, I just winked at Father — for we had had a talk.

It had taken place that afternoon, while he was standing at a window of our suite looking into the street through which flowed the old, old river of Roman life. There were, as usual, swarms of loathsome, ragged beggars; plumed and booted officers were strutting in that throng, and now and then he saw a pimpled conscript; there were women with baskets balanced on their heads, their figures showing them to be enceinte; there were priests.

When Father spoke he said: "See how cruelly these people load their donkeys."

A minute later he asked the question that was in his mind, putting it to me point blank: "Daughter, are you going to marry this prince?"

I knew he did not want me to, and just to tease I asked, "How much money does he want?"

Father said, "He hasn't asked for any — yet."

(Mother was not in on this at all. I never did confide in Mother.)

"Look here," said Father, as if suddenly determined to wind the matter up. "There is going to be a lot of pressure put upon me! Didn't Fanny Reed take money for helping on the wedding of Anna Gould with Count Boni de Castellane? I'd spend a million twice a day to buy happiness, but I just can't believe you'd get it. What do you say?"

Poor Father! He was weighing in his mind the relative disadvantages of an Italian prince in search of dowry and Ned McLean.

"I'll tell you what, my papa," I said. "I'd rather have a red Mercedes any day than Altieri. If you will telegraph to Livy Beeckman up in Paris he'll buy and ship the car for us."

R. Livingston Beeckman had become one of our friends. Afterward he was Governor of Rhode Island; then, he was a charming companion who made all acts of living part of his fine art.

"Sure you don't want this prince?" persisted Father.

"Cross my heart! I'd far rather have the car. And we can start right off for Venice."

"It's a go," said Father.

We left, as I recall it, a few days after the dinner, and I avoided any farewell with Altieri. I had no intention of keeping that affair aboiling as Katherine Elkins later did with the King of Italy's cousin, the Duke of the Abruzzi. As a matter of fact I was sick and tired of a certain prince.

We reached Venice about noon and Maggie Buggy unpacked everything. Father and Mother went out. Our sitting room overlooked the Grand Canal, and I was looking down upon its unclean water when among the sharp-prowed boats I spotted a gondola in which the single passenger was, of all people, Prince Altieri. He stepped ashore at a place which was practically in our hotel.

I let out a roar at Maggie to declare that I was out. Then I jumped into bed.

I absolutely refused to speak with him for two days. He saw Father first, and introduced to him a red-haired lady—who promptly started in to flatter that old miner, Thomas Walsh. Well, he had dug gold long years before she began; but she was, in her way, more expert. In no time Mother had her hands full, and Altieri's flowers were delivered to me every morning in even bigger boxes than he had sent in Rome.

"Now you look here," I said to Father late one night, "you'll get yourself in trouble if you don't watch out."

"Why, what do you mean?" He looked completely guilty.

"I mean that red-haired hussy; that's what I mean."

Well, we both agreed it was time we ducked away from Venice. I was entirely cured of all romantic notions about a titled marriage.

And now Mrs. John W. Mackay was in Paris with her grandson, that pale dark Prince Colonna who first had introduced me to Altieri back in Rome. The old lady was then a great figure in society, especially in London. She had known my parents for several years.

"Tom," she said to Father, "you want to give this girl an education, and Monte Carlo is a proper place for her to begin. I'm going down. Let me take her along. I'll take my grandson and be their chaperon."

As we motored south through France Colonna seemed to think his place in life was just to make me forget all about Altieri. He was half-American, he would remind me; but I could see that the other half was pretty much like Altieri.

Mrs. Mackay stayed in bed all morning. She was made of rolls of fat, but when she stepped forth to begin her day she was beautifully made up. With that dark red wig she wore, and with a veil, she kept herself looking pretty smart. Right after luncheon she would go to the Casino and play until she had lost a certain sum; if she was winning, of course, she hated stopping. In the evening after dinner she would waddle back and lose or win some more.

Once I chided her: "You always lose."

"Oh, no, " she said, "I spend money for certain wares you do not see. I am buying excitement with my money when I gamble. That makes my blood course faster, and that itself is better for me than if I constantly gave doctors great big fees to tell me what was wrong with me."

My own excitement was feverish. Father and Mother had come to Monte Carlo and as he, too, came to gamble, I was free to ride around in my red Mercedes, escorted by Colonna and chaperoned by Maggie. That was fun; but I had twice the fun when Altieri appeared on the scene. Almost at once those two princes began to squawl and bicker over me. I am not vain enough to think it was entirely me they quarreled about. There were stunning beauties on the Riviera, lovely creatures who tempted by design. But even so, I can see even more clearly now than then that in pursuing me those two were doing, in their Continental way, what Tom Walsh had done when he went prospecting for gold. Indeed, Altieri said one day that Colonna had, in effect, jumped his claim. Those were not his words, but that was his meaning. The three of us were having lunch at Cannes, and suddenly Colonna's pale face turned purple at something Altieri said in Italian. He halfrose from his chair, and snatching up a wineglass threw its contents in the other man's face. Altieri was no coward and I, who thought this all quite comic, do not know how they ironed it out.

A few nights later Colonna was sitting in our suite. Generally the half of him that was American was uppermost in what he said and did. Maggie had gone to bed and in the adjoining room my mother was in hers, reading. I have forgotten where we had been, but I do remember that in those days it was considered hardly proper to leave two young people by themselves. In Europe the rules were strict, and a girl was constantly being warned by her elders to give no cause for talk.

All of a sudden there came a knock on the door and I heard Altieri say, just like the Wolf, "Can I come in?"

I don't know what evil spirit prompted me, but I whispered to Colonna, "Get in there, quick" — and pushed him into the worst of all hiding places, my bedroom.

"What are you doing here all alone?" asked Altieri.

"Just thinking," I said.

Well, then he acted as if we were engaged or married. He was raging as he pointed a trembling finger at a hall bench and said, "You are thinking in the company of someone who wears a hat and coat."

"What of that?" I told Colonna to come on out, and then I crossed the floor with the stride of Duse and opened Mother's door and spoke to her.

She answered, Yes, darling girl?

I looked at those two young men and knew, inside, that I was wishing I was home in America.

"Get out!"

And they went.

The truth is, I suppose, it was my own fault; but I will not take the blame for a mediæval kind of thinking that justifies the men of European nations in supposing that a girl is the reverse of good if she's not watched from hour to hour.

We Walshes went to Biarritz and Prince Colonna came tagging along. (I don't know where Altieri went.) Then Colonna began to get excited telegrams from his grandmother. She said his mother was ill and needed him. Mrs. Mackay wired my father please to send the young man home, and Father told me to start Colonna going. I had lost all interest in princes of whatever kind. Everything they did and said made me know that I would be awfully lonesome with any one of them.

We had a farewell luncheon at the Casino. Maggie sat near by to keep our little party regular. I told Colonna to be on his way before his grandmamma sent gendarmes after him. He grew perfervid then, and once or twice Maggie Buggy snickered. (When we were by ourselves we used to mock the manners of the Princes.) Then he said good-bye, and started off.

It was raining, and I decided to send Maggie after some money, as I wanted to play roulette.

She went into the adjoining chamber and there was the little Prince, still hanging around. Maggie laughed at him. Well, the American part of him disappeared and his rage was all Italian. He rushed at Maggie and jumped with both his feet, hard, on her corns. She shrieked so loud that I came out to see who was being murdered. Next day my father escorted the young man to a train and put him on it.

When we got back to Paris, at the Ritz, he came to call—but I was entirely out of patience by then. Father talked with me from time to time, and although he rarely interfered I could see that he was relieved that I had decided I did not want a title.

"The way I see it," he once said to me, "these foreign marriages do not work because the man and woman have such different points of view. But don't you forget this: the greatest luxury that I can buy myself is the knowledge that I have secured for you and Vincent corridors of security extending far into the future beyond the time when I can be here as your shield."

CHAPTER XI

A Tollgate on Our Road

WASHINGTON, D. C., was a little town, comparatively, in 1905. My brother Vin and Ned McLean were far from liking one another. If they saw each other, driving, that was excuse for a hard, fast race with motorcars. Vin had become a first-rate driver, and he had lots of nerve. Quite frequently he was pursued by some policeman on a bicycle. It seems to me his favorite car that year was a Pope Toledo; he had one that could be changed in something shorter than a jiffy from a roadster with bucket seats into a sedate family car with a large tonneau.

One day he and Monroe were gasping in the garage yard at 2020 after making such a change, when a cop rode up and coyly fluttered his fingers at a kitchen maid, who beckoned him to enter. He was streaming perspiration, and pleaded for a drink of something cold. (He had been there before.) Suddenly he looked into the yard and saw Vin and Monroe beside the car, half-overcome from their exertions in disguising it.

He gaped, then stammered, as he perked his finger toward a bent fender: "I'd swear this was the car that I been chasing two miles or more, except that one I chased had some other kind of hind end." He scratched his head, replaced his helmet, and with his hand squeezed from his thick mustache whatever fluid it was our maid had given him to drink. When he had departed on his large-sprocketed bicycle. Vin and Monroe hugged and punched each other just like two maniacs. It was more fun, they said, then they had ever had. Vin was seventeen then.

The year before, in Colorado, he had shot a bear. Its skin became a rug of which Father was mighty proud, although ordinarily he was opposed to killing animals or birds. Anything that Vinson did, or I, was apt to seem all right to our indulgent father.

Father was proud, too, when Vin, after playing hookey about half the time at the Washington School, had settled down at Pottstown to make a fair record at Hill. Up there his ambition was to become a member of the staff of the *Dial* the school paper. To win he had to get some paid advertisements, and Father wrote a lot of letters to New York tailors, to George Boldt of the Waldorf, and to others who had enjoyed his patronage. He invited them to come across, each one, with $30 for a page in the *Dial.* Not one refused, and Father was delighted.

My red Mercedes was something that made Vin whistle with astonishment and joy. With goggles on, just like a racing driver, he was bound he would make that car deliver all the speed there was in it. While we had been in Rome, I now gather, he had done some speeding in his own car.

I found a letter in Dad's papers dated January 28, 1905, and sent from Sligo, Maryland, by the keeper of the tollgate there. In a scrawly hand the man had written Vinson demanding sixty cents for toll fees. That ancient letter now reads like a threat: —

You went North through Toll Gate No. 1 at Sligo at half past three o'clock A.M. at not less than thirty miles an hour. The Maryland law says you must not go more than six through any village and I taken your number as you passed me when I haled you to stop and pay toll.

There were other unheard voices hailing us to stop and pay our toll just then.

We worried about the ones we loved more than we did about ourselves. Father used to say to Vin, "Now, son, don't go so fast you can't see where you're going." He took pride, though, in the fact that his son was such a skillful automobilist. As for me, I was astonished, every time I looked at him, to see how little Vin was growing into a tall, good-looking youth who was sure to have a welcome in society. Yet it had been no more than the year before that the two of us at 2020 had slit a small hole in a painted canvas screen that covered a gap above the dining room wall. (The actual wall itself was not carried to the ceiling, so that the musicians could be heard from their platform on the other side. This was a part of the landing of the staircase in the reception hall. That night Secretary William Howard Taft, Archie Butt, the White House military aide, and nearly forty other friends of Father's were dining. We watched them drink champagne awhile, and then took turns poking a bean shooter through the slit. I myself blew the bean that made Archie Butt get up from the table and start on a search for the culprits.) However, we were much more circumspect by the summer of 1905, when we went to Newport.

Newport society was kind to us that summer. Mother had talked with Father about a party they were to give at 2020 in the winter season, to present me formally to all their friends. I was not pleased indeed, I was fearful of such an ordeal as a debut. But at Newport I lived through, and to some extent enjoyed, a tea that was given in my honor by Mrs. James L. Kernochan. Born Eloise Stevenson, she had become a celebrated cross-country rider, a woman who knew dogs and horses as well as she knew all angles of society. Three years before while following hounds she had fallen so hard that she was forced to give up riding. The next year her husband died. This charming young widow was our great friend and counselor at Newport. She was living there as the guest of her mother-in-law, Mrs. James P. Kernochan.

Father decided we needed a big place in order to entertain. Just south of Mrs. O. H. P. Belmont's marble home on Bellevue Avenue is "Beaulieu", of brick and brownstone. The house was built in 1862 by a Peruvian named Frederic Barreda, reputed to have made his money out of guano. When he lost it his niece, Maria de Barril, went to New York and for years thereafter made a living acting as a social guide. Eventually that house became the property of William Waldorf Astor. The place was spoken of as "hoodooed." Before she became our friend, Mrs. Potter Palmer had lived there for two brilliant seasons. It was in that house, in 1899, that her niece, Julia Grant, was married to the Russian Prince, Mickel Cantacuzéne. Next, it had been leased for a term of years by Cornelius Vanderbilt (not the young fellow—his father) and Father rented it from him. I never had more fun that I did those months at Newport.

On a day in August,—the nineteenth,—Vinson and I went to the Clambake Club to a luncheon given by Mrs. Clement Moore. We had gone in my Mercedes, driven by Emile Devoust, our imported chauffeur; but when we were leaving, about four in the afternoon, Vinson wanted to drive.

Mrs. Kernochan, Herbert Pell Jr., and Harry Oelrichs rode with us. Devoust sat on the step in front. Vinson drove us swiftly past the other automobiles and turnouts getting away from Mrs. Moore's. We climbed the grade behind the beach, then started down Honeyman's Hill. We were going fast when I heard something like a pistol shot and the Mercedes began to sway and pitch. A rear tire had blown out. One of us screamed, and in that second we struck the flooring of a bridge that carries the road over a creek. I heard the chilling sound of splintering wood, and then our car bounced through the rail and threw me into a dreadful darkness. My face was pressed into mud and water; I could, with tremendous effort, bend my neck. I tried to think, but each thought was engulfed by waves of pain. I spent many, many years in that position with something like a painter's torch cooking all my nerves. I remember hearing my own groans and those of others,then a voice of some man saying, "God! She's under the car."

I know the car was levered up with fence rails and that I was pulled out; that was agony. A doctor gave me something from a glass and said, "Lie still; your leg is broken." I struggled against his hand and over and over cried out, "Where is Brother?" Some gentlehearted liar said, "He's all right." I was ghastly cold from pain and creek water, but my brain kept turning out a relentless logic: if my brother were all right, he would be with his sister. I tried again to rise. Everything seemed to happen with an incomprehensible slowness. I saw Alfred G. Vanderbilt bending over the creek bank. I called for Vinson and someone said he was hurt a little. Actually, right then his mind was blank and he was dying. Eloise Kernochan, one hand to disordered hair and with her summer frock all torn and stained with mud and blood, was being helped into a trap. I saw the docked tail of a horse switching nervously and the lines that held the animal were clenched in the hands of young Pauline French. I promised someone not to scream if they would show me Vinson. His hurts, I heard, were being dressed.

That was a time when an automobile driver occasionally was impaled on a steering post. As two policemen put me on a stretcher, I demanded that I be carried past the broken Mercedes to a place where I could see the steering wheel. It was not broken, but slanting through that car from end to end, just like a monstrous spear, was a heavy, wooden timber, the railing of the bridge. It seems to me that

Blanche Oelrichs, Harry's sister, and their mother, had come upon the scene. Then Fifi Potter Stillman leaned down, and I breathed her fragrance as she touched me softly on the face. I shivered, and she took off a lovely coat of Irish lace and placed it over me. I have loved her for that action ever since. As the police ambulance started rolling behind its trotting horses, I begged the policemen to squeeze my wrists—for the sake of that same mercy we give a horse by putting a twitch upon its lip to distract it from some other pain.

I kept conscious until I saw my mother. I tried to tell her Vinson was in better condition than I was but had been taken to the hospital. I did not know it then, of course, but he died about the time I was placed in the ambulance. The fact of his death was kept from me. On the day of the funeral my father and mother came into my room in ordinary clothes, forcing themselves to be sweetly cheerful, and then, out of my sight, put on their black. I finally learned that Vin was dead through a letter of condolence sent to me. Mother had read aloud from it just a line or two, that expressed hope for my complete recovery. She was called away and put the letter on the table. I asked a nurse to hand it to me. She did, and I read a phrase that spoke of our great affliction in the loss of one so young. Well, after that my mind was vague for weeks and weeks. They gave me morphine whenever I had need of it.

The house we had leased from the Vanderbilts was closed and we left Newport, going to the Garden City Hotel, on Long Island. I was in a cast and made the trip in a lonor deep basket. Katherine Elkins came and was a comfort to us then.

I suffered the tortures of the damned before that injury was healed. Even now that wretched part of me, my crippled leg, knows how to give its owner fits.

Because the great big house at 2020 Massachusetts Avenue was filled with souvenirs of Vinson that, it was feared, would keep us weeping, Father took a floor in the old Shoreham Hotel when we returned to Washington. I was in such agony there that I could not sleep. I had a graphophone beside my bed, and it was kept playing, generally, all night long, and much of the day. Every pulsation of my heart gave me fresh aches as blood was forced through clogged-up channels. They gave me more and more morphine until I was receiving ten grains a day, and even then my pain would prowl about my system until it found a nerve not quite dead to gnaw on.

Two months later my right leg, as I stood upon my leg, swung inches from the floor. It was limp. When I tried to rest my weight upon it, I screamed so loud I think I could have been heard a half -mile away. There is no use now to blame the doctors who had bungled. I had no need of X-rays to tell me that two broken ends of bone were unmatched in my thigh.

I had one friend just then who was especially sweet. That was Ned McLean. The gawky youth had become a mustached man. He found that new records for the graphophone gave me just about my only pleasure. He would bring up all the new ones he could buy.

One day there was a great argument between my parents, Mother said, "Which would you rather have her do: lose her life or lose her leg?"

Father said, "The girl herself should make this decision."

I told Ned about that dilemma and he dashed off, half-frenzied, to get his father. Old John R. McLean was the oddest hybrid of gentle friend and fierce monster that I have ever known. In Washington he exercised a power almost like that of a political boss. Owning two newspapers, his most effective trick in life was to discover something compromising about a highly placed individual—and then not print what he had learned. He kept such secrets as loaded guns. In secret caches he had all sorts of facts. This strange man came to call on us, and out of his assorted knowledge produced a fact that saved my life.

"There is," he said, "a marvelous doctor at Johns Hopkins. He saved Ned's life when he had appendicitis. My brother-in-law, Admiral Dewey, swears by him. He'll make this right."

Confidence, to my way of thinking, generally is all the magic needed to work miracles. John R.'s faith decided us. So Dr. Finney came. John Miller Turpin Finney was about forty-two, and he had a skill that only now and then is given to a surgeon. He did not try to fool me for a second.

"You have an even chance of living if I operate."

"It is up to you, daughter," said Father, and caught his graying mustache in his teeth.

That was on a Tuesday. I said: "Friday is a lucky day for me. Let's make it Friday; but I want it done in Twenty-twenty." (I could not tell them that I simply did not want to die where I might become a young ghost doomed to haunt the old Shoreham's corridors.)

We moved back home on Thursday. I never shall forget that night. Little Annie slept with me during that period, and believing I was going to die in the morning I chattered on and on until the pink damask on my wall was taking on a glint from the rising sun.

Dr. Finney and his associates had decided to use my white tile bathroom as the operating chamber. It is about six times as large as any ordinary bathroom. I had refused, the night before, to see Ned or any of my callers. I was afraid my nerve might break.

Quite early, one of the doctors entered my bedroom and announced that they were ready.

"First," I said, "I am going in to see the knives and saws Dr. Finney's going to use." I walked in on my crutches and my excited chattering made white-smocked Dr. Finney so nervous he had to go outside.

Soon after that, they gave me an anesthetic and then Finney worked four solid hours. He cut out necrotic bone and riveted the semihealthy broken ends together with a fifteen-inch splint of silver plate. My thigh, of course, was opened wide—as one might split a mackerel—to give the doctor room to do his cabinetmaking and silversmithing job.

When I woke up I was back in bed. The crippled leg, fixed in a cast, was held up on a scaffolding by ropes, counterweights and pulleys, so that it pointed at the ceiling. I remained that way for five months; and while they had me flat on my back the new doctors set to work to cure me of my worst affliction: I had become a morphine addict.

"Dope fiend." I was shocked to realize it, but even that could not keep me quiet when I wanted to be drugged. I was pretty well spoiled anyway (I make no secret of it), and those doctors had a time with me. One day, regardless of that cast and harness and the delicate structure of silver and half-made bone, I tried in madness to fling myself out of the bed. (I never read about those poor devils who get in trouble through robberies or other violences designed to gain for them the drug they crave without a throb of pity. I know that aching hunger. I know how cunningly it magnifies the slightest twitching of a nerve into a pounding, crushing, all-pervading sense of pain.)

There was one night when Dr. Jim Mitchell and Dr. Briggs stayed in my room until four o'clock in the morning.

I have forgotten what I said or did; but I remember hearing Jim Mitchell, his jaw stuck out, say to me: "Yell your head off if you like; but you won't get it."

I hated him so much I could have killed him if I had held a gun in my twitching hands.

Once when Father sat beside my bed in 2020 and held my hand I said, "What a price I'm paying just because I find myself alive."

"I cannot bear to see you suffer," he said, "and I'd do anything to spare you. Why, do you know that if I could have our boy alive again and you well and whole I'd undertake to spend eternity restoring to that Colorado mountain every bit of gold and rock. I'd wad the tunnels of the Camp Bird mine until the place was just as we found it that day that you and I . . ."

He stopped talking then, and tried with a smoothing gesture of his hands to straighten out a grief-contorted, ageing face. That made me ashamed, I suppose, of the way I had carried on. Until then he had hardly mentioned in my presence the load of sorrow that he bore.

I buckled down from that day on. I listened carefully to the advice the doctors gave me. As best I could, I cooperated; and finally, except for a haunted place deep in my mind, I had smothered my fantastic craving.

A letter I found stored away among old papers recalls the date I was released from the thralldom of the cast. It was March 20, 1906. Vinson had been dead for seven months.

This letter was one that Father wrote to Grandma Reed: —

Dear Nannie:
Well, our darling had the cast removed for good two days ago and everything was found in fine shape; a positive union of the break. She is able to move the limb from the hip in all directions. To make assurance doubly sure she will rest for 8 days more so as to give the

bone time to harden. Then we look for the dear child to get around very quickly. The limbs are practically the same length. We are accordingly happy or as happy as we can ever be again.

Then he spoke of what we had been through as the "long, dark night."

One late spring afternoon when birds were chirping in the grass beside the house Dr. Finney came. I had been rolled into a sitting room, and sat there talking with my mother and little Annie.

"I want to see you take a step," he said.

I had become completely invalid from months of lying down, and so they had to lift me as they would a flabby baby until I was erect and found myself looking down from what seemed a terrific height at a threatening floor that reeled and pitched like a ship's deck in a storm. With an effort I stiffened my good leg until I was balanced on it. Then I put my other foot a stride forward on the rug, free from pain, felt it bear my weight. Dr. Finney has had one of the finest surgical careers, but I'll wager that never has any patient felt more gratitude than I felt at that moment, when I knew for sure that he had given back to me my life and my leg. It surely would be ungracious of me to mutter, now, that I had lost an inch and a half from that leg and that, ever since, I have had to have a support built in my shoes to compensate for the shortness. Wearing such a device, unless I'm tired I walk without betraying lameness. I marvel at Finney's skill. What he performed on me was very like a miracle.

My seven months of invalidism had left the back of my head as smooth and yellow as a duck's egg. My appearance has always been a matter of supreme importance to my ego. I love to nest my body in soft and frilly things. I like (and who does not?) to be admired when I am seen. So it was most disturbing—after seasons spent in fashionable company in Washington, Paris, Rome, and Newport —to be going back to Colorado to see the home folks, looking, from the rear, a fright.

We went back to Colorado that summer because of a real ache in us to breathe mountain air, hear Western intonations, and mingle with old friends. As a flavoring among our reasons was the fact that certain Republicans had suggested to my father that he might appropriately consider himself as a possible United States Senator from Colorado. They thought he ought to run, they said; while they spoke as friends, I am inclined to think they were not unmindful of what was called his "barrel." My mother was disposed to agree, I think, because she knew that politics, or something like it, was saner filling for his mind than what was there incessantly—dreary thoughts of his dead boy and of the feebleness of money in any contest with Fate.

Once, in a family council, someone said that by going home to Colorado we might change our luck.

We moved to Wolhurst, an estate near Denver that my father had leased. Later in that year records seem to indicate he bought it for $150,000. The place had been a part of the estate of Senator Edward O. Wolcott. There were five hundred acres, numerous buildings, stables, a fine house, well-made roads and extensive gardens. I was less in love with Wolhurst than Mother was. I have always liked the excitements of city streets, of throngs, as Father did. At Wolhurst my great problem was my half-bald skull, especially when soon after we arrived I was invited to be one of the guests of honor at a Denver Country Club dinner dance.

The other ladies wore elaborate evening gowns, cut low, and there were lots of jewels flashing. When I entered they all looked at me and in their shock revealed surprise. Not knowing I was nearly hairless, they did not understand what strange new fashion notion made me wear a simple, high-necked gown and a close-fitting lingerie hat.

They talked so much—gossiped, really—that the fact was commented on in the Denver Post, which said:

Miss Walsh's costume though simple was striking, and the fact that she has been welcomed to Westchester, Burlingame, Renlay and Nieuller clubs was quite convincing that she was about correct; at least the number of wash dresses and lingerie hats which have since been worn to the club indicate that the "thirty" have since arrived at that conclusion.

Such things were exciting, but right on top of that we had another scare.

Almost the day we arrived in Colorado, Father had started out from Colorado Springs aboard a special train to Hartsel, a new mining camp where dry placer gold mining fields had been discovered. The craze for finding gold or silver in the earth was still a part of him. John W. Benson went with him, and they spent half a day trying to guess how much gold was hidden in old river gravels there. The special had traveled a mile on the homeward journey when it collided with a freight train. My father, seated in about the middle of a railroad coach, was flung into the aisle by the crashing stop. His face was deeply cut below his eye; a jaw was badly bruised, and he was terribly shaken up. John Benson, thrown backward with great force, lost consciousness but was not badly hurt. The freight's fireman was killed; the engineer was terribly injured. For many days Father was unstrung, although he protested he had not been hurt.

I am superstitious. I had a notion he was courting trouble every time he went afield for gold; yet he kept on going, as if he were bewitched. The least little rumor of some fresh strike could always catch his close attention.

"I never expect to find another Camp Bird mine," he said. Nevertheless, he had put some money then into a syndicate that was hopeful of finding gold in Siberia. William Randolph Hearst was likewise in that syndicate. Father had other gold properties in British Columbia, and was buying machinery for them that summer in Denver. He was also full of plans, which he talked over with John Benson, about a careful exploration of his other claims in and around Ouray. Much of his correspondence dealt with mines, claims, exploration syndicates—until one might have supposed that all he thought about was cashing in on vaster riches than those he already had. But that would not have been fair to him. Mother and I knew that what he wanted was some anodyne to ease his pain of mind. That is why we entertained so much that year.

One of the first affairs we gave at Wolhurst was a luncheon to the leading Republicans of Arapahoe County. It was only one of the signs that if the Legislature and the people of the State should insist upon it Father would not refuse to go to the Senate. There were a half-dozen candidates, but Simon Guggenheim, who was called "the smelter king" in Colorado, was out in front. As I look back now it seems to me that Father was trying to make the Guggenheim campaign something less of a sure thing. I don't pretend to know the inside of that struggle, but I do know that Father let it be known he was not trying. Nevertheless, he talked like a candidate. Some months later Colorado's junior Senator was elected by the Legislature. They chose Simon Guggenheim. However, Tom Walsh had almost stopped the smelter king by speaking out in such a way that what he advocated for the masses was headlined by the Denver *Post* as "modified socialism."

Mind you, what Tom Walsh said was said in 1906; and yet to me it sounds much like the prophetic words I hear almost any time I turn on a radio.

We find men with such accumulated wealth that they are puzzled to know to what use to put it. We find men so rich that they are unable to give anything like an approximate estimate of their wealth. Accumulated and concentrated wealth, both corporate and individual, is crushing from the masses the life of individual ownership, individual independence and, almost, individual existence. A simple and practical example is the department store, where is concentrated under a single roof every human product. They stand as terrible monuments to the thousands of commercial lives that they have crushed out.

A continuance of these monopolistic conditions means that all the commercial wealth of our country will be concentrated in a few hands, and the masses of the people left without an atom of ownership.

We should establish a new basis for compensating the masses.

CHAPTER XII

Romance in Washington

I WAS the only living human who ever exercised control over Ned McLean. Certainly he never ruled himself. His father was limp and spineless where his only son was concerned. He loved Ned as much as he was capable of loving anything other than John R. McLean. His mother, Emily Beale McLean, was the leader of Washington society, but she never was able to give her son any of that courage with which the Beales were so richly endowed; all Ned received of that part of his heritage was recklessness in dissipation.

In a measure I seemed able to strengthen Ned. From my childhood I was greatly attached to his mother and liked to please her. Whenever she saw me she would embrace me and say, warmly, "Here is my girl." I think that sympathy between us, between an older woman and a young girl, influenced me to try to make Ned behave himself. However, during my illness after the automobile accident he drank so much that he was on the verge of seeing things. We had broken our engagement over and over, but when he was in such a state of nerves from drinking that he had to make a handkerchief sling to steady the hand with which he lifted his glass I had sense enough—for a little while—to stop even associating with him. I broke with him absolutely in 1907, and did not speak to him for many months. During the following year I was repeatedly half-engaged to several men. There was Bradish Johnson; I thought he was too old, but liked him enormously. I gave a picnic once on Pike's Peak for Viscount de Chambrun and was, for a little, quite wild about him. Just to be a French countess? Oh, no, indeed; because I liked Charley. We broke off in London in a cab. Then there was another man I thought I might marry.

First, however, I ought to tell about the ruptured romance of Katherine Elkins and the Duke of the Abruzzi. As I recall it, they met in 1907, when Prince Luigi Amedeo of Savoy-Aosta, Duke of the Abruzzi, arrived in America in command of a squadron of Italian warships. He was the sort of man to make any woman lose her reason and become a creature ruled entirely by emotion. It was not simply titled glamour that made Kitty Elkins look at him, and look again, and listen when he talked. Here was no ordinary, swarthy, foppish Italian nobleman; this was a man who seemed to be the essence of nobility. He was tall. The brown of his eyes was set in rings that were as white as marble. His skin was richly olive from the tanning of mountain sunlight as well as from the open sea. His nose was a proper feature for a man born to speak commands. His full lips were just the kind that invited women to be fools and they were modeled on a line as straight as a needle.

He was every inch a man. Besides all this, there were his uniforms of blue cloth glinting with gold stars.

When Katherine met him he was thirty-four and she was, my guess is, twenty-one. She was long of limb, erect, the very model of that American fineness Charles Dana Gibson tried to capture in his drawings. She had great pride, and warmth equally great for those she liked. The faintest glow of interest in her eyes would have been quite enough, it seems to me, to make the wandering Prince her slave, even if old Senator Stephen B. Elkins had not owned railroads and coal mines in West Virginia.

Wrapped up inside the two of them there was a concert of the voices of all their ancestors shouting. That is the thing we call instinct. It seems to me that even the least of the human race is touched with genius when mad with love. Katherine was my close friend. I saw her eyes and said straight out, "If I were you I'd take him on any terms, with royal marriage or without." I saw them almost day by day, watching what flickered in their eyes while the families were bartering. His royal relatives were divided; this man stood in line for the throne of Italy and his life was much less his own than, for example, mine was. Yet, if it comes to that, we have at best but precious little weight in controlling circumstances that mold and shape our lives.

The Duke might have renounced his royal privileges, or, if Katherine had said "yes", he might have married her with, so to speak, his left hand. She thumbed her nose at that. John R. McLean told me that old Senator Elkins could have fixed it all on a regular basis if he had been willing to pay $2,000,000. The newspapers were at that time more excited about the romance of Katherine and the Duke than about almost anything else. Why, I remember that one night, when I was going to a small dinner party Katherine was giving for the Duke just before he was to return to Italy early in 1908, Mrs. John R. McLean called me on the telephone.

"Evalyn," she said, "everyone thinks Katherine is going to announce her engagement at this dinner party. Don't forget we own the *Washington Post* and the *Cincinnati Enquirer.* Such a scoop, my husband tells me, would be worth an extra. I want you to slip out as soon as you learn and telephone me."

I had been engaged so often to her Ned that I called her "Mummie", and I agreed to telephone. The dinner was beautifully arranged. Mathilde Townsend was there, and Martha Hitchburn. I wore a plain black velvet princesse dress. Abruzzi was completely charming that night, but there was no announcement and finally when I was sure there would be none I slipped upstairs and used the telephone.

When I told her, Mummie McLean said, "She's a fool."

The Duke sailed for home and Billy Hitt was sometimes seen out riding with Miss Katherine Elkins in her smart trap. Something of great importance in that affair for me started on a day at the Chevy Chase Country Club. Katherine Elkins was there with Marjorie Gould, who was her house guest; and I was there. Ned McLean was in our party; we were not speaking, but from time to time I caught him looking my way, wistfully, and when I so caught him I was looking wistful too, I suppose. Billy Hitt and Katherine had been spatting, with the result that Joe Leiter had taken this chance to give her a rush.

Joe was a great big fellow who quite perfectly matched in spirit the pretentiousness of Leiter Castle, his widowed mother's home at 1500 New Hampshire Avenue, on DuPont Circle. Levi Leiter left a lot of millions, made in partnership with Marshall Field. One of his daughters became Lady Curzon, wife of Lord Curzon of Kedleston, later Viceroy of India. (She had died two years before this day I speak of.) The Leiter girls were all Anglophiles: one was Countess of Suffolk and the third became Mrs. Colin Campbell. But Joe was a delightful companion. In 1898 he had tried to corner wheat, and with so many millions at his beck and call might have succeeded but for the stubborn fight of P. D. Armour, who turned ships around at Liverpool and broke the winter ice on the Great Lakes so he could deliver more wheat at Chicago than there were Leiter millions to pay for.

By the time of our party, Mrs. Leiter had become a horticulturist. She mixed some pollen and named the resulting blue verbena after Alice Roosevelt. Later on she brought about a yellow verbena that she called "Ethel Roosevelt." Still later, she produced a pink one that she named for Helen Taft. Besides these marriages fixed up among the flowers, Mrs. Leiter had a passion for society romances. (It was she who brought the Duc de Chaulnes and Marguerite Shonts together, so we all believed.) In the late spring of 1908 she was trying to help Billy Hitt win Katherine Elkins from the glamorous Duke of the Abruzzi. Mrs. Leiter's plan, no doubt, was highly patriotic, but her son Joe himself liked Katherine.

Suddenly, that day at Chevy Chase, I heard Katherine Elkins say to Leiter, "Joe, I'll never speak to you again until you apologize."

Joe and I left then, and went to "Cabin John's Bridge", a roadhouse.

"Evalyn," said Joe, and twirled the thin stem between fingers that were fat and somewhat hairy, "I'll bet you a thousand you can't split up Katherine Elkins and Billy Hitt."

My glass was tilted and in my nose constellations of champagne bubbles were exploding. I quickly swallowed.

"I'll take you, Joe. That's a bet." We shook hands, and then began to plan just how to start the ball rolling.

That same evening Katherine was giving a dinner party for Marjorie Gould. I suggested to Joe that he give a midnight party that would be our bait for Billy Hitt. I knew Billy only slightly, but I called up Fritzi Scheff, who was playing in Washington, and made a date for after midnight. Then I went home to dress for the Elkins dinner.

Joe Leiter, of course, did not attend Katherine's dinner, because of their row; but after midnight he was in rare form as a host at the Willard. Fritzi sang the best of her songs but when she sang Victor Herbert's "Kiss Me, Kiss Me Again", I felt somebody take my hand. That was Billy Hitt, who had been placed next to me by

Joe Leiter who wanted very much to lose his bet.

I feel older now by about a thousand years, and I have quite forgotten what tactics I employed to keep young Mr. Hitt attentive. At any rate, he came to lunch and came again. We had a lot of talks together concerning many things. We went for drives, and out to the races. I warned him: "Now, Billy, you must not talk to Katherine. I could not bear it." Then, when he said he would not, I collected my bet from Joe Leiter. By that time, though, I thought Mr. Hitt was what I really wanted. We were going West to spend the summer at Wolhurst, and Billy agreed to come too. (However, I am quite sure now that all the time he was mooning over Katherine.)

Then Ned McLean called up: —

"I hear you're going out to Colorado, and that Hitt is going too."

"We are leaving in two days, Saturday afternoon," I told him.

"Well, I want my letters back," he said in a sulky tone. "You send them."

"Like hell I will; you come and get your letters."

"Damned if I will!"

We were like that always; fighting when our hearts were half-sick with loneliness and love.

Mother and Daddy were having a big dinner that Thursday night for Mabel Boardman of the Red Cross. Our house was filled with guests and flowers and the music of a group of Italians perched in their place above the dining room, with their violins, their flutes, and a harp.

I was wearing a Worth gown of emerald green. Billy Hitt had gone to New York to see his mother off for Europe; I knew I was not wearing that costume for him. Ned was coming; Ned McLean. It is not thinking that goes on in a girl's mind when she keeps her attention fixed upon some young man. I answered vacantly when either of the two men who sat beside me at table spoke polite phrases against my ears. The musicians played some songs that made a wild mood of mine much more intense.

I ached with a strong wish that Ned McLean were more than rich and handsome, that he were noble in his manners and courageous in his soul.

We were moving from the table into our Louis XIV salon when a butler whispered to me that Mr. McLean was in the reception hall. Then I spoke pleasantly to Ned, just as though for months we had not been pretending we could not see each other. We went to the second floor in an elevator, and to my sitting room. When the door was closed Ned put aside his half frozen manner.

"It's no use pretending, Evalyn: Won't you marry me? Sure, I'll give up drinking. Please! We've always loved each other. You can't marry Hitt! When are you going to stop this?"

"When you stop drinking," I replied. I felt a thrill just then that was beyond all reason. I made myself believe I had the power to mold him into everything I wanted from the race of men. For the twentieth time, I made up my mind right there and then; but what I said to Ned that night was, "You will have to ask my father."

In half an hour he had gone home and I was left alone to think that he was only bluffing. He was so shy and he was so sure my parents would not stand for him that I was more than half-inclined to think he would never meet that simple test.

In the morning I told my father.

"There must be some good in the boy," said Father, "or you would be able to forget about him. This time, though, let's have no shilly-shallying about it. I don't want you like you were before—ready to marry him one day and vowing on the next that you would like to have him shot. Are you decided?"

It was about a quarter to two when Ned showed up at 2020. I kissed him and said, "Now you are in for it, because Papa's waiting for you."

My sweetheart said, "My knees are knocking. You know I love you, Evalyn, because I'd rather swallow poison than appear before your father. Well, maybe he won't shoot me."

Then Ned went in. They stayed and stayed. I saw the butler responding to my father's ring. Then the servant went upstairs and soon returned, preceding by a pace or two my mother, who was white-faced after a morning of trying to accept a situation that was hateful to her. Soon Mother left their conference and followed me to my sitting room. She was really brokenhearted, but she never said a word to show her state of mind. Then Father came out just ahead of Ned, who was smiling with a hangdog air.

"The boy and I," said Father, "have fixed it up. You will have an announcement of your engagement later, and after that be married. But just now he is going to follow us to Chicago and then go on to Colorado with us."

Ned then went out to see his family at Friendship and report what he had done. In a little while his mother called me and expressed complete satisfaction—"You and Tom and Carrie all come on out here."

The families drank a toast to us, and then there was a lot of speculation about our future. Ned and I left them together, and as we had done so many times as kids strolled down beyond the cabin, his playhouse, —where afterward my children played, —and stood beside the spring. We had not taken any champagne. We rather solemnly drank water. For at least an hour or two Ned had stopped drinking anything but water.

Ned McLean's enormous basket of orchids on the seat beside me as the train left Washington for the trip to Chicago reminded me of something—Billy Hitt! I sent him a telegram to let him know as tactfully as possible that he had best forget my invitation to come out to Wolhurst. I explained that I was engaged again—I am sure it must have been the fiftieth time to Ned.

Father was a delegate-at-large from Colorado to the Republican National Convention in Chicago, and he was enthusiastically committed to the candidacy of William Howard Taft. Ned was acting in the role of cub reporter, but he would not have recognized a piece of news—not even if the man who bit the dog likewise bit Ned McLean. He showed me some copy paper and some pencils in his pocket,

EDWARD BEALE MCLEAN

About 1908

but I guess he was less of a pest to the other reporters of the *Cincinnati Enquirer* and the *Washington Post,* because he was so much more concerned with me than with news.

It seems to me that Ned was staying at Joe Leiter's apartment in Chicago. We went to many parties, and there was one to which he was asked on my behalf by Alice Longworth.

Politics in those days meant less than nothing to me. It was something you played, as any other game, for excitement. (Perhaps that still is true.) Ned's work was justification for his trip to Colorado. He wore his pencil in his vest when we went on to Denver. The papers laughed at him in type that pointed out that he had arrived many days in advance of any other reporters to cover the Democratic Convention. Those days we spent delightfully. He dressed up in a cowboy suit— high-heeled boots, curly black-haired chaps, a wide, brass-studded belt, a holster with a forty-four, a red bandanna at his throat and on his slicked hair a large tan hat. I posed him on a keg and took his picture. I still was lame, and about half of each day I helped myself along on crutches.

An appropriate time was picked to announce my engagement to Ned: July Fourth. We celebrated with champagne and firecrackers, to the dismay of all the birds that Father's gentleness and no-shooting rules had induced to come there to roost. (One time at Wolhurst, I have discovered from his papers, Dad spent $700 just for birdseed. I know I am extravagant too but that seems to me to be a lot of birdseed.)

Louise and Crawford Hill were there that Fourth, and the news of our engagement was announced in Crawford's paper, the Denver *Republican,* under headlines which referred to Ned as "a Washington editor." The boy surely had a rise if this was true! In Chicago, he had modestly admitted in an interview that if he could hang on a while he might get to be a cub. Crawford, being fond of us, promoted Ned to be the *Washington Post's* managing editor. (After all, I suppose that sort of thing occurs right often.)

This fiancé of mine was not an editor nor was he a cub reporter. He was a rich man's son, twenty-two years old. He never had been other than rich—or else he might have been an editor. I have a photograph of Ned when he was eight or perhaps no more than seven. It shows him mounted on the tin seat of his goat buckboard. His team of goats had halted on the gravel of the Park across from the McLeans' I Street house. The button shoes he wore extended halfway to his knees. There were brass buttons on his coat, befitting a grandson of General Beale who helped to win California for the United States. A tiny, round cap is perched above a frowning little face. Three small girls in garments trimmed with fur were photographed with him that day, and I can imagine that the little boy they played with was a friendly little cuss. This picture has the power to give me an ache deep inside my heart. The gentle lad out driving his team of black-and-white goats was still peering out at me above the brown mustache my Ned wore on July 4, 1908.

A telegram from Ned's mother urged us to plan for a large wedding in the East;

she proposed that we have the ceremony performed at Bar Harbor. Ned seemed to shrivel in his clothes at that suggestion. My own preference, generally, is for show. I should have been quite willing, if anyone had proposed it, to be married while hanging by my knees from the crosspiece of the spire of any well-known church. If I had a dog, I wanted him to be a dog people turned to stare at; it was the same with any of my possessions, and with many of my acts. From that standpoint my engagement was a success. Messages of congratulation began to pour in on us. I heard from the three girls with whom I had been closely associated in Washington society: from Mathilde Townsend, Katherine Elkins, and Isobel May. Mathilde, just then, was planning to entertain the Duke of Alba at her mother's home in Bar Harbor. (She afterward married Peter Gerry, and is now Mrs. Sumner Welles.)

In their convention the Democrats nominated William Jennings Bryan. Alice and Nick Longworth had arrived for that affair and came to Wolhurst for luncheon. Before Alice had gone out to the Orient in a party headed by Secretary of War Taft, and on the trip fallen in love with Nick, one of her favorite beaux had been Ned McLean. She was sweet to us that day, but Ned was always grumpy where Alice was concerned.

"She is our loyal friend," he would say, "because we have two newspapers and one of them is in Cincinnati. If Cincinnati turns Nick down in some election she'll be exiled from Washington. With Nick it's different. You can count on Nick." Ned always was suspicious.

One afternoon in late July—it was the twenty-second—while we were driving miles from Denver in my car, attended by a chauffeur and Maggie Buggy, Ned said a reckless thing—"Let's get married." Precisely because it was a daring thought, I liked it. I agreed. Ned went into some store that had a telephone, to call up Crawford Hill. After just a little coaxing Crawford said he would fix everything and meet us, with a ring and a license, with Louise, his wife, and with Colonel Billy Stapleton, at St. Mark's Episcopal Church. So far as I was concerned it would have been all right if we had gone down the aisle to the altar of some Hindu temple. That day I was wearing a dress of white broadcloth and a high straw hat thickly feathered with snowy ostrich plumes. Ned was wearing a light gray serge suit and a cloth cap.

I remember kneeling in front of St. Mark's altar, with my eyes fixed on a golden cross made luminous by candlelight. I saw the scuffed shoes of the rector, Henry Foster, peering at me from the bottom of his hastily tossed-on cassock. I heard the words about as clearly as one detects the separate words uttered by a droning bee that hovers noisily above a flower. Yet, if anybody should believe that my harum-scarum qualities implied that I would be a harum-scarum wife, they are mistaken. The part of me that draws through Thomas Walsh the whole genius of the Irish race is fixed by instinct when a marriage vow is said. The scent of just about a peck of violets that Ned had bought for me escorted into my nostrils, into my brain and being, a strong desire to have this bond of marriage last forever. Kneeling there,

I recognized with gratitude that Ned loved me and cared but little for my father's money. Another girl in such a fix upon her knees would, I supposed, have prayed, but I was thinking that a few feet down beneath the church floor was Colorado earth, the generous earth that had opened to my father his great store of gold, and now, close to that earth, I was coming into something richer.

Crawford Hill gave me away in place of my father.

I remember kissing Ned, Louise, Crawford, and Billy Stapleton, and then a strong embrace from loving Maggie Buggy.

The next thing was our return to Wolhurst; as our car turned into the tree-bordered, gravel driveway I was aware of being grateful that Father was away in Kansas City. I could not bear to see his eyes when I must leave with Ned.

Mother was not pleased but she was pleasant. A society wedding would have been excuse for musicales, receptions, dinners, dances. However, she ordered a wedding feast and we sat down with several house guests. Ned and I drank water while the others gulped down champagne. Right after that we two excited people, Ned and I, were driven to the station and took a train for Colorado Springs. At the Antlers Hotel, where we had taken a suite, we found the restaurant closed; so we went out and in an all-night restaurant that advertised coffee and doughnuts for five cents we ate our real wedding supper: lamb chops and salad and ginger ale. We were not drinking stronger things. We stayed at the Springs about a week.

CHAPTER XIII

A Fantastic Honeymoon

A QUEER, queer fellow was this Ned McLean that I had married. The simplest way to make him comprehensible is to show that he was just about a dozen men packaged as one jealous husband. He was so changeable that at times I felt quite polyandrous. We spent some weeks at Bar Harbor with all four of our parents beaming on us. Then, so we could be alone, we went back to Washington and stayed at Friendship. Joe Leiter and his bride, the former Juliette Williams, were with us for a while. Finally, however, Ned and I decided that we would not have a honeymoon unless we went roaming over Europe. Our fathers matched each other in extravagance and gave us each $100,000.

"Now, children," Mother said, "be careful." My father grinned a bit and said, "Get yourself a wedding present if you see anything you like."

On that fantastic honeymoon I was attended by dear old Maggie Buggy, and we also had a chauffeur, Platt. On the way across Platt told us he thought we ought to have something besides our Packard down in the ship's hold. That car was yellow with red striping. It was a roadster, and in the rear there was a rumble. Its tires were about twice the size of garden hose. Platt, in a chauffeur's visored cap and fur-lined coat, seemed to suggest that the Packard would be about right for him and Maggie.

"I think we ought to have a Mercedes," I said to Ned.

The one we ordered sent from Paris on the day we landed in Holland was waiting for us on the dock at Amsterdam a few days later. It cost us 15,500 guilders, but I have forgotten how much money that was in those days. I had never seen a bigger car. It had two seats and all the rest was hooded engine. I swear it looks as big today—a kind of domestic locomotive. I have it still, in a barn at Friendship; I keep it as a souvenir of our honeymoon madness, just as another woman might keep a champagne cork or faded violets.

That pale yellow automobile on the dock at Amsterdam certainly looked like a wild contraption.

"Can you run that monster, Ned?"

For answer he just helped me to my seat, tucked me in, climbed in himself, and signaled Platt to crank it. Platt and Maggie were to follow in the Packard with most of our small luggage. Ned pressed the clutch and yanked a lever.

"Now," he said, "you're going to Berlin."

We started with such a mighty lunge that we were off the wharf before I had time to stiffen my neck and brace my legs. In 1908 good roads were not so common as they are now, but when we headed into Germany we bowled along on smooth gray crushed rock roads that would have seemed sinister, if we had been gifted with the wit to understand. Those roads were as gun barrels pointing towards England, Holland, Belgium, France.

Near our journey's end we decided late one night that we would leave the small town inn where I was having trouble sleeping and push on to Berlin right away. We swiftly pulled away from Platt and Maggie. We drove and drove and lost our way repeatedly. At last a policeman stopped us with a yell. Happily he spoke some English — otherwise even then we should not have known that we really had reached Berlin.

"You are McLean?" The policeman asked the question so deeply in his throat it sounded like the growling of some huge dog. "*Ja?* Your other car passed three hours ago!"

Berlin, I thought, might be the place to get my wedding present; but I could not find quite what I wanted. I did buy a chinchilla coat—a fur so soft that I cannot imagine any more delicate sensation than the feel of it against my cheek. Its gray was most becoming, and usually I wore it decked with fifty marks' worth of violets.

Ned bought me a present that now reposes high on a closet shelf in 2020; a traveling case of gold, the twin of one made for the Crown Princess of Germany. It contained just about every utensil for the toilet that could be invented, all massed in green plush drawers that lifted out on slender extensible metal arms so that its ordinarily compact two cubic feet or less may become a wide expanse of green plush utility. Maggie found it just another nuisance among her many chores, but for a while I liked it.

Dresden, Leipzig, Cologne, Dusseldorf—each one to me stands for a shopping spree.

One day, in Leipzig, we lost patience with the fact that we had only one Mercedes and went overnight to Paris and bought an extra one for 24,000 francs.

We had meant to go to St. Petersburg to visit Ned's Aunt Mamie and Uncle George Bakhmeteff. Bakhmeteff, a Russian diplomat, was an entertaining gentleman. Aunt Mamie had been Marie Beale, Ned's mother's sister. These two girls and their brother, Uncle Truxton Beale, were the children of old General Beale. For years he had been American minister at Vienna; later he became American envoy to Greece, where Aunt Mamie had been a great favorite in Athens. Her close friend there was Queen Olga, formerly a Russian princess.

In Berlin Ned told me of a scheme that had been hatching in his head. The family was hoping to bring about the appointment of George Bakhmeteff as Russian Ambassador to the United States. That, of course, would be perfectly wonderful for all of us, but most of all for the social dictatorship of Emily Beale McLean. (As I look back on it I feel inclined to think that Ned, with all his diplomatic fixing, was trying hard to impress me, his bride with his importance. I do not remember now, but I have a suspicion that I urged him on.)

He began his negotiations with a telegram to Bakhmeteff at the Czar's capital. That telegram was so discreet and cloudy in its phrasing that it could not be understood even by Uncle George.

So Ned dictated to the public stenographer of our hotel in Dresden a letter, less discreet. (I came across all the correspondence tucked away with other souvenirs of our wild honeymoon.) He wrote Bakhmeteff:—

The matter which I telegraphed you about and which by your telegram you say you fail to understand, is this:

I was told from America to find out if anything could be done through money, if so how much and would there be any surety of it being accomplished if conditions were complied with.

Very much disappointed that you both could not come to Vienna as would have loved to have seen you personally and then it would have been so much better to have talked it over together.

America wants definite information if it is possible to arrange for you to come to Washington.

I have a list of people, that was given me, to see about the matter and who could exert great influence in the proper quarters, influence which is very powerful and which you do not know of.

As soon as you get this letter telegraph me to the address which I shall wire you in Vienna. Then if you think that I personally could put any weight to help you in Petersburg, just frankly say so and we will both come at once.

You know how anxious America is to have this accomplished.

The impudence of it becomes a laughing matter now, and yet when I read George Bakhmeteff's frantic telegram of reply I can see how close to ruin Ned's letter must have seemed to bring Bakhmeteff's long diplomatic career. (I have forgotten many of the details, but I remember well that it was supposed by certain of our relatives in the United States that money could buy the place Bakhmeteff wanted.) What Uncle George wired from St. Petersburg was:—

LETTER RECEIVED STOP I MOST POSITIVELY INSIST ON YOUR NOT TAKING ANY STEPS WHATEVER IN A MATTER WHICH CONCERNS ME ALONE AND I MOST CATEGORICALLY REFUSE MY CONSENT TO YOUR INTERFERENCE WHICH CAN HAVE THE MOST FATAL CONSEQUENCES STOP BAKHMETEFF.

Ned went into a rage at that, of course. This was, to him, the Koh-i-noor of all ingratitude. He wired back:—

HAVE NO ANXIETY OVER ME EVER TAKING ANY STEPS CONCERNING YOU.

But even after that, Ned got a wire from his father saying, "STAY OUT OF RUSSIA"

In later years, when the Bakhmeteffs were in Washington (he was there for the last five years of the Czar's reign), we had great fun together; but on my honeymoon I had small hope that we should ever become reconciled, so deeply was Ned wounded. Neither of us, then, had the slightest conception of the risk to which Ned's blundering, well-meant efforts had exposed that couple. Poor Aunt Mamie! She was more observant of court etiquette than any Russian. She had joined the Greek Catholic Church when she married and became, to the best of her ability, a Russian. When I came to know her well I loved her.

Ned and I went on to Vienna and saw the Legation building where the Beales had lived so long. Near by was a little park enclosed by a tall iron fence, and Ned told me how when Bakhmeteff was a young Russian attaché courting Marie Beale the two had once strolled inside the gates of that park. When they decided to leave it they found the gates locked. Poor Aunt Mamie supposed, so strictly were such things regarded, that she was hopelessly ruined. I have forgotten just how they escaped. At any rate it was there at the Viennese court that my mother-in-law acquired the poise, the tact, and the other qualities that enabled her to become the boss of Washington society. One factor was, of course, her husband's money and his great power; but she was an extraordinarily gifted hostess, with a flair for pomp.

Our next stop was Constantinople; we went there — so we wrote home — in pursuit of culture. We arrived in a period when the Young Turks were trying to work reforms that could only be accomplished by unseating and unhareming the old Sultan, Abdul-Hamid. Our Ambassador at that time was John G. A. Leishmann, whose next post was Berlin. He was more than kind to us.

I told him that I had grown tight in my skin from the pressure of two wishes that he might grant. He was the friend of both John R. McLean and my father, and as wishful as an enslaved and grateful djinn to do my bidding.

"I want to meet the Sultan, since he is, I'm told, the Caliph of all Mohammedan faithful."

Mr. Leishmann's eyes began to gleam with merriment. He looked me up and down, a girl of twenty-two, and then said, "He may tap you for his harem."

"The way they tap a boy for some society at Yale? Is that the way he gets 'em?"

He grinned and pretended it was so. Then he arranged, with what effort I do not know, for Ned and me to go to Yildiz Palace. In the streets that we drove through on that very day there had been shooting, the Sultan's loyal troops against throngs incited by the Young Turks.

The Sultan had pouchy, bilious eyes, an ugly nose and lots of trimmed bristles, red with henna, for a beard. He was stoop-shouldered and kept on his head a fez ornamented with an emerald for which my fingers itched. The coffee we had with him was served in tiny eggshell porcelain cups, each one in a golden filigree holder set with diamonds. Those diamonds caught my eye at once. There were so many cups I was half inclined to slip one in my muff and, in my mind, went through the motions many times until I thought I saw a eunuch watching me from behind the Sultan's chair. Of course, I have no way of knowing positively that he was a eunuch, but he was there and watching. There were thousands of those mutilated creatures in Turkey, and such extreme care to guard the Turkish ladies made me feel that they must be ten times more lovely than ordinary creatures that make men jealous.

"The other thing I'm set on doing if it can be arranged," I said to Mr. Leishmann, "is to see a harem. The Sultan's harem."

The Ambassador frowned at that and said it was impossible, or at least very difficult.

"You know this is not precisely like going through Coney Island or any other play resort. These people are highly civilized, even though you may not perceive it."

"My dear Mr. Ambassador," I pleaded, "I have a jealous husband and I want to know the worst that is in store for me."

Lord knows, I was jesting, but anyway Mr. Leishmann fixed it. I was received within the imperial harem; but what I saw was disappointing.

Our next stop was Egypt. We went ashore at Port Said, saw all its filthiness, and then went on to Alexandria. The consul there was D. R. Birch who endeared himself to us by acting as a friend. He simply made us go and see the things that were important, the gigantic artifacts of ancient times that used to make my father ponder—but which generally made me impatient to go out before it was too late and buy something I might want. In Egypt I bought a lot of junk I sometimes wish I had left there—things inlaid with mother-of-pearl, and not-so-good rugs. These were offered with such excitement that at the time I seemed to think each was precisely what I wanted.

We had a frightful trip by boat to Jaffa. For nearly three days, it seems to me, our boat was tossed around. Two sick passengers died aboard, and one woman was flung from her berth and badly injured. They said her back was broken.

Ships did not land at Jaffa; they anchored, and by means of small rowboats passengers were sent ashore or brought aboard. From Jaffa we went by train to Jerusalem.

As soon as we were established in a hotel there, I went right out and bought some Arab costumes. For Ned there was a cream-white burnous that fell to the ground unless he held it as a woman holds her skirt. I got an appropriate silk and woolen swathing, rainbow-striped, to wrap about his head and shoulders, and for his head a small green hat that we were told should not be worn by anyone except such pilgrims as had been to Mecca.

"My favorite saloon in Cincinnati," said Ned, "is a marble barroom called The Mecca. That makes me eligible. You are now looking at Hadji McLean." With that he covered his unreligious head with the green lid.

For myself I had bought a red velvet, richly embroidered. Such things are done nowhere as finely as in Asia Minor. The jacket was studded with turquoises. I had a pillbox hat which was fixed upon my head by a netting fashioned out of thin gold coins with other coins worked into a strap that passed beneath my chin. Thus clad we rode as much as possible on camels.

"What shall we do next?" asked Ned one day.

"How about the River Jordan?"

We set out with two victories; ours was drawn by four horses, and we had an escort of nine Arab horsemen—armed with rifles, swords, and I don't know what else—to defend us. They wore cartridge bandoleers across their chests. We had with us also a courier, a very funny German named William somebody. We were passed from tribe to tribe with ceremony—and the payment of small bribes. On our second day we saw a number of small clouds of dust approaching. A score of horsemen were coming at a gallop.

"Let's throw the women to 'em," said William to my husband. "We can save our more precious necks."

We were sure they were bandits; but they proved to be quite friendly show-offs who scampered up and down the treeless stony hills on their small Arab horses. Those creatures were keenly interesting to Ned, who had an eye for horseflesh. The chief of the band, a reckless brown-skinned fellow with a thick mustache and beard, was thrown. The other riders seemed to think this was a matter between the chief and Allah; they made no move to help him.

I insisted on his drinking from a bottle of whisky that Ned produced. We had a case or two for just such an emergency.

The Arab, forbidden by his creed to drink alcohol, put his hands before his eyes, palms outward, and waved me off. I urged him just a little more, and then he took a stiff drink. When it hit his stomach he let out a yell that was far less Arablike than Indian.

"Just be quiet now," I said. I had Maggie bring me two soft pink satin pillows, smelling enticingly of sachet powder. I lifted up the man's head. I really thought he was dying. He was suddenly alert, and watched me closely like a captive hawk. When he saw the pillows he began to yell and curse and struggle. He seemed to think I was trying to put some kind of spell on him. So, with a wide gesture designed to foil whatever sorcery I might be working, he climbed back, bleeding as he was, into his saddle.

Late that evening we reached a small inn, a barren place where for years Christian pilgrims had been coming just to touch their hands in Jordan water. The river seemed a sickly stream; we had expected at least a Mississippi. But we were impressed when told that we stood where Christ had preached.

I felt the force of that, and so did Ned. So, when we were told that bathing in the Jordan was a permanent cure for colds we decided to go swimming. We drove out to the river, and had the tops of the victories raised to serve as dressing-rooms. As soon as we were in our bathing suits I stepped to the ground and walked into the river.

I could not swim for a nickel prize but, of course, I had to show an Arab audience what a great swimmer I was. The current proved to be terrific, and before I could muster up a grain of sense the thing had me. I felt my feet go out from under me and swallowed enough holy water to last an ordinary sinner a lifetime. I shrieked, but the sound I emitted was just a snort. Happily Ned saw me and grabbed for my long hair. With that for a rope, he towed me to the muddy shore. (I have not thought about it much before, but I really wonder that I am alive after so much feckless living.)

We suddenly decided we had better hurry out of Palestine. It was not suited to our mood. We hired a special train to get us back to Jaffa to catch a ship that otherwise we might have missed.

About ten days later we turned up in Paris, with not enough money to pay our next hotel bill. Ned cabled his father and I cabled mine. My father sent me a fresh credit and his love. Ned got a message that said: —

BETTER HURRY HOME JANUARY FIRST FOR WASHINGTON POST MEETING.

Then I remembered that I had not bought my wedding present. So I went to Cartier's at 13, rue de la Paix (I need no guide to find that place) and told them my predicament. They were lovely and, of course, they knew me and my Dad.

"We have just the thing for you," said one of the firm. Then he hypnotized me by showing me an ornament that made bright spots before my eyes. (Anyway that's what I told my father later.)

A line of diamond fire in square links of platinum where it would touch my throat became a triple loop and from the bottom circle was depended an entrancing pearl. It was the size of my little finger-end and weighed 32¼ grains. The pearl was but the supporting slave of another thing I craved at sight—an emerald. Some lapidary had shaped it with six sides so as to amplify, or to find at least, every trace of color. It weighed 34½ carats. This green jewel, in turn, was just the object supporting the Star of the East. This stone, a pear-shaped brilliant, was one of the most famous in the world—92½ carats. All lapidaries know it.

With fingers that fumbled from excitement I put that gorgeous piece around my throat.

"Ned," I said, in mock despair, "it's got me! I'll never get away from the spell of this."

"A shock might break the spell," said Ned. "Suppose you ask the price of this magnificence."

"Well," I said to the man at Cartier's, as I put my index fingers in my ears, "how much?"

He whispered, "Six hundred thousand francs, madame." "You mean a hundred and twenty thousand dollars?" He cocked his head to one side so that his nod was made obliquely.

"After all," I said to Ned, "this is really an investment. Besides, this is December fifteenth and I can tell my father it's a double gift, to cover both my wedding and Christmas."

So we signed a receipt, and Cartier allowed us children to walk out with the Star of the East.

It made me half-drunk with excitement every time I put it on in Paris. I wore it everywhere—into all the fantastic places one goes when seeing Continental night life.

"How can we pay duty on that bauble when we reach the Customs?" Ned had just a trace more caution then than I. He never had been allowed so much as I. Indeed, that $100,000 of his that we had blown along with my own $100,000 had been intended by John R. to set us up in life. He was, according to Walsh standards, tight.

"Never mind about the duty, Ned; I'm going to sneak it in."

The day we sailed I walked into a cabin that Ned had had lined, walls and ceiling, with orchids. He was a dear when he was sober.

"Did you buy a wedding present, Daughter?" Father asked when we were home. I told him to hide his eyes until I put it on. When he had looked he blinked a time or two, and said, "That's fine. Did you pay the duty?"

"No, I smuggled it."

"You take the cake," he said, and laughed until he almost cried.

We went to dinner that night at the McLeans', in the famous I Street house. (John Russell Pope was the architect who transformed what had been a comparatively small, old-fashioned house into a place for giving regal entertainments. We were in the dining room. Its ceiling is covered with the work of some great painter. The table is always guarded by four massive columns that rear themselves like pagan altars, each decorated with sculptured vines and grapes and bearing a basket piled with fruits. Each column and its basket is a cunning contrivance to diffuse the light that touches the faces of those who banquet there.)

We were served by Grafoni, a butler who was himself a jewel. While Grafoni was handling the lesser servants with something of the silent zest of a concert master, my father spoke to old John R.

"I have a surprise for you: see what Daughter bought herself as a wedding present."

I bent my head and, by then much practised, quickly fastened it about my neck. The champagne glasses out of which we had been toasting one another were a foot tall, crystal vessels with golden bands where one's lips touch. This luxury of Ned's home was quite as fine, I'm sure, as could be produced if all the wrecked civilizations of the past were brought to life. So what I showed upon my throat and bosom seemed to us Walshes quite appropriate. Yet Mrs. McLean, who had no really fine jewelry herself, looked at it almost sourly, and said no word until she was pressed to speak. Then she burst out with an opinion much too frank for that occasion.

"Hideous thing for a child to wear! That's what I think. I must say it looks Jewish, and since you ask my advice, I say: send it back."

I am generally most concerned to spare the feelings of those about me. I cannot bear to wound anyone in so sensitive a spot as the naked ego. If I were less considerate, be sure my household servants would not be with me year after year. I am careful of others' feelings because I myself am most sensitive to such things.

"How much duty did you pay on that thing?" said old John R.

"Didn't pay any. I sneaked it in."

"Great God! Don't you see my Ned becomes involved because he is your

ON THE HONEYMOON

In their Packard
On Camels In Jerusalem

husband? This thing would be ruinous to me. Think of the hostile headlines in rival papers!"

"Don't worry," said my father. "I'll send my lawyer down to-morrow and let him declare the trinket. Hell, I am glad to buy it for my Evalyn. There won't be a bit of trouble. I'll send word to the customs men that she is not all there."

CHAPTER XIV

The Hundred-Million-Dollar Baby

My pointless, pampered life of spending began to have a point in April, 1909. That was when I discovered I was going to have a child. My partner in this enterprise of being sorcerer was gentle with me then. He tapered down his drinking. He gave Platt, the chauffeur, strict orders to drive with exaggerated care. My Ned, I knew by then, was the most plausible of liars; but I had no wish to contradict him now when he was telling me how lovely he was finding me.

That was a happy summer. Ned kept me breathing the fragrance of the most costly blooms he could find. I am not a gardening variety of lady. I want my flowers cut and gathered for me, but I wanted very much to be the gardener of my child. The channel of my care of it was my own throat. I stopped all drinking. I ate precisely what the doctors ordered. Likewise, I rested regularly. Yet underneath my conscious mind, in realms where there is stored in any woman all the pasts of all ancestors, I was most active. I knew this every time I tried to sleep.

Deep inside me, quite beyond the foolish surface touched by bungling teachers, indulgent parents, lavish friends and my own behavior, there was going on a chemistry I wish I fully understood. How ultra-wise I should be then! Yet I insist that every time I have been pregnant I have been presciently aware that I was engaged in the greatest of all magic. I? Perhaps I mean that God was doing this. At any rate I knew that incomprehensible forces within my being were building up a human entity. What best of Ned, what best of me had been imparted to my child? I used to lie awake and ponder even as I felt the baby growing.

My Tipperary father had qualities I hoped were fixed in me, and these I knew I wanted for my baby; warmheartedness and a genius for persistence in any endeavor. My mother had a gift for music. I wanted that. Ned's charm I often thought of; it would be a better world, I used to think, if a woman in my state could control the formula of her child's being. What had been taken from Ned and passed along to this one who was our son? (Of course I never had a moment's doubt but that I would have a son.) Ned's father's sister, Mildred, had possessed charm enough to capture at the peak of his glory the hero of Manila, George Dewey. Ned's father was a potent, crafty man—a newspaper proprietor who had a trick of getting his own way with men or women. I wanted my son to possess charm and sweeping power; but I wanted more for him than had shown itself in Ned. Through Emily, his mother, the great traditions of the Beales were funneled into Ned—and there, somehow, smothered. I hoped to bring to life again in my own son those great ones. There was Ned's grandfather, who as a navy ensign helped to wrest California from the Mexicans and grabbed for himself a big ranch; there was a line of soldier and sailor leaders printed in his blood.

Whatever was done about it inside my body has been done before some billions of times. Still for me this was a unique process, my personal miracle.

September, 1909, was a glorious month for my father. Consequently I remained in the East and got my information about the Western trip of President Taft from family letters and from the newspapers.

As a former national committeeman from Colorado, and also a friend, my father had strong claims on William Howard Taft. Father wished to rename Wolhurst: he had selected as a name for it "Clonmel", that Tipperary village where he was born. Mr. Taft had agreed to come for a visit (he had been there a time or two before) and rebaptize the place.

That was one time when I wished human gestation was a swifter process. I wanted very much to be out home for that affair. President Taft and his party came the eighteen miles from Denver on a special train. I have forgotten what sort of renaming hocus-pocus they went through, but my father sent me a copy of Mr. Taft's speech. It contained a story that I like. He said it had been told him by a Lord justice of the Court of Appeals of Ireland: —

While holding the Assizes in County Tipperary, a man was brought before the Lord justice under indictment of manslaughter. The evidence showed that the deceased had come to his death through a blow from a blackthorn stick in the hands of the defendant. Medical testimony disclosed that the victim had what is called a "paper skull." When found guilty and brought before the Lord justice for sentence, the defendant was asked if he knew of any reason why the sentence of the Court should not be pronounced on him.

"No, your lordship; but I would like to ask one question."

"What is that, my man?"

"I would like to ask what the divil a man with a head like that was doing in Tipperary?"

Father wrote me that when the President told this story his vast paunch shook from something like an earthquake of merriment. Mr. Taft always laughed with fresh enjoyment each time he told a funny story.

The bulk of William Howard Taft was well nourished at the breakfast served by the Walshes in his honor at Clonmel: his meal included mountain trout, bacon, eggs, broiled chicken, chops, peas, corn, biscuits, and waffles. I have, besides that menu, some photographs that show my father smiling with his friend Taft. My mother was the heroine of each picture, plumed as a Hottentot and tightly laced. Archie Butt was there, in blue with gold braid and black riding boots, and so was Jimmy Sloan, the secret service bodyguard, closely watching all who came. (How blind they seem to me, because not one of them could see what is now so clear: my father as he smiled was dying.)

At Bar Harbor Ned and I had taken a fancy to a summer place known as the Sears Estate. My father bought it for us. He had furnished Ned's office and given him whatever money "the boy" seemed to need. Ned's own father gave him a strict allowance, a salary of $1,000 a month. Yet Ned was not living on such a basis, and never had. In August, 1909, he got from Father $10,000. In October he got $7,000. It was like that, month by month. Father had more than plenty. The Camp Bird mine that very year produced for him, on the sale agreement and in dividends on his stock, $554,136.13. One day in January Father gave my mother $100,000 for whatever she might be needing, and on the same day advanced to the father of his grandson another $50,000.

My child was born December 18, 1909, in 2020 Massachusetts Avenue; and the two of us were close to death. Those months of being fixed immobile in a plaster cast had taken tone from muscles that I needed to expel my child into the world. Dr. Whitridge Williams, dean of Johns Hopkins, saw that he would have to use great forceps. Hour by hour Ned implored other specialists to come. Dr. Williams was with me four days. He sent for Dr. Harvey Cushing, the brain surgeon, to reshape my precious baby's head. There had been a heavy snowstorm and Cushing rode from Baltimore on a special engine. Ned's mother, thinking the baby could not live, baptized the infant and named him, for my brother, Vinson Walsh McLean.

He was called in newspaper headlines "the hundred-million-dollar baby", and if that was an exaggeration as to his prospects as an heir it seemed to me gross understatement of his value. He had a golden crib, and in it he was sheltered from all drafts by a lacy, quilted canopy depending from an arrangement like a crown. This crib was a gift from King Leopold.

The strain of having him had exhausted me. I had no bit of strength, and very little poise. Much of my vitality had gone into this little son. I worried unnaturally about his safety. This was made worse because they would not let me more than touch him.

At this time my father vanished out of Washington. As I grew better I was told that he and Mother were down in Palm Beach. Perhaps it is life that is cruel, but I have always felt that there was needless cruelty on the part of the doctor who harshly, or at leastly bluntly, transformed my gentle, sweet-tempered father into a condemned man. I knew nothing of his situation until one day Wayne MacVeagh came to see me. His daughter was one of my best friends.

He gave me the facts: my father had a cancer that was devouring his lungs. In Florida he had suffered a severe hæmorrhage.

I telegraphed my mother to ask what she was going to do, and heard that she had started West with him for San Antonio, Texas. A doctor had gone South with them, but now had been left behind; and on the Western trip decisions were being made by a woman Christian Scientist who had my mother's complete confidence.

The morning Ned and I reached San Antonio I went straight to the little cottage where my parents were sheltered. I was weak and ill myself. I wanted more than anything to see Father, but Mother and this woman talked to me. Everything was lovely, beautiful; they were made up as if for a dance, and would not speak a word concerning sickness. Nor would they let me see my father.

I was too weak to argue, and went back to the hotel; but as soon as I had eaten breakfast I stormed back and demanded to see him.

He asked for something as I entered, and I saw a sullen nurse, instead of handing it to him, throw what he had asked for on his bed.

"Get out," I said to her, my eyes blazing, and that is when my father knew I had arrived. Tears rolled down his cheeks as we reached for each other.

"I knew you'd come," he said.

That Spartan boy who let a fox gnaw at his vitals had been no more silent under hideous pain than had my father. Those two, my mother and the practitioner, were honestly persuaded that by mumbo-jumbo his frightful sufferings could be nullified.

I took charge. I arranged for a squad of nurses, and with Ned's help found the best doctor in San Antonio. Then I turned on my mother's friend: "I understand that it is against the laws of Texas to practise as you have been doing here. I give you just one hour to get out with your bags and books. Leave Texas!"

In an hour she was gone. My mother, weeping, abandoned everything to me. My nostrils were still flaring from my rage, but I felt more nearly like myself than I had for days. My father was asleep, his limp wrist held by a physician who kept his eyes fixed on his watch. I am not religious, I almost never pray; but with my emaciated fingers clutching the bed rail I thanked God, with all my heart, for morphine that could give my father ease from pain.

I do not think he suffered so very much after that.

Ned and I had taken the house next door to Father. Arthur Buckman was in charge for us in Washington. Many times each day I had telegrams from little Vinson's bodyguards and nurses. Will Duckstein, Ned's secretary, was on hand; also there was a nightwatchman and one other man. Besides these, there were the nurses, and a doctor who was constantly in attendance.

I could not sleep soundly, because I worried. I feared some of the threatening letters that had come to us were more than mere threats from cranks. A wire would come saying "TWO-THIRTY A.M. STOP BABY IS NOW ASLEEP." Then I would sleep. Later, another message would arrive and soothe my fears a little by reporting "BABY REALLY LAUGHED THIS MORNING", or I would try to nap after reading a telegram that said "BABY ONLY CRIED TEN MINUTES TO-DAY STOP HE IS FINE." Even though I had a message every hour I did not have enough, because I was tortured by a fear that almost drove me mad.

All my nightmares for twenty-six years have had to do with my plight as the mother of a kidnaped baby.

My baby Vinson was just two months old when I saw the first of those loathsome threats—a scrawled message on soiled paper; of course, it was anonymous. Then others came; there were telegrams sometimes, and messages by telephone as well as the notes that came by mail. Sometimes these contained directions as to where

TALLYHO WITH VICE PRESIDENT FAIRBANKS
THOMAS F. WALSH AND OTHERS

PRESIDENT TAFT RE-CHRISTENING THE WALSH
COLORADO ESTATE

to deposit money. Sometimes there was just a cold-blooded statement that at such an hour, such a day, my baby would be slaughtered. These threats were most hideous to me when the writers did not ask for money. They were expressions of an envy I could not be expected to understand or share. The others, the blackmail threats and those that demanded, in advance, a ransom, began to lose some of their frightfulness in time and seem to me to be the bugaboo performances of futile people trying to frighten me. Ned took that view even while he hired more detectives. He would try to blast away my fears with just a word or two: "Crackpots, that's all they are."

I think Ned was right; and yet I realized that a crackpot with no more than half a mind might take my baby. In Texas I tossed off orders every day by telegraph, trying to tighten our defenses against the mental misfits, the criminally envious, the scheming ones who threatened us.

Right here I want to say most earnestly that it never pays to give a nickel to a blackmailer. The way to deal with them is fight! Quite obviously they are cowards, or they would take some bolder way of criminality. I say quite flatly that if ever I have one of these creatures within my reach I hope to shoot him. I have told all those I love: "If you start paying blackmail you will never stop. Fools pay to hush things up. No matter what wrong thing you may have done let it come out and pay no heed, but focus all your feelings on the blackmailer. Fight. Don't pay." That is what I have told my children.

In Texas all the days of early March were bleak for me no matter how brightly the sun was shining. My father was dying, literally by half-inches. I wanted to pour out all his fortune into one great effort to restore him. Somewhere, I felt, there might be a doctor who could perform a miracle of science.

My poor mother's argument was that Christ had raised men from the dead. She cited Lazarus and repeated other stories from the Bible. I told her with all possible gentleness that we ought to try both systems. I told her to pray and not to feel that God would be so unjust to her and to Father as to deny relief merely because I was having faith in doctors as the direct instrument of His power. She went into a darkened room and closed the door. I had Ned send more telegrams. By those wires we fixed upon the doctor who was regarded as foremost among those who dealt with cancers. This was Dr. Lewellys F. Barker of Baltimore.

"He must come down here," I said to Ned.

Dr. Barker's fee was fixed at $1,000 for each day away from Baltimore. He left Baltimore on March 14th and devoted ten days (including travel) to my father. I say it earnestly: he might have had everything that had come from the Camp Bird mine if only he could have cured my father. We knew he could not do that, but wanted him to exercise his skill with morphine. Dr. Barker decided that a certain solution he knew how to mix would have more potency than the injections Father had been receiving. My conscience was soothed of its least pang at having taken

126

charge and deposing Mother when I saw my father's pain-racked face relax and show its gentleness once more as Barker gave him treatments. There were others: all first-class men. There was no excuse for hope. We knew that even while we hoped.

We decided at the first of spring to take Father North to 2020 so that he could see my baby and then die at home. John W. Gates's private car was hooked to the "Ohio", the McLean private car, and these two formed part of a special that carried baggage cars for weight. I never left my father's side throughout the ride from Texas to the Capital. I could not sleep. The train, so we were told, was breaking every record, and looking out from time to time I could believe this. The landscape rushing past to shrivel into a distorted background was not more crazy in its seeming behavior than the actuality of the world.

I have not led a contemplative life; and yet there has been time for pondering. The thing I wonder most about is why the universe is geared to cruelty?

My father found in the earth a treasure of which all men wanted pieces; so my father, in turn, could trade his treasure for what he wanted. Thereafter he was as he had been before: gentle, generous, and fair to all. It pleased him to be accepted as the friend of presidents and of a king, and of their friends. Although an errant Catholic, it was a thrill for him to bend his knee before the Pope. Surely such recognitions, such acceptances would be pleasing to any immigrant lad who had crossed in the steerage in search of fortune. He bought all manner of costly things, and by his buying scattered much wealth. His spending gave employment to unnumbered people. His wants created activity, and thereby more wealth for others.

I cannot see the justice of it. Why should he have been so frightfully afflicted?

Beyond that, I am puzzled at the envy of others, who seem to suppose that wealth is the perfect anodyne for human misery. Perhaps I'll find the answers in some world to come, if there is any.

Each day at 2020 my father gazed at my baby, — named for his dead son, — and as he looked found relief and satisfaction quite as potent as the treatments of Dr. Barker. It used to seem to me — still sleepless — that our plight, his pain, my worried state, and my mother's wretchedness on his account had been going on for years and years.

On the night of April 8th, when I went to his room to kiss him, he roused himself and gripped my hand. I looked deep into his eyes and listened.

"Take care of Mother, darling." That was all he said.

I waited in my own room for several hours. Then someone came to beckon me to return to him. I sat beside his bed and held his hand. I could feel his pulse and knew his heart was pumping. I could hear his breathing. Presently he ceased to breathe. The flutter of his pulse against my fingers was the only signal that he was living; when that stopped there were no other signals.

There is a magic in old papers that can evoke visions of the past. A letter from a Washington store, a thing I read once and put aside, can now do this thing for me.

Enclosed please find samples of the very best dot muslin suitable for nursery curtains that we can obtain.

The date it bears is the date of my father's death. Turned over, that letter reveals a note I penciled there to be sent as a telegram to Mathilde Townsend.

Dearest Mathilde:

Mother, Ned and I are so delighted to hear of your happiness. We send you hearty congratulations and best love.

Affectionately,

EVALYN McLEAN

That "happiness" was the announcement of her engagement to Peter Goelet Gerry whom she later was separated from and then divorced. But did I send a telegram from 2020 to 2121 Massachusetts Avenue? The answer is supplied so swiftly I can believe that all experiences, however trivial, are kept on record in each mind. After the funeral Ned, mother and I went to Atlantic City.

Mother and I were so broken up by my father's death, after the strain of his long illness, that we did not attend the funeral. Instead, as our friends began to gather at 2020, three doctors of that group, Finney, Guthrie, and Jim Mitchell, took us to the garden on the roof. Mother was in a state of trance. I remember that one of the doctors invited me to see how blue the sky was, but looking up was just an excuse for me to try not to hear the clatter at the porte-cochere and the noises of automobiles moving slowly.

Afterward Ned tried to tell us how he had handled everything for us. (He reached one of his peaks of fineness on that day.) From Ned we learned that President Taft had been among the mourners, and that Speaker Cannon had been seen to stoop behind Supreme Court justice McKenna so that none would see him bite off a piece of dry stogie to chew in a situation that forbade smoking.

I heard Ned speak of these and other pallbearers: Admiral Dewey, John R. McLean, Myron Herrick, whom we loved, Senator Charles J. Hughes of Colorado, and David Wegg, who for years had been his partner.

Mother hardly nodded even when asked a question.

CHAPTER XV

Drink and Drugs and the Hope Diamond

WE went from Atlantic City, after about a month, to our place at Bar Harbor; but even there my mother kept to her room, the blinds drawn tightly against all light. She said, quite without dramatics, that she wished to follow Father. I tried to talk with her of business matters. Father had left his fortune in trust for us for ten years, half to Mother, half to me, with a joint survivorship arrangement. Even the details of this did not rouse her. She was so weak she had to be carried to her bath. She ate sparingly or not at all. However, there was one by whom her interest was aroused for a little: my baby had that power—she adored him.

I talked about her case with several doctors, and we hit upon a scheme for making her custodian, for a little while, of Vinson.

"It is up to you, Mother," I said to her one day. "I am putting full responsibility for my baby in your hands. Ned and I are going to France."

She got right up, and in a few days she was out and in the garden. She was almost like herself by the time we sailed.

One night we drove down to Vichy in our yellow racing Fiat. I felt an urge to gamble. Unless I gamble more than I should, there is no flavor for me at the tables. Well, at the Casino I bought the bank. For me the best of all gambling patterns is Russian bank.

Sitting next to me that night was a dear old man, who helped me run the bank. I had begun to play at about ten-thirty in the evening. When I stopped, at four in the morning, I had won about seventy thousand dollars. Ned had gone to get a drink, and I followed him.

"Where's that money?" Ned asked.

"That old man is looking after it," I said.

"Who is he?"

"I don't know."

We started back to the tables without our drink. The old man had vanished, and with him all my winnings.

For about three minutes Ned and I were wondering just how loud to pitch our voices as we shouted that we had been robbed. Then I saw the old man again. He was approaching, smiling broadly, and had all my winnings, changed into bills of large denomination and neatly packaged. As he handed this to me he introduced himself as the owner of Angostura Bitters. But for all I knew before he might have been a crook.

I talked of going back to the Casino to make another killing, but Ned demurred.

"I'll tell you what we're going to do," he said, "we're packing now and driving back to Paris. If you stay here you'll lose all you've won and more."

We had a consultation about the chauffeur, who was feeling ill. We put my maid on the fast express to Paris, and then Ned told the chauffeur to get in the back of the car.

Ned was most skillful at the wheel and drove with élan, with daring. That day the roads were thick with summer dust and the driver of a car ahead of us was reluctant to let us pass. So Ned opened up the Fiat. Dosed with laudanum and whisky, I did not care about the risk so long as we were not riding in the other fellow's dust. Ned blew three or four times and then went by, our fenders scraping the other man's with a screeching clatter.

When we pulled up in front of the Hotel Bristol in Paris Ned looked at his watch. We had beaten the fast express by ten minutes. For a minute we exulted and then noticed that the chauffeur had not jumped out to help us. I looked around and there, lying behind us, half on the seat, half on the floor, wide-eyed and slobbering, was the chauffeur. The hotel porter at my cry reached in and touched him. "My God," he said in French, "this one has broken his pipe."

He meant that the chauffeur was dead; and he was right. The man had suffered a heart attack. We had not known before, but apparently he had been suffering from heart trouble for a long time. If he had driven us that day, and died while driving, we should have had a pretty smashup.

Pierre Cartier came to call on us at the Hotel Bristol in Paris. He carried, tenderly, a package tightly closed with wax seals. His manner was exquisitely mysterious. I suppose a Parisian jewel merchant who seeks to trade among the ultrarich has to be more or less a stage manager and an actor. Certainly he must be one great salesman. Of course, M. Cartier was dressed as carefully as any woman going to her first big ball. His silk hat, which he swept outward in a flourish, had such a sheen that almost made me believe it had been handed to him, new, as he crossed our threshold. His oyster-colored spats, his knife-edged trousers, his morning coat, the pinkness of his fingernails, all these and other things about him were made by him to seem to be for me—for Madame McLean—one French compliment.

Ned was still abristle with a day-old beard, and from the folds of a peacock-colored lounging robe was blinking at me across the breakfast coffee cups. He had ordered ham and eggs, but he could not bear the sight of them, or of me, or of Pierre Cartier.

"You know about the Turkish Revolution?" said Cartier, and tapped his polished fingernails upon his package in the manner of a Kellar or Mulholland about to do a trick.

"Why," I told him, "we were in Constantinople when there was shooting in the streets. We went there on our honeymoon. I was admitted, thanks to Mr.

Leishmann, to the Sultan's harem—just a lot of fatties, except for two or three who wore Worth gowns."

"Ah, I do not forget such things. You told me when you bought from me your wedding present, the Star of the East. I remember very well. It seems to me you told me then that you had seen a jewel in the harem, a great blue stone that rested against the throat of the Sultan's favorite. A lovely throat, eh?"

"I guess I did." It was too early to argue and, after all, I had seen jewels on Turkish ladies that made my fingers itch.

"Of course you did," said Cartier. "Such things impress one and, besides, not many Western women have been inside such a place."

"It seems to me I did see that stone."

"Naturally. We hear the woman who had that jewel from the Sultan's hand was stabbed to death."

All my boredom vanished as he went on.

"The beginning of this stone's history, as we believe it, was its appearance in Europe when Louis the Fourteenth was King of France. A man named Jean Tavernier had brought it from India at a time when maharajahs and rajahs kept their wealth in jewels. In that day the world's greatest jewel markets were in the Orient. This stone when it was sold to Louis the Fourteenth was called the Tavernier blue diamond. Marie Antoinette wore it, so we understand; we know positively that there was just this one big blue diamond among the French crown jewels. Marie Antoinette was guillotined and the Revolutionists seized all the wealth. The crown jewels were inventoried, and the Tavernier blue was listed there. Then, along with other important items of the royal regalia, this big blue diamond vanished—stolen, so we think."

By this time Cartier had me on fire with eagerness to see what treasure was sealed up in his package. But, shrewd salesman that he was, he did not open it. He just went on talking, tracing out the jewel's history (or what he freely acknowledged were his beliefs concerning that history). He said he understood that Tavernier had stolen the gem from a Hindu, perhaps a Hindu god. My recollection is that he said Tavernier afterward was torn and eaten by wild dogs. I might have been excused, that morning, for believing that all the violences of the French Revolution were just the repercussions of that Hindu idol's wrath. M. Cartier was most entertaining.

In after years Sir Caspar Purdon-Clarke, who had been Director of the Metropolitan Museum of Art in New York City, confirmed some of the diamond's history. In 1830, he said, a diamond dealer named Daniel Eliason offered for sale in London a big blue gem that weighed 44 ¼ carats. The Tavernier blue diamond had weighed 67 ²/₁₆ carats; but obviously that stone could not be sold in its old form anywhere in the world with a clear title. It was property stolen from the French Government, and as such would have been attached and made the object of legal struggles that would have devoured any pseudo-owner's equity. In 1874 another stone, the Brunswick blue, came on the market, and that stone was said to be the lesser part of the Tavernier. The larger stone Eliason had sold to Henry Thomas Hope, a London banker. Hope's wife was a Parisienne named Bichat, who kept the big blue gem until her death in 1887. Her daughter had become the Duchess of Newcastle, but when the banker's widow died she left her wealth not to her daughter, then a dowager duchess, but to her daughter's younger son, Lord Francis Pelham Clinton. On one condition, she left to him her country-seats, Deepdene, near Dorking, and Blayney Castle in County Monaghan, her other wealth, and her collection of jewels, the prize of which was the blue Hope diamond. The condition was that he should thereafter call himself, "Lord Francis Pelham Clinton Hope." This he agreed to do. Lord Francis squandered his fortune and got deeply into debt. In 1894 he married May Yohe, an American actress. She used to wear her husband's jewels on the stages of music halls where she was singing. They could not sell or pawn the jewels without risking jail, because Lord and Lady Francis Hope had only a life interest in them. However, when Lord Francis Hope was declared bankrupt the jewels had disappeared.

Some time after that Sir Caspar Purdon-Clarke received a visit from an old man who made a business of trading bits of jewelry that he picked up at secondhand stores and pawnbrokers' shops. Out of his bag onto a cloth-covered table he dumped an astonishing collection of jewels, so dirty as to be without lustre. The old trader accounted for his possession of these by saying he had bought them at a sheriff's sale in Brighton. They had been among the effects of a music-hall actress who had vanished from her lodgings, with her husband, without paying her landlady or any of the other creditors who had been keeping the couple practically in a state of siege. None but the old jewel trader had supposed the ornaments in the actress' abandoned trunk were other than shoddy imitations, stage jewelry. The cheap lodgings bore out that idea.

When he realized the enormous value of his bargain, the trader went for advice to his old customer, Sir Caspar Purdon-Clarke. The antiquarian at once recognized several items as belonging to the Hope collection, but he most easily recognized the Hope blue diamond; he knew there was not another like it in the world. He advised the trader to get in touch with the trustees of the Hope estate. The old man did so, and for surrendering the collection received a fair reward.

After that the Hope diamond was sold to an American syndicate. "Selim Habib" was the name of the customer who took it off their hands. Did the Turkish Sultan, Abdul-Hamid, ever own it? I do not know for sure. Cartier told me his firm acquired it from a man named Rosenau in Paris.

But I could wait no longer. "Let me see the thing," I said impatiently to Cartier. He breathed quietly without movement for at least a minute, as a concert pianist may do before striking trained fingers to the keys of his instrument. That pause was eloquent, and made me feel—as he wished me to—that I was being privileged beyond most persons in being shown this gem.

No word had been said of price; this was just a visit from a jewel merchant to a friend whom he admired.

Finally, he stripped away the wrappings and then held before my eyes the Hope diamond. No other gem I know of is so rare as a real blue diamond; I have never seen another the precise blue of the Hope diamond. The blue of it is something I am puzzled to name. Peking blue would be too dark, West Point blue too gray. A Hussar's coat? Delft? A harbor blue?

Sometimes when I have looked at it, I have felt that Nature, when making it, was half-inclined to form a sapphire, but its diamond hardness dispels that thought, and, really, it has no more than a quarter of the blue of soft sapphires. That very rareness of color is the thing that convinced me the Hope and Brunswick were once a single treasure of the French crown.

The stone was set in diamonds, and, as I looked at it, M. Cartier told me things he did not vouch for: that it was supposed to be ill-favored, and would bring bad luck to anyone who wore or even touched it. Selim Habib is supposed to have been drowned when his ship sank after he had disposed of the gem. We all know about the knife blade that sliced through Marie Antoinette's throat. Lord Hope had plenty of troubles that, to a superstitious soul, might seem to trace back to a heathen idol's wrath. May Yohe, Hope's wife, eloped with handsome, feckless Captain Putnam Bradlee Strong; maybe that was not bad luck, but it was embarrassing. There were others, too.

You should have heard how solemnly we considered all those possibilities that day in the Hotel Bristol.

"Bad luck objects," I said to Cartier, "for me are lucky."

"Ah, yes," he said. "Madame told me that before, and I remembered. I think, myself, that superstitions of the kind we speak about are baseless. Yet, one must admit, they are amusing."

Ned held the jewel in his hands long after I had put it down.

"How much?" he asked, although I do not know why, since he almost never paid for things until forced by threats of suit.

Before Cartier could answer I declared myself. "Ned—I don't want the thing. I don't like the setting."

We sailed for the United States aboard the *Rotterdam* in October, and the jewel I was thinking of was no blue diamond but my precious little son.

A tide goes out, a tide comes in; so I would describe my leaving him and my coming back. I take no credit for the wild, uncontrolled love I had for little Vinson. I am, myself, the merest speck of life, but I think its fullest force exerts itself whenever life breeds life. I cannot remember when I did not hunger after thrills. That is the key to all my recklessness, I fancy. For some thrills I have paid terrific prices and, properly, I almost paid the biggest one of all for Vinson.

In the McLean private Pullman car we hastened from New York to Bar Harbor. We found the baby strong and smiling, a nine-months-old man, gurgling, laughing, showing just the suggestion of a tooth. What exquisite joy it was to feel his roselike ear printing itself against my neck, to test the vigor of his kick against my stomach!

But Pierre Cartier had not forgotten me. Mother, Ned, the baby and I were back at 2020 in November when we had a letter from the Cartier establishment at 712 Fifth Avenue. It was addressed to Ned.

Dear Sir: —

We have the pleasure to inform you that Mr. Pierre Cartier has arrived from Europe this morning on the "Lusitania." He has brought with him the documents concerning the Hope diamond. He has a book written by Tavernier himself, who, if you remember, sold the stone to King Louis XIV.

Besides, he has a book written by the great French expert of all jewels of the crown of France and you will have there all details you require.

Mr. Pierre Cartier will be glad to be honoured with an appointment, so as to be able to give you all further details you may require.

Awaiting your kind answer,

We beg to remain, dear sir,

Yours respectfully,

CARTIER.

Ned talked with Pierre Cartier and reported that the jewel merchant simply wanted me to keep the Hope diamond in my custody from Saturday until Monday. I agreed, of course, telling Ned to put the gem on my dresser.

For hours that jewel stared at me. The setting had been changed completely to a frame of diamonds, and there was a splendid chain of diamonds to go about my neck. At some time during that night I began to want the thing.

Do I believe a lot of silly superstitions, legends of the diamond? I must confess I know better and yet, knowing better, I believe. By that I mean I never let my friends or children touch it. Call it a foolish woman's fetish if you like; after you have said so without contradiction, let me say that I have come to feel—not think —that I have developed a sort of immunity to its evil. What tragedies have befallen me might have occurred had I never seen or touched the diamond. I have sense enough to know that fortune-tellers gain fame as prophets by habitually predicting probabilities. My observations have persuaded me that tragedies, for anyone who lives, are not escapable.

Pierre Cartier came to call on Monday morning, but the deal hung fire for several months. The price was fixed at $154,000. I agreed to pay $40,000 before long and then, in the space of three years, $114,000. I had an emerald and pearl pendant with a diamond necklace that pleased me less, and Cartier accepted that as part of the price. Then I signed a note and Ned signed too. I put the chain around my neck and thereby seemed to hook my life to its destiny of good or evil.

I knew Ned's mother would try to stop me. That was why I hurried to make the purchase irrevocable. When Cartier had put our note inside his pocket, I called Mrs. McLean on the telephone.

"Mummie, I have bought the Hope diamond."

With her at the time was Mrs. Robert Goelet, who told me afterward that my mother-in-law almost fainted.

What I heard her say was, "It is a cursed stone and you must send it back. Worse than its being freighted with bad luck is your buying of it—a piece of recklessness. Money is a trust for better things than jewel-buying."

She lectured on and on and only now and then did I break in to say, "But, Mummie—"

She did not let me say much more, because she had a thousand objections bursting forth.

Finally I said firmly, "But, Mummie, everybody has bad luck. You never know."

She reported then that Mrs. Goelet was joining in her entreaty to save me from a piece of madcap folly. Mrs. Goelet actually spoke to me over the telephone. Then they drove around to see me, continuing to urge a change of mind even while they handled and admired the gem. So, at last, knowing I was obliged to be a nice daughter-in-law, I sent back the stone to Cartier.

And Cartier quite promptly sent it back to me.

Bad luck? Within a narrow space, just about a year or so, both women died: Mrs. Goelet was stricken on her yacht; Mummie died of pneumonia at Bar Harbor. They had to die sometime, as we all do. Nevertheless, lacking other philosophy to meet such events, I made mine up when needed out of odds and ends of superstition and common sense—as do most people, I suppose. In me were half-sprouted faiths in saints concerning whom I had no teachings. Perhaps I simply scared myself for fun; at any rate, I did believe that blue diamond was a talisman of evil.

Every day I received letters from persons near and far who had read that I had become the owner of this stone. A man wrote to me about how he had nearly drowned when the S.S. Seine went down. He implied the Hope diamond was aboard, but did not explain who saved it when he asked me to compensate him for some of his later troubles, which he blamed on his former proximity to the thing that was hanging on my neck. I had letter after letter from May Yohe, now trying to recoup some bit of happiness from the ruin of her life. She blamed the diamond; as one woman to another, she begged me to throw it away and break its spell. Every time I got a dozen letters I got fresh thrills, but in spite of myself I began to have about my life some of that feeling with which we await the rising of a curtain at a play.

One day I said to Maggie Buggy, "Can't we get some priest you know to lay the curse?"

"A priest will bless the stone," said Maggie, "and be sure that will foil the devil in it."

We set out in my electric victoria for the church of Monsignor Russell.

"Look, Father," I said to him, "this thing has got me nervous. Would you bless it for me?"

We were in a small side room of the church, and Monsignor Russell donned his robes and put my bauble on a velvet cushion.

As he continued his preparations, a storm broke. Lightning flashed. Thunder shook the church. I don't mind saying various things were scared right out of me. There was no wind or rain; just darkness and these lurid lightning thrusts. Across the street a tree was struck and splintered. Maggie was half-frantic with her fear; beads were clicking through her fingers. I wished I could have such faith; Maggie was calling on Personages with whom I rarely reckon in my thoughts.

Monsignor Russell's Latin words gave me strange comfort. Ever since that day, I've worn my diamond as a charm. I kid myself, of course—but I like to pretend the thing brings good luck. As a matter of fact, the luckiest thing about it is that, if I ever had to, I could hock it.

Grief over the loss of my father brought me back, temporarily, to morphine. I was becoming more cunning than an animal in hiding my supply of morphine.

A squirrel saving nuts is limited by its undeveloped imagination when it buries such winter treasure in earth holes or hollow trees; but I was not so handicapped. A squirrel, for example, is debarred from sending money to some greedy doctor or druggist and making arrangements to have a bit of powder sent each day by mail. (That was a trick of mine that worked until Ned had all our mail deliveries switched from 2020 to the *Washington Post*.)

Thin packages were cached beneath my bedroom carpet. With a pair of scissors I would make skillful cuts in obscure places in the furniture and then, as far in as I could poke my thinning arm into the stuffing of chairs, couches, sofas, I would put a small brown bottle, hoping thus to impregnate my future with the drug I craved. I seem to recall that I had one big bottle stored away inside the pipe organ.

I was always popping into drugstores, although on most shopping trips I would simply flick a finger at some servant as a signal to begone upon my errand. In those days a woman, diamond laden, could buy laudanum by the quart if she would simply pay the druggist what he asked. I always went provided with some sort of prescription.

Months went by, and what with dope and drink I had no trace of appetite. I could not keep a thing on my stomach so I would fill myself with narcotics and go, completely dazed, for two or three hours of driving.

There was one advantage for me in the habit. Ordinarily I worried incessantly about the money—about all the things that formerly my father had dealt with; but when I took morphine there were no worries, no cares. Of course I paled until I looked like a ghost.

If by some bad chance I could not get the stuff the instant I required it, I would take a dose of chloral, or anything narcotic that I could buy in the drugstores. Then one day I confessed to Ned.

He was shocked, but sweet. "Can't you stop?" he asked me. "Suppose you try real hard. You know, we've got the baby; we must think of him."

"I'll stop." But I was quite unable to keep my word without help, so one day I called up Dr. Hardin. I told him I had been taking morphine again, that it was beyond my control, and I wanted him to cure me of the habit.

He came, asked some questions, and left beside my bed a big green bottle from which I was supposed to take a small and measured dose whenever I could not control my nerves. Well, during that night I drank everything in the bottle.

It must have been about ten days later that I came to what we may call my senses. When I could focus my eyes, I saw two women sitting in the room; they wore white starched uniforms. Dr. Barker was in charge of my case then.

I also learned that, during those days when I was blathering and dazed, Dr. Barker had wanted me locked up in some sanitarium. That was when Ned McLean did something fine for me.

"We'll have a sanitarium right upstairs," he said, "on the top floor of this house. If she were to come out of this locked up somewhere, she never would recover from the shock. She stays here!"

I was meant to "taper off." At times I felt such pains as must afflict a creature while a bigger beast eats and claws at its middle. God-awful things were hiding underneath my bed, and it was no use telling me they were not there—I knew they were, and felt their dreadful ever-changing shapes.

One day I telephoned for Barker.

"I am ready now to fight this thing myself. I will do as you say—that is, I will try, and certainly I will submit myself to any rule you make. Just to prove me, put a vial of morphine tablets on the table here beside my bed. I won't touch them, and I won't drink or smoke a cigarette."

I do not know whether it really was morphine that Dr. Barker left with me, but I believed it was. Wrestling with myself to keep resisting, I would become drenched with perspiration. I did not win the fight for hours.

I know there was a month when during any night I did not pass more than a half-hour in bed. We used to walk around that mammoth house throughout the night, the nurses and I. We would circle every gallery as, so many times, I've paced the decks of liners. We would go from the top floor to the ground, each nurse holding tightly to an arm; and when we would round a corner or go into another room I would start and tremble.

"What's that crawling on the wall?"

"Now, now, that's just a shadow, darling."

"If that's a shadow it has legs with substance and a slimy, writhing tail."

Don't ask me to account for it: I really saw the things the nurses said I fancied out of shadows. I have had lots of time to think about the matter. It is my belief that out of mental records of my past the impression of some lizard or garden snake no bigger than a pencil came crawling into memory, and that in my delirium these old impressions were enlarged and projected against the wall and ceilings of my home.

Eventually I seemed to find myself with a lessened craving but whenever Barker came he warned me: no drinks, no smoking.

I had the help of all who loved me, including Ned. We used to talk of my affliction without a trace of passion. He wanted me to discipline myself for the sake of our baby; but he was .unwilling to discipline himself.

One night, about the time Barker was becoming proud of his cure of me, Ned did not come home. I sent his secretary to the Post to get him. When the secretary failed to produce his boss, I called up Ned and ordered him to come right straight to 2020.

"I'm not coming home to-night."

"Unless you come I'm going to pour myself a nice big drink." There were terrific implications there. Need I confess again that I was warped and spoiled?

"Go on. Take your drink. I'm not coming home."

I was in the fix of a man who draws a gun and lacks the nerve to shoot. I called up Barker over in Baltimore, and told him Ned and I were fighting and that I was about to take a drink. The two nurses, Miss Shearn and Miss O'Brien, were still staying with me, although I was supposed to be quite cured.

"Listen," said Dr. Barker: "don't you dare touch a thing. Get your hat and coat and come straight to me as fast as you can come. I'll be waiting. Mind, now."

I ordered the car and told the two nurses to get ready. Mother had learned of this commotion. She pleaded with me to calm myself and stay at home. I would not listen, flouncing out the door to where the car was waiting under the glass-roofed porte-cochere.

"You open it up," I said to the chauffeur, "and if you fail to pass each car ahead you can be sure someone else will drive for me to-morrow."

I guess I made him mad, or hurt his pride; at any rate, he broke some records for the run from Washington to Baltimore and lost a fender.

Those two calm nurses were anything but calm when we arrived. The Irish saints they called on for protection were pretty nearly a Catholic education for me.

A suite had been engaged at one of the hotels.

Dr. Barker was waiting in my sitting room. He is an admirable man—handsome, effective, self-contained, and forceful. I owe him much.

"I'm through." I said to Dr. Barker. "Ned's acting up, terribly. He would not come home to-night and I am through."

Barker raised his eyebrows a little and looked at me.

"Now," went on the dramatist in me, "I'm going to order three cocktails, and cigarettes. I'm pulling wide the throttle on the road to hell."

Barker seated himself in a comfortable chair and merely looked at me.

Presently a hotel servant came and placed the tray of cocktails and the cigarettes on the mantelpiece. The door closed and we two again were alone. I rubbed my hands. Then I walked up to the cocktails—three Manhattans.

I could not reach out for a glass. I told myself that Barker had me hypnotized. Probably the truth is I could not bear to see a man so fine gaze at me with contempt. It was then about half-past nine.

The Hope Diamond

We were there until three-thirty in the morning, and if Barker spoke two words I do not remember them. He simply watched me. Repeatedly I went to the mantelpiece and stopped, just as if I were a clock that had been wound too tightly. Whether Barker really hypnotized me or whether he simply aroused my self-respect I do not know. At some time before dawn the nurses put me to bed, and Barker gave me something he said would make me sleep. It did.

That was the last struggle I had with morphine. I think the credit goes half to Barker, half to little Vinson Walsh McLean.When I returned home I discovered that Ned was still off somewhere on a drinking spree. My nurses remained with me for some time after that, and even when they left I continued to be careful. My bout with morphine was over forever.

CHAPTER XVI

My Relatives-in-Law

THERE never has been another cast in the mold of Ned's uncle, Truxtun Beale of San Francisco. Born rich, he never had to lift a finger. In 1891, at the age of thirty-five, this brother-in-law of influential John R. McLean was sent as Minister to Persia; thereafter he was, simultaneously, Minister to Greece, Roumania, and Serbia; and after that he traveled in Siberia, Central Asia, and Chinese Turkestan. As one of the family, I can testify that he really was an envoy extraordinary. I suspect he is, or has been, worth about four millions. All his life he has been a sort of lightning rod attracting trouble.

Uncle Trux is now almost eighty and still a fascinating man; but he has the darnedest habits—the old firebrand. Sometimes he leaves his cluttered house at 28 Jackson Place (it is packed with objects of art and other treasures) in such a hurry that his clothes are pulled on over his pajamas. He has been known to stay that way for weeks with a cravat "dressing up" the collar of his pajamas. God knows where he often sleeps! Possibly in a moldy chair at the Metropolitan Club. His first wife—I adore her and she is often my house guest now is Aunt Harriet, the daughter of James G. Blaine. This marriage ended in divorce, and, in 1903, he married Marie Oge of San Rafael, a grandniece of Salmon P. Chase.

Long ago, in New York, Uncle Trux went out for an evening in the company of a young beauty and her husband, a Pittsburgh playboy. They were eating and drinking on the roof of Madison Square Garden when the husband left abruptly.

Suddenly Uncle Trux heard something pop; people jumped to their feet, women screamed. Just then the young husband came back and said, "Here, Truxtun, you take Evelyn home. I've just shot Stanford White." In his hand was a pistol that still exhaled a burned-powder odor.

Uncle Trux was petrified. He was still, he hoped, a person eligible for diplomatic honors, and there he found himself smack in the middle of a page-one scandal.

Uncle Trux was not feeling gallant then; he hustled the former Evelyn Nesbit down to the street, boosted her into a taxi cab, and himself raced off to catch a train for California. It was he who sent, in place of flowers, the California lawyer, Delmas, to defend his friend. Uncle Trux never came back across the Rockies until the trial was over, and Harry Thaw was safe in an asylum.

I do not know for sure what Uncle Trux was mad about the time he had his trouble with Taft's Secretary of the Navy, George Von Lengerke Meyer. Of course, the old man always has been jealous, but he was apt to take fire just as much at a harsh word. (Once, on Marie's behalf, he shot a California editor.)

This particular day at 2020, after luncheon a servant informed Ned that the Metropolitan Club was calling him; it was urgent. Ned bounced back from the telephone and grabbed his hat. His excited eyes showed circles white as eggs-on-spinach.

"Come quick," he said, "so we can see the fun."

"What is it?"

By that time Ned was at the porte-cochere, leaping at the Fiat.

"Uncle Trux," he roared, "and Secretary Meyer are fighting in front of the Metropolitan Club. They began by pulling each other's noses on the club steps, and now they are locked together rolling in the gutter. The House Committee thinks I ought to come and separate 'em."

They had been pulled apart before Ned arrived, but he was there in time to hear his Uncle Trux say: "Now, you this-and-that, come on across the street to the hotel. We'll get a room and finish."

Ned phoned me later: "Uncle Trux was the winner." Ned, naturally, was partisan. Since I do not know the inside of the story I am willing to call it a draw. Marie Oge Beale is very handsome, as vivid as a poppy.

John R. McLean was always "Pop" to Ned. To me he was and will remain a mystery. I know he had an acid stomach, but I can't see why he had to have an acid heart. His father, Washington McLean, built up the *Cincinnati Enquirer* and accustomed his children to a life of riches. (John R. used to tell how he eventually got the paper for himself and then made his father pay to subscribe.)

Mrs. Washington McLean was just about as fussy as she would have been allowed to be as Empress of Russia. Four horses were harnessed to her victoria. With two men on the box and two outriders, she demurely rode alone in the seat and probably pretended to herself that in her veins was nothing less than royal blood.

John R. went to Harvard, then to Heidelberg. He loved power and nothing was too much trouble when he saw a chance to extend his reach and his control of other men. When I came into the family he was at his peak. He would be sweet and gentle with some callers and when they had departed he would say, "Now, what do they want out of me?"

The McLeans had the big house in I Street where afterward I was hostess. It covered half the block. John Russell Pope, the architect, had nobly fashioned it for entertaining — nothing else; actually the modern part is like a palace, but this pretentious front is hooked onto a small, old-fashioned home of crumbling brick. (That was the old McLean place where I used to go when I was little.) Around the corner in Fifteenth Street was the original Shoreham Hotel. I Street is paralleled by H Street, and there John R. had another house in which he had his office. This was the place that later on, in the Harding Administration, was called "the love nest" by Harry Daugherty.

One day when my boy Vinson was a baby, Mummie McLean herself took me to see that place. Elsie De Wolfe had supervised the decorations; it was one of the first things she ever did. Below the street level were the kitchen and the pantry. At the rear on the first floor was the dining room with stone serving tables and a small fountain. In front of that there really was an office, a room with panels of buff satin. John R., the head spider, could sit behind the curtains in a big bay window and observe all who passed along H Street, knowing that none in the street could see him. Upstairs were two bedrooms. The rear one was in lovely chintz; the front one was a gorgeous place, everything covered with pale pink taffeta. The gilt bed was sheltered by pink taffeta draperies and pale pink taffeta curtains hung at the window. It was alluring.

The other day I thumbed through a book of tissue copies of letters and came across one to Brewster and Company, the carriage people, in New York. John R. was arranging the details of a gift, an automobile for his wife. Her name, Emily, was to be put in silver letters somewhere on the inside of the car. He had sent to Brewster's more than a dozen objects to be installed: a bottle for salts, address book, pin-cushion, mirror, hairbrush, hatbrush, and memorandum pad. All those things were silver, and John R. was meticulous in his specifications: "Remember, Mr. Brewster, I want this to be very nice, and I look to you to make it so for me." Another time, in 1909, that book reveals him writing to Tiffany and Company.

Gentlemen:—

I have just received by U. S. Express Company this morning the emerald and diamond pendant, which I ordered from your company in Paris. But the combination collar and bracelet which I ordered there for Mrs. McLean has not reached me yet, and as my time for giving it to her is growing short, won't you kindly cable over there and find out when it will reach this country, and when I will get it here, Washington Gas Light Company, D. C.
Sincerely yours,

JOHN R. McLEAN.

He wrote to Peter Schwab at Hamilton, Ohio:—

Dear Peter:—

What you must have heard was that I wanted to sell Enquirers. As for selling the Enquirer, why, I would as soon think of cutting off my right hand. My father made that paper, as you know, and I never will sell it as long as I have a drop of blood in me. The Cincinnati Enquirer is for my son. No money could buy it. So glad to hear from you.

Just about everything John R. had he seemed to hold for his son. In those days, though, I thought he was a skinflint. Ned received $1,000 a month. I fully realize that to many this amount would seem magnificent, but it never lasted Ned more than a few days. I paid all our living costs and bought my own clothes (in 1911 I had a sable coat that cost $60,000); on top of that, I made up Ned's deficit when he got into jams and needed money. A letter from Pop McLean to his boy Ned simply complicates my efforts to understand John R.:—

Dear Ned:—

All well here. Tell Pop the truth, how are you? Are you over your cold or not? Everything is going here all right at the *Post*. All you have got to do in this world is to keep well. Pop will take all the responsibility. I am only holding the *Post* for you. I just sent you a telegram. Hope I will get a good answer.

He would write like that and mean it, but when Ned went deeply into debt, and was threatened with bankruptcy, this man who had encouraged him in idleness let me be the rescuer. I got every dollar I could get from the Trust Company. Once I pawned a ruby bracelet and other jewelry. Another time I paid $300,000 cash to release my husband from the clutches of his creditors. To me old John R. had few redeeming qualities; Ned's wastrel characteristics were blandly tolerated by him.

And yet, poor devil, how horribly he died!

Mummie was a creature of entirely different stuff. She was a gentlewoman in every fiber; she was foolish on only one subject: her son. I felt her fineness on the day the torpedo boat destroyer *Beale* was launched into the Delaware River, at the Yard of William Cramp and Sons Ship and Engine Building Company. That day soft brown fur of her coat collar was about her throat. She had changed a hat that was white with ostrich feathers for a smaller one of dark straw and ribbon much less apt to catch the wind. A bottle of champagne in a gold wire net was held by the neck as a kind of wand in her white-gloved hand. Her cheek was deeply dimpled, and her smile was a young girl's smile.

"I name thee *Beale!*" she cried, and with an arm that knew a tennis racket and how to swing it in a circle she swung the bottle hard against the prow. A giant figure 5 was painted where that champagne made a christening foam on the thick paint of the new hull.

The Beale for whom the ship was named was Mummie's father, who had been Lieutenant Edward Fitzgerald Beale of the United States Navy, then had resigned to become a brigadier general of the Army. Somehow as a boy, an ensign, while helping to win California for the U. S. A. he also won for himself a million-acre ranch.

After the Civil War, as a friend of President Grant, he had his third career as a diplomat at Vienna. He was born in 1822 and died in 1893. My, but Mummie was proud of him, and so was his other daughter whose eyes that day were full of tears: Aunt Mamie was present with her husband George Bakhmeteff, who late in 1911 arrived in Washington as the Czar's ambassador, little dreaming that he would be the last to represent his emperor in America.

The Bakhmeteffs were temporarily at the Shoreham when I first went to call on them. I found a fat and dumpy little woman whose dyed red hair was pink in spots, as mine is now. Her nose was sharp. Each move she made was accompanied by the clink and clatter of a pound or two of barbaric jewelry. Her hat was thickly

A Banquet At The I Street House

feathered; Aunt Mamie adored feathers. I liked her right away. She was, beyond dispute, an ugly woman. Uncle George's face was deeply pitted with the scars of smallpox. He always wore a monocle. They loved each other more than any couple I have ever known. They were completely devoted, two beings in a perfect union, unhappy every minute they were apart. He had a caustic wit; to illustrate it offhand I have to skip ahead to 1917.

When the Russian Revolution was under way, while the Czar was a prisoner and Kerensky had become the head of the government, President Wilson asked Uncle George a question.

"This Bakhmeteff who is being sent over here to represent the Russian people in your place; he is a relative?"

"He is related to me," said Uncle George, "in just about the way that Booker T. Washington was related to George Washington."

Mr. Wilson roared at that.

The Bakhmeteffs were the guests of honor at a dinner I gave at 2020; that was February 2, 1912 — the same day we settled a lawsuit with Cartier and paid a part of the $154,000 for the Hope diamond. I wore the stone that night but would not let any of my friends touch it on the ground that they might not be immune to its curse.

That was a party! There were forty-eight for dinner, and the cost of the whole entertainment was $40,000; much of that was for orchids and for four thousand two-dollar yellow lilies, brought from London. I wore the Star of the East in my hair. Among the guests were Admiral Dewey and his wife, Ned's aunt.

I can't think when I first met Millie Dewey. She had great blue eyes, and was as dainty and as scratchy as a cat. A doll! That is the only word I can think of to apply to her. She was completely feminine and saved each thing the Admiral gave her in the manner of a girl who hoards her emotional souvenirs—dance programs, faded flowers, and similar objects; I remember being puzzled over her concern for the safety of a china ornament, a yellow cat on a purple pillow.

I loved Admiral Dewey. He used to take me for drives, and driving was the old man's hobby. One day we went to Arlington and rode through all those twisting avenues between the curving rows of graves of soldiers and sailors, mostly officers. Admiral Dewey showed me precisely where he wanted to be buried.

With both hands he preened his snowy mustache. "I'm going to have a tomb in here that will make that ugly mausoleum of Admiral Porter look like hell."

Aunt Millie used to say to me: "You go with George. He wants to hold the reins himself and does not enjoy being driven. I am content in a victoria or a brougham, but I am nervous when I ride close to the horses."

She would tell me how she dreamed and thought of her mother constantly after old Mrs. Washington McLean had died. She grumbled all the years I knew her about her mother's will — "that unjust will." Sometimes her grumbling had a quality that suggested she was talking less to me than to her dead mother. Such a conversation would run on like this: "Cutting me out with only a life interest! Humph! And I should have had one third of Mamma's estate—it all came from Papa and I have been juggled out of it. I do not blame poor little Mamma. It must have given her many unhappy hours. After all, I was the last person on earth she spoke to, and I was the only child she kissed and blessed."

Mrs. Dewey and her sister, Mrs. Mamie Ludlow (her son, Frederick Bugher, was Police Commissioner of New York for a while when Hylan was mayor), squabbled endlessly; they fought like sparrows, with chirps and pecks and screams. Mamie was the widow of Rear Admiral Ludlow. The constant umpire was John R.

Aunt Millie used to tell me how she quivered when she and the Admiral, soon after their marriage, were being criticized in the newspapers. Two months after their marriage, in November, 1899, they had moved into a place called Beauvoir, in Woodley Lane. The man who destroyed the Spanish fleet at Manila Bay took pride in a little sitting room decorated in Delft blue and white. His admiral's flag hung against the wall, with pictures of Cavite and also photographs of two Spanish ships that his guns had sunk.

Aunt Millie was really dwelling in the past for all of her last years. She had been a beautiful widow in 1899 when Dewey came home from the Orient a hero. He was acclaimed almost as a god. But Mrs. Washington McLean and her widowed daughter, Millie, came to the conclusion that he was not a god, but quite a man. The night he proposed the old lady was poised upstairs awaiting her daughter's call. She hustled down, kissed the Admiral, kissed her daughter, almost before she had heard a signal. Then the nation gave the Admiral a house in Washington, D. C., at 1747 Rhode Island Avenue, N.W.—and he, dear man, gave the house to his new wife. What a clamor that caused! I barely remembered any of it, of course; but after I was married and often with the Deweys, they continued to speak of this period of disfavor as something much more dreadful than the war that made him a hero.

"The New York *Journal* had a whole page of lies," she told me once. "All about my disputing for precedence with Mrs. Nelson Miles, how I rose from table before my hostess to show I was a 'hero's wife', how I fought for my rank at luncheon and dinners. There was not a word of truth in those silly charges. Miles was just a lieutenant general, while George was Admiral of the Navy. There was no question of his rank. Yet all that abuse distressed me horribly, because I was, and am, so sensitive. It almost killed me!"

Poor Aunt Millie! She had little force with which to meet calumny. She was easily wounded, even by a fancied slight. Later on Ned did something that she thought was outrageous and Admiral Dewey, through me, sent word that he never wanted to look on Ned's face again.

I found a letter in our files that I had not seen in twenty-three years. Mrs. Henry Cabot Lodge, the wife of the Senator, wrote it to John R. McLean in 1912, when Taft, Roosevelt, and Wilson—and their supporters—were in a mad, triangular campaign, It seems to me that Mrs. Lodge wrote beautifully of my husband's mother:—

No one had, or ever will have, her grace and charm of figure and movement. To see her cross her own ball room or sit at the head of her table; to have her come as she so kindly did sometimes to my house, when I could no longer go to her, and enter the room with that beautiful gliding motion was always an enchantment to me.

And then her lovely hands with those flashing diamonds which made her fingers even more fine and slim, those eyes of hers and hair! I have to say these things to you because I know that you appreciate all Mrs. McLean's kindness and the warmth of her human sympathy; but I want you also to know how I admired and rejoiced in the outward and visible signs of her many inward gifts and graces.

This reminds me of a time at Newport when I was full of eagerness for the morrow — I was to help Aunt Mamie Bakhmeteff with her garden party at the Russian summer embassy. Between times, when I rode in a car or drove in a smart cart to Bailey's Beach, I had beside me on the seat my big French poodle, Sarto; he was white, woolly as a sheep, and devoted to me. That *caniche* could almost talk. So sensitive was he, I swear his tail and spirits drooped as I read a telegram from Bar Harbor that told me Mummie McLean was confined to her bed with a bad cold. I hated that summer home that John R. owned in Bar Harbor— it had uneven floors and other antique discomforts; but as I expected Aunt Mamie forthwith canceled all arrangements for her Russian party at Newport and we set out for Maine.

When Mummie was not on parade she was accustomed to move around the house in a little, old flannel gown, with her hair pulled straight back into a braid held fast with a string of ribbon. She was thin, dark of skin, and in her brilliancy as hard as any diamond in my jewel casket. When young she had been better than good-looking; that could be realized by anyone who saw her eyes and dimples. But when I made her into a grandmother she was old, but of unrevealed age. Her age was guarded by her as a bitter secret. In September, 1912, 1 feel sure that there were years that she despised and hated among her probable sixty-five. Perhaps it was bitterness that flavored the witty remarks with which she could keep a table roaring with laughter. I have heard her do so a hundred times, especially at her regular Sunday luncheons out at Friendship where, at one time or another, everybody came who helped, through politics or business, to run the nation. She was ghastly-looking when Ned, Aunt Mamie, and I reached her, but what she had was still "a cold." John R. was already there.

I stayed beside her several days, and once or twice we thought she was getting better. Then abruptly she began to breathe much harder. An oxygen tank was brought and we began to put in calls to Baltimore for Dr. Barker. He was away somewhere in the mountains. I do not recall all the details of the search for him, but at last he was found at a point on Lake Toxaway in North Carolina, more than thirteen hundred miles from where Mummie was trying with frightful wheezings to get air into her lungs.

John R. said, "Get him." The man who spoke was one long accustomed to authority. The messages went forth by telephone and telegraph. Three special trains would be needed to get Barker to Maine: one from North Carolina to Washington; one from Washington to New York; then a third train that would travel over several lines to Bar Harbor. The McLean payroll was a long one. All kinds of talents were detached from other employment just to weave for this one occasion a swifter path for Barker. At the beginning he had to come for hours down the mountains in a wagon, and while he was being jolted along Mummie McLean was dying.

"Send off a wire," said John R. to me as he halted in his pacing, "to Tiffany or Cartier—whichever you think best. I want a string of pearls. I have been after them some time to locate a string."

In the next room my Sarto, grotesquely barbered (I paid five dollars for his haircuts), lifted up his long snout and howled. I shivered.

I find some letters: in one John R. asks one of his editors to get two hundred decks of playing cards with unglazed surfaces. He wrote: "Mrs. McLean's eyes cannot stand the shiny cards." In another, written much more than a year before this time, he was asking one of my favorite jewelers to be on the lookout in Paris for a string of pearls in case he wished to buy one when he came over. Why did he not go through with that?

I hated my father-in-law and yet I want to be fair. The old man with his soft blue eyes, his cropped mustache, was always a businessman. A string of pearls? A hundred thousand dollars? Why, that would buy the presses for the weekly paper he was now conceiving, now aborting in his mind. He knew much better than I could ever know the force of money, what true wealth was and how to store it. The business manager of *the Enquirer* received from him a note expressing genuine delight: "Do you really mean you have on hand $22,000 worth of white paper and that it is all paid for?" Another one to W. F. Wiley, his Cincinnati editor, reveals a business mind turning over just about as fast as big Hoe presses.

How would it do to use more white paper on the week days and give me all the chance possible on Sunday? Last year we printed more Sunday papers than this, and yet this year we used over 18,000 pounds more of white paper than last year. The increase for the weekly amounts to maybe 4500 pounds. Now I would do more with the daily than what we have been doing, but turn less white paper in on Sunday. It's the terrific use of white paper on Sunday that is my great expense. The additional page on Sunday, as you know, far outranks the additional page on a week day. I have no competition to speak of on Sunday, but competition on the other six days. Just for a trial let us turn it around — save on Sunday, and spend a little more on week days. Kindest regards.

Such a mind would envisage a string of pearls and right beside them 600-pound rolls of white newsprint in a mound big enough to run his papers for a longer while than I can calculate. He would be concerned because, with Congress in session, less gas was being consumed in Washington than his engineers had estimated. He would send word to Mamie Ludlow:—

> The man who now runs the Arlington will give us $15,000 per year for the rent of the Normandie, provided we put on $25,000 worth of repairs for work that he thinks necessary to make the hotel all right. You see he has a full equipment of cooks, maids, men and etc. and can move right in. Now the question is, are you willing to put in ⅓ of the $25,000. I am if you are. Milly says she is. Please let me hear from you at once? There seems to be no danger about the mines.

Aff.—

JOHN R. McLEAN.

God knows what happened to him on the route to fortune. He left Harvard early —after being injured, so I always understood, while playing baseball. Then, after some years abroad, where he became infected with the harsh, ruthless philosophy of Kant and Nietzsche, he returned to take over his father's paper. He made it boom. He made it into what I consider one of the greatest papers west of the Hudson River, and he made it sensitive to news by free spending on telegraph tolls.

I imagine that in his youth he was more gentle and that he put on a harder shell as he grew older.

Dr. Barker reached the other side of the bay just before eight o'clock on September 8th, Will Duckstein met him there with a fast motor boat, and brought him across through a streak of spray. When he entered Mummie brightened just a trifle; her faith, as mine, was high in Barker. I hated my Hope diamond when he turned away from the bed. If anybody could have saved her Barker could; but Barker shrugged his shoulders. I did not know what to blame. We needed her, each one of us, for she was sane and good.

Outside the wind shrieked against the house that had withstood so much harsh weather. A shutter banged. Sarto lifted his head as he would do when someone played a violin off-key or sang soprano. Then he began to howl. Another superstition? Hell, I am not saying. All I know is that while Mummie lay dying Sarto howled.

Ned threw himself upon his mother's body, and although he had grown to be over six feet tall and weighed more than two hundred pounds, I could detect in his heartbroken wails the grief of the sweet-faced, wholly charming little fellow whose photograph, aged eight, can help me orient my mind when I am inclined to think, sometimes, that the McLean I married was always a half-lost soul. I often wonder what he would have been, what he might be, if he had never had much money.

But we had the money, or rather it had us. We were held fast in its clutches, captives to it as I had been to morphine. Indeed, I think that is the way to say it: we were the slaves of an infernal habit. This habit stole our will, subtly metamorphosed our point of view, thwarted our creative powers, and quite constantly made us the victims of such awful shapes of greed as would defy the fancy of such persons as we Walshes were until after I was ten. I will prove my case with something that I ordinarily forget; this was the experience that to remember even for an instant chills my blood with horror.

Among the letters that poured in on us, extending sympathy and love from all our friends and Mummie's, there were several that were vile. I shall not dwell upon this grisly subject. The point is that John R. found he had to hire two men to guard his wife's tomb by day and night. The armed watchman who came on duty as darkness settled was escorted to the mausoleum by the superintendent of the cemetery. This official unlocked the tomb, and when the watchmen entered locked it again. The man was a prisoner there all night. For several years this was continued; and all this unnatural seeping out of fear was caused by letters asking money to placate the threat of some greedy fiend who signed his letters with one word: GHOUL.

With Mummie buried, a half-dozen women began that winter, 1912-1913, to struggle to achieve the leadership of Washington society. The newspapers always speak of the wife of the current president as "the First Lady of the Land"; my experience is that she has little chance of being First in Washington. No matter what her skill, her grace, or her family background, when she moves into the White House she moves into a social strait jacket. She never enjoys anything like freedom in making up her lists. Her husband's problems must come first. His politics keep interfering and, moreover, the manner of their entertaining must never cause dismay among the churchgoing small-town voters. That winter our friend Mrs. Taft was preparing to depart, and the new mistress of the White House was to be the first Mrs. Woodrow Wilson—gentle, cultured, almost an invalid, far outside my reckless orbit.

The ones who struggled for the ruling social place in Washington, a place linked up with Palm Beach, Bar Harbor, and Newport, were very rich women: Mrs. Levi Leiter, Mrs. William F. Draper (I have her photograph taken with a coronet, each point blunted with a pearl approximately half as big as my thumb), Mrs. Edson Bradley, and some others. Marshall Field's widow was in Washington that year, and she was in an entrenched position.

Because of our mourning, Ned and I were completely out of things.

CHAPTER XVII

Newport and Palm Beach

WE had our customary pre-Christmas party for Vinson on his birthday. His parties — as my own — were everything that White House parties cannot be. Champ Clark was devoted to my little boy; so was Admiral Dewey, who gave him, one year, a birthday cake that was a pastrycook's idea of the battleship *Olympia.* The Deweys also had given him his first team of goats. He had one toy I had selected, a life-sized burro made of the skin of one of those creatures of the Colorado mountains. There was nothing I could think of that our son lacked. His Christmas parties were a treat for others. Each little boy would get an electric railroad train or something like it; each little girl, the most expensive doll. I think I never spent less than $15,000 for one of his parties.

Somehow, Ned got the idea that Vinson would be spoiled by too much attention from his elders. As a matter of fact, the child did talk in the manner of grown-ups.

"Say," Ned exclaimed to me one day in a rebellious voice. "I had a Negro boy to play with when I was little. Vinson needs a change from this association with detectives, nurses, and others. He does not see enough of children. He'll be a snob if you're not careful."

I argued. Ned retorted: "Last year we provided him with a private showing of the circus. My plan is to change things a lot. Let's find him a Negro boy to play with. When he grows up the Negro boy can be his valet." I had a notion, for a while, that the scheme would be amusing.

We could not buy a colored boy, of course, although it was our habit to buy anything we wanted. But Ned made arrangements with the parents of a little five-year-old named Julian Winbush to let him come and live with us. They relinquished all control of him for ten years, and signed some papers to make it legal.

The Winbush boy was shiny black with teeth that anyone would envy. I dressed him up to match Vinson, and then we headed South in the private car. The colored Pullman porters all the way to Palm Beach were just about hysterical at the astonishing prospects of Julian Winbush. Aladdin, Sindbad, Ali Baba rolled into one would not have been as interesting to them as the little colored boy who, they thought, was being reared as a brother of the so-called "hundred-million-dollar baby."

In winter and in summer most of Vinson's little things came from Paris, from Worth's — like his little carriage robe, his hat, his coat, all made of ermine. I liked that little colored boy, at first; but I could not bring myself to a point where there was pleasure for me in dressing him in clothes from Paris. Yet, since Vinson played with him, he must be clean and sweetly scented. He was playful, friendly, roguish. His big eyes that rolled like agates in his little head gleamed with amusement when I placed him and Vinson in a wicker rolling chair at Palm Beach and pushed them, seated side by side.

As far as I can recall the experience, Vinson was none too well pleased. So far as he was concerned, I would have done as well to have borrowed a playmate for him from the zoo. My Vinson was remarkable for something I have not detected in my other children. He was puzzled, almost as soon as he could talk, at being alive and by the queerness of that situation. If God made us, he asked me once, then who made God? I could not answer, so he posed the question to his dancing teacher, Miss Hawks—but she was no better informed than I.

By the time we were ready to come North from Palm Beach our experiment with the little colored boy was nearly finished. We canceled ourselves out of the deal with money. I have wondered, once or twice, what black-skinned Julian Winbush thought about it all, or thinks about it now. Some day, perhaps (God help me!), he will write his own memoirs and speak his mind concerning rich white folks.

Vinson had one little chum whose visits made him rapturous—Shirley Carter, a sweet and lovely boy on whose countenance was printed all the fineness of the great old family of his father, Dr. Carter, that reached in an aristocratic line far back into the history of Virginia. Those two little boys, together, were wholly charming, in microcosm what the race of grown-up men should be; at least, that was the way I felt. Most of the time, of course, my Vinson's companions were the heavy-shouldered guards who were his outdoor nurses and to whom he was attached. The way he talked with them and their manner with him was the reason, I suppose, for his young intelligence having such a strong appeal for some of his distinguished friends. Between my little boy and Speaker Champ Clark there was a real friendship. The old Missouri politician would walk, sometimes for an hour on end, about the grounds at Friendship with Vinson's tiny hand clutching his lowered index finger; linked in that way, they exchanged thoughts—the old man and the little boy.

Among the papers I have looked over in my effort to awake the past is a typewritten list, part of an expense account of a guard named Murphy as turned in by Arthur Buckman , who was then our steward. The list relates to a couple of days when Vinson was sometimes with me in my box at the Laurel race track. In my fancy now I can follow him into the paddock, under the stand, everywhere a little boy's keen curiosity might take him. When he saw anything he wanted (provided it was not forbidden as injurious) it was promptly bought. Apparently he purchased apples and chewing gum on sixteen separate occasions in those two days; he also admired, somewhere, a pumpkin, and that was bought. The price was a quarter. Another quarter was given to an organ man. Heigh ho! it is a long time since that day, but I find rising inside me a tiny hope that the organ man was the escort of a dressed-up monkey that once made my Vinson laugh. He met the organ man a second time, I now discover—for the expense account lists another quarter. There were quarters handed out four other times by Vinson, through his almoner, to someone called Billy. He also handed out a quarter at Friendship to someone he liked whose name was Joe. I cannot remember, now, just who the "Margaret" was for whom he bought (aged not quite five), on two occasions, apples, gum, and candy.

I remember that in 1913 we went back to Newport and in Black Point Farm found a place that took our fancy. It was the property of Mr. and Mrs. Reginald Norman, and our near neighbors were Alfred and Reginald Vanderbilt. I much preferred Newport to Bar Harbor; besides, with the Bakhmeteffs living there, I was holding trump cards in what always is a tricky game—society. Ned, of course, wanted nothing to do with society; he hated it for himself and hated worse, I think, to have me concerned with it. At heart he was an outdoor man. Jokes and drinking from a flask in a duck blind pleased him much better than jesting and drinking in dressed-up company. Besides, he could not bear to see me dance with other men. He was by inherited instinct a jealous person, but even while it irked me I realized that his jealousy was a warped expression of his love. He never trusted me a minute; I trusted him too long. That is the precious thing we lost by being too damned rich: a trustful love.

I never lost the thrill of hoping we were going to have smooth sailing in our marriage. I used to listen eagerly for his shout at homecoming—"Hey! Evalyn!" If a child was sick Ned could be as tender as a woman; but he could also be, when his mean qualities were brought up by drink, a complete beast. I went to our ducking camp time after time to be with him. I learned to drive horses in a show ring to be with him. I stayed away from big parties to be with him—to lull his half-mad jealousy. That first summer at Black Point Farm I left a lot of social engagements to go off to Quebec to fish and shoot. We caught salmon until I was worn out and then proceeded deep into the woods where I shot two caribou and dropped a moose, an enormous bull whose weight was calculated to be eighteen hundred pounds.

That winter, Lady Duff-Gordon designed and made for me a superb coat of tailless ermine with a deep-shaded flounce of broadtail. This was draped from my shoulders to a point below my ankles. The collar was a strip of fur finished with a heavy tassel, and was twisted once about the throat in the manner of a hunting stock. The hat I liked to wear with that coat was black velvet made smart with black aigrettes.

I used to send telegrams to her New York shop, where she was doing business as "Lucile." A wire from me would read: "PLEASE HAVE LADY DUFF-GORDON MAKE THE LOVELIEST DRESS SHE CAN FOR ME STOP HAVE 200 IMPORTANT PEOPLE COMING TO DINNER DECEMBER 31ST" or "PLEASE MAKE ME AN ORANGE THEATER GOWN AM DESPERATE." It seems to me, as I finger old bills and excite my memory, that during some months there was hardly a day when I was not receiving additions to my wardrobe. An enormous room on the top floor of 2020, much bigger than some shops, contained

*Goat presented as a Valentine to Vinson by his
great-Uncle, the Russian Ambassador*

VINSON WALSH MCLEAN

rack upon rack in something like a wilderness—my clothes. I used to give commands to those I dealt with to send my things by something swifter than express or parcel post. I ordered Madame Tappé: "PUT A MAN OR GIRL ON TRAIN AND SEND MY DRESSES AND HATS TO ME RIGHT AWAY." I paid and never haggled, so I usually got the haste I asked for. Years and years ago my father said to me: "Daughter, women who complain of service have only themselves to blame. They don't know how to tip. Be sure to tip beyond the amount to be expected. Those people make their living out of tips. Be generous in such matters. You can afford to do so. Pinch down in anything but tips."

In 1914, as all the world was plunging into war, we three—Ned, Vinson and I —went back to Black Point Farm. We had a staff of thirty people most of the time. I will try to make them real again by writing down their names: William Schindele, Arthur Buckman, Simeon Blake, Leo Costello, Ernest Heil, Henry Verdelman, Herbert Wright, Hedwig Tack, Alice Buggy (that was dear Maggie's sister), Laura Jenkins, Rosie Jenkins, Thomas Murphy, Angus McInnis, V. Bracaloni, William Rideout, Rosie Mengel, Helen Wright, G. M. Terrell, Harry Kohler, Gurley Weynzer, William Holmes, Adrian Icart, D. H. McVicker, Fanny Grandy, Alfred Schiffner, Bernice Jackson, Anna Berthold (the second cook), Henrietta Jenkins, Maggie Harkum, and some soul called simply Tony.

Some months our household payroll, with expense accounts, reached $2,700; by rearranging jobs Buckman got it down to $1,800, and once or twice the total was only $1,600. Of course, this does not take account of those who worked on the farm as laborers. To cooks, maids, laundresses, and cleaning women we had to add an extra three or four just to do work for the other servants. The staff would grow in spite of attempted curtailment but, even so, we liked to be surrounded by those people. The men, to us, were men-at-arms. I almost always have had devotion from the people who have worked for me.

Those were wild times we had, during the two summers we lived at Black Point Farm and went to Newport parties. Ned was the wild one then, not I. But do not misunderstand me: I was never just a quiet matron.

I remember a curious experience on a Fourth of July. In the afternoon Reginald Vanderbilt came over to the farm to continue his day's drinking in Ned's company. He said to Ned, "Let's go over to Narragansett Pier and celebrate our Independence, hey?"

"Now, now, I said, "you'd better not go. Anyway the last ferry has gone. It's past four o'clock."

"Does that matter?" Reggie challenged. "We'll hire a ferry."

Our motor that year was ultrafast, an Isotta-Fraschini. In next to no time, we were on our way; I had about a pound of diamonds and some evening clothes in a bag. The two men had evening clothes. We hired a ferry, and when it came into its slip we went ashore in the whizzing manner of a skyrocket. We went to the hotel (since then it has become a boarding house), cleaned up, and went to the

Casino for dinner. Uncle Truxtun Beale joined us there; also Preston Gibson, who was two or three wives younger then and spent some of his time writing plays. John R. McLean was living in Narracransett that summer, to escape a ghost that might have bothered him in Maine; but I was careful not to tell my father-in-law that we were there under the same sky.

Ned, Preston, and Reggie kept on drinking, and were feeling pretty good. I kept my promise to myself; black coffee was the strongest thing I took. Therefore, I was cold sober when I heard them say we ought to gamble. I loved gambling; I love it still.

"Come on," I said, "I'll stick with you."

"Not me," said Uncle Trux. "I almost know when I've had enough."

So just we four headed down a side street of the town and entered what looked like an entirely innocent little cottage. Then, inside, we were ushered through a sort of tunnel into a chamber where, as I remember, there were three tables. Ned and Preston settled down at roulette; I headed for one of the other tables, and Reggie went with me.

Reggie played heavily; I played just a little. Then, in about an hour I got up and walked over to Ned's table. He presented a strange appearance; his lower lip hung slack, his eyes were glassy. Ned was a tank, and I knew he did not easily pass into such a complete daze. I looked at the table and saw a vast mound of chips just thrown around his elbows where they might seem to belong to anybody. That was not regular.

"Here," I said sharply to the croupier, a thin lipped fellow wearing a green eyeshade. "What are you doing? What has been done to my husband? How much has he lost?"

There was silence for a few seconds all over that room. Everybody stopped to listen. The bouncers moved quietly into sight, just like an opera chorus getting ready to perform something that has often been rehearsed. Finally the croupier lifted his eyeshade an inch and spoke.

"This man has got into the house for fifty-five thousand dollars. And now you ask what we done to him? Lady, that ain't nice."

"You had no right," I shrilly stated, "to let him play in this condition. Any child could see he does not know what he's doing."

While this went on, Ned was pawing his chips around as if they were sand; he drooled a little and his eyes were half-shut, vacant of any expression. I hurried back to the table where I had played.

"Reggie," I said, "come over here. There is something queer going on." Reggie got up promptly and went directly to the proprietor, an elderly wolf.

"You should not let him play," he said, as if to shame the man.

"He owes me money," growled the keeper of the den.

I spoke up to Ned then, as I shook him by the shoulder, saying, "You are going to stop right now; come on, Ned." He half-rose to obey me, but the head man came up with paper, ink, and a pen.

"I'll tell you something, lady. He's going to sign these notes before he goes out of here. I'm not going to let you out until these notes are signed."

In the pit of my stomach there was a feeling of chill that was merely, I knew, the bottom of my rage. I was not scared a bit.

"You know this is Mr. Ned McLean. You probably know his father. Maybe you think you know how to fix things, but if you do, you don't know old John R. Now listen: If you try to make my husband sign a single paper I begin to scream. You've never heard me scream? When I scream the whole police department of Narragansett will come a-running. Anyway, you know damn well such notes won't be legal."

Somehow I had got Ned's stiff straw hat into my hands. I banged it down on his head as if it had been a tambourine, and with a shove started him toward the door. I gave Preston several shoves and got him going. Reggie gave me a pair of approving pats on the shoulder. "I should not have had the nerve," he said. He was a sweet fellow. The other hats and coats were left behind and we started out. I pushed Ned step by step; Reggie handled Preston, who was growing limp. That passageway that was so much like a tunnel seemed to me to be the cover of a long, long journey. I did not know what minute that gang would come after us with guns or something. Reggie and I shoved Ned and Preston into our machine and took them back to the hotel. We found that both of them had been doped.

Afterward, the gamblers tried their best to make Ned settle for his losses but they could not make him pay a penny.

But if I had not been with Ned that night he would have signed anything.

When I went rummaging in my house in 2020 Massachusetts Avenue I looked through my clothes room upstairs and fingered silks, satins, furs, all kinds of fabrics that in the past had been a part of me. I saw a score and more of long-forgotten trunks, and each held its store of garments. There was one trunk that I had opened by my maid, Inga. To my surprise it was filled right to the lid with sable collars, other trimmings, and a gross or more of ermine tails. Each item on that floor excited a fresh flood of memories. I had not thought of it before; but I believe I might take that store of things and garment by garment use them deliberately to revive experiences that likewise hang forgotten in my mind.

One object I found up there in the closed-up house my father built caused me to blush and feel afresh the chagrin that I first felt in Newport back in 1914.

That was a terrible affair: Ned got us into a regular feud with the Vincent Astors. The thing I found was a wig of Chinese hair, the black and glossy strands elaborately coifed and ornamented across the top by a half-moon shield of embroidered silk that dangled, just beside each ear, four strings of green jade beads. The embroidered Chinese shoes were there on a table beside that wig, and in a near-by box was the Chinese gown, and with it was my ivory and peacock feather fan, a priceless object when I bought it. That was the costume that I wore to Mrs. O. H. P. Belmont's big Chinese ball in her playhouse, an enormous and faithfully copied Chinese pagoda with real sun-dogs guarding its entrance.

However, all the trouble occurred not there but at the dinner party which preceded the ball, at the home of Mrs. Stuyvesant Fish. She was a social queen at Newport then. If she became angry with anyone, that person's life in Newport would not, thereafter, amount to much. Mrs. Fish had her dining room all hung with red brocade satin, decorated with stunning gold dragons. She herself was lovely, but was watching everything just like a lady hawk. I suppose she had at least a hundred and fifty guests for dinner, and all the tableware was gold; that was, it seems to me, the last of her big parties.

Mrs. Belmont's ball was keyed to this dinner party, or *vice versa.* At any rate, Mrs. Belmont's son, Harold Vanderbilt, bridge expert and yachtsman, took me in to dinner. It seems to me he was dressed as a mandarin, but, mandarin or yachtsman, Harold Vanderbilt is Mike to his friends. My own face was yellow with a Mongol tint of grease paint; my black brows slanted upward from just above my nose. On my forehead I wore my biggest emerald; it is just a trifle bigger than either of my eyes. I have forgotten who the Russian grand duke was who sat with us that night; he was visiting the Bakhmeteffs. Mike's sister Consuelo, then Duchess of Marlborough, was on hand. In fact, everybody who counted in society was there that night, or wished to be. That was where it happened; I saw nothing of it but only heard when it was too late.

The Vincent Astors that summer were newly married; their wedding, I think, had been-in April. Anyway, she sent word, so I was told, to Mrs. Fish that unless Ned McLean was made to leave the house she would leave. I knew nothing of this, as I say, until later when I heard that Mrs. Fish had sent word back that she would have no guest of hers removed, and if Mrs. Astor did not like it she could go herself. However, when I got into the motor after dinner to drive to Mrs. Belmont's I plainly saw that Ned McLean was much too drunk to be at a party. I tried to persuade him to go home; he would not; he was sullen and suspicious. So I took him to the dance, and about two o'clock in the morning I left him there and went on home.

The next day I went to see Aunt Mamie Bakhmeteff. I rushed into her presence and said, "This is frightful. What will we do?"

Aunt Mamie clucked a time or two, and caught a pair of tears on her cambric handkerchief before they could streak her make-up. She shrugged, as if to say it was beyond her.

"I'll tell you what," I said. "I am going straight to Mrs. Fish and let her know how dreadfully all this makes me feel."

Mrs. Fish was a very quick, high-strung woman. If she liked you she liked you, and nothing mattered.

"Mrs. Fish," I began, "I feel heartbroken about this thing. I feel that Mr. McLean and I ought to get away from Newport."

"My dear child," she said to me, "you let him go, but you stay here. Stick it out. It is not your fault."

John R. McLean was full of wrath and thumbed Ned out of town just like a traffic cop. Ned never said a word, but for him from that time on Newport was not on the map.

I went to Mrs. Belmont too. She was a comfort to me.

"It's not your fault. You just sit tight. We are all back of you. Now listen: I am giving a select dinner for the Duchess of Marlborough, and I want you to come."

I went: this dinner took place a few days after the Chinese ball. Of course, it made me feel much better. There were only twenty or twenty-two at the small Marlborough party. Soon after that, I gave a party for the Duchess of Marlborough. I had it under a big tent on a green bluff overlooking the ocean. After that I was ready to leave, and I told Arthur Buckman to close up the farm. Just recently I found a memorandum dealing with that move; it brings back sharply some of my distaste of that moment for Black Point Farm and all that was connected with it.

The carriage house was filled with rigs on which we had spent a lot of money; vehicles designed to make us feel like country folks. Buckman asked me how to ship them.

"Ship them, hell!" I said. "Sell them."

A list tells me what I never gave a thought to then: a little straw wagon brought $75; a yellow station wagon brought $100, as did one other wagon; Vinson's pony cart went for $35, and a gig for $50.

At Palm Beach that winter, for good and sufficient reasons I scolded Ned, and so he left the place. My playmate then was Mrs. Quincy Shaw, 2nd; Nanine was the close friend of Mrs. Harry Payne Whitney. Quinney Shaw, as I recall it, left Palm Beach when Ned did. So, the first thing we two wives did was to go to Miami Beach and hire ourselves a yacht.

I remember that the first person we met down there was Harry Black and we told him we were going to charter a handsome little vessel called the *Bluebird*.

"Girls," he said, "don't you hire a yacht. I have chartered a perfect beauty, and am all ready to sail to Nassau. Come on with me and save your money."

We told him good-bye right there and that same day we went aboard the *Bluebird,* telling the skipper to take us back to Palm Beach. We came inside by what is called the canal route. I remember we tied up somewhere against a marshy bank just under a revolving beam from a lighthouse. Of course I had to climb up the tower and inspect the lighting mechanism. Nanine was furious with me. Then we went to sleep.

I woke up in a fright; Nanine was yelling from a corner where she had fallen from her berth; and the ceiling, I could see, was slanting. We were convinced the boat was sinking and rushed on deck. What had happened was that the tide had gone out leaving us aground, on tidal mud. For the rest of that night we sat in the stern on cushions, playing a graphophone.

One of our acquaintances at Palm Beach was old Mrs. William Rhinelander Stewart, who by this time was the widow of James Henry Smith, who was known as "Silent" Smith. She was past sixty, and all her life she had been accumulating jewelry. Tiffany might have started a branch with what she wore even when she was going swimming. Because we both were constantly encrusted I was perfectly terrified at times that, with a drink or two, she might lose some in the beach sand and then say that my jewels were really hers. (At night when she retired it was her habit to grope in darkness on the floor until her jewelry was cached beneath the carpet.)

One day there appeared, on the most exclusive section of the beach, a young fellow in a pale pink bathing suit, a pretty good imitation of flesh color. He was strolling with a white and-gray Russian wolfhound. Quite boldly he was making eyes at this old woman, and his eyes were big and fringed with long lashes. He got a quick response from the elderly widow.

Under her breath she spoke intensely: "Meet this fellow. Then invite us both aboard the *Bluebird.*"

My motto is, "Oblige a friend at any price." Consequently, when I met this chap I invited him to come to dinner on the yacht; then I invited old Mrs. Smith. The affair, I thought, would be amusing.

As I recall it, Colonel Edward Bradley introduced me to St. Cyr one night when I was playing hazard at one of Bradley's tables. As it happened that was an occasion when I lost about everything I had.

Bradley had taken off the $50 limit and we were playing on the cuff at $500 a throw. I went in the hole fast, and went in deep. However, I was superstitious and I concluded the croupier was giving me bad luck. Bradley changed the man for me, and I began to win. I won a lot, and kept on until I had played off my loss. Word of what I had been doing there must have reached Ned through some detective spy. I got a telegram from him: —

HOPE YOU AND MRS SHAW WERE NOT ARRESTED IN BRADLEYS DO YOU WANT US TO GO BAIL AM SENDING IMPORTANT PAPER SIGN AND RETURN AT ONCE TO MY FATHER DEAREST LOVE TO YOU BOTH

In the space of just about two weeks I had from Ned a total of sixty telegrams, all of them designed to accomplish just one thing: to get me back with everything forgiven.

I have a magpie habit of saving things: bright objects, all photographs, old letters, programs. I suppose the habit has been encouraged by the multitude of servants always around to file away what I want saved, and likewise by the storage space in a half-dozen houses. At any rate, among other things, all those written mementoes of that fight I had with Ned in 1915 have been preserved; his telegrams to me, my telegrams to him, and the telegraphed reports from his man Arthur Buckman. Ned always used a code of some kind because he was invariably suspicious.

One telegram I got from Ned asked me to come to him at once without the servants. He said my signature was needed on some papers. There is in the file another message, one I never saw before, from Buckman back to Ned: "SHE RECEIVED IT MADE NO COMMENT." Then there was another from Buckman concerning me: "GONE TO SLEEP WONT SEE ME THINK CAN FIX IT IN THE MORNING." A sample of the code remains: "BYWOI HY CRUD NYWH CU KI HTWEM E SU VIEX EH EW KYLWEWB." Decoding that to-day would be beyond my powers, and yet what I am trying here to do is to decode emotions that long ago were printed in cipher on my mind. I can recall how hungrily I waited for Ned's morning message. I was angry, but I loved him and could be happy—then, at least—only when I was sure that he loved me. His frantic pleas by telegram were far more satisfying at that time than anything I could buy with all my money.

To his request to come and leave the servants, I replied: "CANT GET ACCOMMODATIONS WHY COME ALONE EVALYN."

I had another telegram from him: "HAVE SEEN WIRE YOU SENT MY FATHER AM TRYING TO STICK TO MY PROMISE AND HAVE DONE SO WIRE ME AT ONCE WHEN YOU ARE COMING."

Why did I not reply at once to that? Let Buckman's message speak: "HAVE STATEROOM SHE IS OUT FISHING."

At six I sent my answer: "LEAVING TONIGHTS TRAIN BEST LOVE EVALYN." But at nine there was another wire from him that made me rage: "DELIGHTED YOU ARE COMING BUT HAVE ARRANGED YOUR SIGNATURE NOT NECESSARY SO THERE IS NO NEED OF YOUR COMING ON BUSINESS UNLESS YOU WANT TO COME NED."

At 11:17 that night Buckman wired him: "NOT BEEN ABLE TO SEE PARTY YET"; and then, four minutes before midnight, Buckman wired again: "IS NOT COMING."

Naturally I was not coming. I had too much spirit to surrender to him so completely. How characteristic of Ned to lead me on, to pretend that important business required us to come together, and then, when I was wild with eagerness for a complete reconciliation, to let me see that all his pleas by wire were just part of a spoiled man's trick to make me show I was the one who cared the most.

I think it must have been the next day that I gave my dinner aboard the yacht *Bluebird* and had as guests, among some others, this strange young man, St. Cyr, and Mrs. Smith. He was so much younger than her son Willie that her interest in St. Cyr's hats might have seemed at first glance to be maternal. I saw her rearrange the yachting cap he wore upon his dark curly hair. I saw the black veins on her aged hand as she let a jeweled finger scrape his ear. That very minute I was sorry I had introduced them. Contrite, I sent a wire to Willie Stewart. He came, and we did all we could to break it up; but we had no chance —what glittered in Willie's mother's eye was something that thirty-five years before could have been indexed as girlish love. The old woman became Mrs. St. Cyr, and when she died she left St. Cyr, as I recall it, practically all of her money.

A few days after the yachting party I had another flood of telegrams from Ned, in code, and the first one I unraveled said, "DARLING GIRL YOU KNOW HOW CRAZY I AM TO HAVE YOU COME BACK." There was another, saying "I THINK YOU WOULD BE FOOLISH

TO GO TO THE COAST AS THAT PERSON HAS CALLED ON MY FATHER ABOUT YOUR LOSSES AT BRADLEYS."
I replied, "DONT WORRY IT IS NOT TRUE ABOUT BRADLEYS WHEN YOU WIRE AGAIN DONT USE CODE AS THEY GET IT AWFULLY MIXED UP LOVE EVALYN." One of his wires that day said, "IF THE WEATHER IS NICE DARLING GIRL STAY UNTIL THE TWENTY NINTH."

At this time I had an entire first floor wing of The Breakers. All night long two men stood guard outside of Vinson's door; by day my little son was in the company of Arthur Buckman. It was not difficult for him to keep Ned posted on what I did, or said that I intended to do. That was a part of Buckman's job just then. He was working earnestly to keep us together.

Ned had word that I was starting North to Hot Springs, Virginia, where I had a cottage. My intention was to make our separation final. One minute I would be sure that was the thing to do, the next minute I would be uncertain.

Ned climbed aboard the train at Jacksonville; and when I heard the shrillness of my little Vinson's joy and saw his keen delight my own emotion declared itself for what it was: complete satisfaction in our reunion.

We went to Belmont Farm. That was the place Ned had bought at Leesburg, Virginia, with some of the money inherited from his mother. He paid $90,000 for the place, and then kept pouring money into the establishment until he was hip-deep in debts. Guns, dogs, and horses were the sort of things with which Ned would want to equip his part of heaven. Down there we had some show horses that were superb, and we were breeding others: but we had switched our devotion to the sport of racing. I had my own string, and with a natural appetite for gambling found the racing atmosphere agreeable. It was fun to plan with Ned how we might make the farm produce a Derby winner, even a horse that could show its heels to any owned in England. The finest stables, the most costly horses entered into Ned's plans. He issued commands, and whole battalions of laborers appeared to change the landscape of the farm, to create new structures to house our scheme; and all the while I was careful. I was going to have, I knew, another child.

My son Jock was born at 2020 on January 31, 1916. His father, grandfather, and great-grandfather in the McLean line held power chiefly through the widespread ability of Americans to read print; for this, along with the common appetite for news, is the earth and water that generate that still strangely modern force, a newspaper. My children's father, Ned McLean as he was an only son, was born face-to-face with opportunity for greatness in the world; that is, the instrument of power was there if he could learn, as Jason did, to wield it. The unpredicted thing that robbed Ned of his chance was lack of discipline: a spoiling mother from his babyhood saw no wrong in anything he did, a doting but a selfish father would not take the time to study, as he studied any problem of business or politics, the problem of his son.

There is tragedy in all this, if only I can show it. All of my life, from the time we Walshes left the Camp Bird mine to spend its riches for whatever we might want, I have been in contact with the chiefs and captains of the world. Beyond dispute, throughout the years my son Jock has been engaged in growing up my world has been restricted to the places where such people play and work. Why, I have nursed that child of mine and then gone, gowned and jeweled, to preside as hostess over tables where all those of consequence in Washington were sitting. How natural, then, that I should feel a hunger for my sons to have their share of greatness.

I think I still believed, in 1916, that given his father's authority, Ned could make the *Enquirer* and the *Washington Post* pedestals for real power of his own. I wanted him to have the admiration and acclaim that go to greatness. I wanted him to rule his father's fortune when the time should come, and above all else I wanted our sons to be fit to play and work with the leaders of the nation. They do not teach as plainly as they should, in any school I ever went to, that these things cannot be bought as swift horses, jewels, furs, and lawyers' services are bought.

CHAPTER XVIII

Washington Scandals

JOHN R. had power apart from money—a kind of power I should like to see my sons acquire for better usage. In 1884, he was a delegate from Ohio to the Convention that nominated Grover Cleveland for the presidency. In that situation, John R. incurred the enmity of Allen G. Thurman; and so in 1896, when John R. was eager for the Democratic nomination for himself, a son of Thurman showed that the feud still lived by depriving him of the essential support of the Ohio delegation. Bryan was nominated. In politics my father-in-law had the ethics of a masked raider.

John R. purchased the *Washington Post* about 1905, and in it had a lever with which to pry himself into stronger power. The Old Dominion Railroad was one of the things in which he was heavily interested. He was also one of the largest stockholders in the American Security Trust and the Riggs National Bank. When he issued a request politicians of both parties usually tried to oblige him. When a new Republican Senator came to Washington from Ohio in 1916, and John R. sent word he would like to see him, Senator Warren G. Harding was rather prompt to go and call at the H Street office of the owner of the *Cincinnati Enquirer.*

I met the Hardings for the first time one night at Alice Longworth's house. We had gone there for a poker game. That evening I decided that the new junior Senator from Ohio (he had beaten old Joseph B. Foraker in the Republican primaries) was a stunning man. He chewed tobacco, biting from a plug that he would lend, or borrow, and he did not care if the whole world knew he wore suspenders. However, whatever Alice cares to say, I say he was not a slob. That night his white-haired wife, whose chin was lifted haughtily each time she scented challenge, served all our drinks and did not play. Warren Harding at fifty-one was full of life and eagerness to enjoy the world of riches that had been opened to him by success in politics; but Florence Kling Harding had been born in 1860, the year Lincoln was elected President—why, in her mind were printed memories of soldiers in blue uniforms coming back to Ohio from the Civil War.

By the calendar she was five years older than her husband; but ill-health and a tendency to worry over what might happen, plus her nagging temperament, had helped to wear her body. With Harding tomorrow was, at that time, just another day. Hers was the ambition; what he had was charm, an ability to get along with assorted persons, friendliness, and a love of jovial companions.

He was the publisher of just a little newspaper—or so the *Marion Star* seemed to Ned and me, who felt we were to rule the *Cincinnati Enquirer* and the *Washington Post.* If it comes to that, I suppose our Ohio paper explains why we had been invited by our friends the Longworths to come and meet the new Senator from Ohio. I was amused to discover that Harding always addressed his wife as "Duchess." That haughty look of hers, a certain spitfire tendency that had not been curbed with age, had made the nickname seem appropriate. He told me, later on, that some years before he had enjoyed a book about a character called "Chimmie Fadden" whose sweetheart was a lady's maid, a French maid; she was called "the Duchess."

Charlie Curtis, who afterward became Vice President with Calvin Coolidge, was at that Longworth party. I remember that he won all our money. Charlie almost always won, and we used to say it was his Indian blood that kept his face a stoic's mask; it fooled us so that we could not rightly guess by his blank face whether he was nursing treys and deuces or had filled a flush. Why, once in later days when Harding was President and they were traveling in the South, they stopped the special train at some wayside station to send a telegram informing us that Charlie Curtis had been taken into camp aboard the train; he had been cleaned at poker. When he lost at cards, that was news.

In a week or two, we had a poker game designed to repeat the enjoyment of that splendid evening at the Longworths'; but, to my disappointment, the Hardings did not come. I asked Alice where they were.

"She is desperately sick," said Alice, "and it is a question whether she will live."

I was shocked, and said that I would go to call on her the next day.

I did. I got into my car and went up to Wyoming Avenue to the house they had rented. As I recall it, their next-door neighbors were the yellow-skinned people of the Siamese legation. A Negro maid opened the door and looked at me in silence.

"Tell Mrs. Harding I want to see her if I can. I hear she is ill."

Word was sent down for me to come right up. Mrs. Harding was lying flat in bed, and her complexion was blue. My roving eyes saw and appraised many things while we sat and chatted. Hanging on a chandelier near the bureau was a rack of neckties.

"I am very sick," Mrs. Harding told me. "I have sent to Marion for my physician, Dr. Sawyer." She explained: it was her kidney; she had but one or else the least effective, floating one was wired in place. It was pathetic, what I saw and heard that day. Her father had been a banker, rich by smalltown standards. Then she eloped with the boy next door, a ne'er-do-well, who drank and had no luck whatever. He became a railroad freight brakeman, and one day fell beneath the wheels. He lost his arm. They had a son. The sequence of those things she told me I have forgotten; but I remember that her father had sent her West, to Reno, where she was divorced. Her father thought she was making a worse mistake the second time she wished to marry. She lifted her chin and married anyway.

She and the young editor (he was twenty-six) rented a house - that frame house in Mt. Vernon Avenue with a front porch that afterward became so celebrated. In the parlor of that house they were married. Thereafter, for some years, her father would not speak to her and was so bitter that he prevented Warren Harding from

PRESIDENT HARDING AND MRS. MCLEAN

being accepted into the lodge of Masons when he first was a candidate. (The lodge afterward was proud to take him into membership.) It seems that old man Kling would go from place to place in Marion repeating some unjust piece of gossip about his daughter's second husband. She told me how hard she had worked to keep the Marion *Star* a solvent enterprise when, about 1906, Harding had what she spoke of as "a nervous breakdown." There was the pattern of a fixed idea in what she said to me that day. I was not the only one she told how she had scrubbed the office, herded delivery boys out on their routes, and performed a lot of chores.

I used to send flowers to Mrs. Harding during her recurring spells of illness. She had been lovely in her youth; anyone could tell that. Her eyes were blue, her profile firmly chiseled, but her mouth was a revelation of her discontent. She was ambitious for herself and for Warren.

"What did they say about me?" she would ask unfailingly each time she met me after we had been together in a group of people of the smarter set.

That was some months after the time when what we had to gossip about in Washington was the hot romance of President Wilson and the widowed Mrs. Galt, whose deceased husband had been the proprietor of a jewelry store. Few of my friends knew Mrs. Galt, but all were frantic to know more about her. They used to chide me because I did not know, right off, the inside story of the White House love affair.

"Please, Evalyn," they would say, "what is the use of having newspapers in your family if you cannot find out all about such matters?"

We knew that Mrs. Galt was good-looking and, in Ned's horsy phrase, well-fleshed. Admiral Cary Grayson probably was never more sought-after in his life by hostesses than during the period when a president was going courting. When anyone was giving a dinner party her best friend was apt to say, "Get someone who knows this Mrs. Galt to come. I'm wild for information."

Woodrow Wilson and Edith Bolling Galt were married December 18, 1915. And how the gossips buzzed! Ned brought home from the office of the *Washington Post* a hint that a certain Mrs. Peck was offering to sell to newspapers her correspondence with the President. It covered a period of years, extending into his past to the time when he was President of Princeton University.

"Editorial dynamite is what it is," Ned told me. That was the opinion of able newspapermen with years of training. The letters did exist—I have in my possession copies of them all; but they were never published. As a matter of fact, I have no way of knowing that Mrs. Peck offered them for sale while Mr. Wilson lived. I do know that everywhere in Washington her then mysterious friendship with the President was just about the most exciting topic we had ever had. Who is Mrs. Peck? Reporters scampered here and there to propound that question in a whisper.

The truth about those letters is that by 1917 various newspaper executives had read them all. Mrs. Peck still retained her copies. There was not in a single letter one statement that was damaging, in any way compromising, to the character of

Mr. Wilson or Mrs. Peck. I have no skill with which to measure the literary value of his letters, but I know the friendship he expressed was something any woman might be proud to inspire in any man. He wrote, for example, that he supposed it was a recognized principle of friendship that one might show one's weaker, even one's weakest side to the friend who will best understand and most deeply sympathize. Few people realize that Woodrow Wilson had such a side — he seemed so cold; and yet he was not cold at all. By a court decision after he was dead, the second Mrs. Wilson was upheld in her contention that her husband's letters, to whomever written, were still his own and, after him, belonged to his heirs.

However, I must admit I got an extra dividend out of the *Washington Post* the year I read — immune to the Widow Wilson's wrath — those letters. The injunction did not stop, of course, the distribution of the sample copies to the newspapers planning to print the letters.

In 1916, though, when Washington still gossiped about the White House romance, Ned and I were much more exercised about another marriage we feared was pending. Old John R. was in a state of mind that gave us great concern. His wealth had filled all our world with conspirators; or so it seemed to us.

In the spring of 1916, the old man developed jaundice and a case of hiccoughs that could not be ended, seemingly. He told us he was going down to Atlantic City; but as soon as he had gone we began to wonder whether we should not have sent along some person to watch out for him (of course, he had his servants). His valet was a man named Meggett, and he also was attended by a nurse. The suggestion was made to us at that time that a certain woman might take advantage of his feeble state and jump herself into the queen row by way of marriage. That was a most unpleasant fear to haunt Ned and me at 2020. A lawyer, retained by Ned, went to Atlantic City, and checked the records of the Marriage License Bureau there; happily there was nothing. Yet when he returned we still feared something was amiss, because John R. was acting quite unlike himself. And his hiccoughs had not abated much. At the I Street house, except for servants, he lived alone in princely magnificence.

Then, one day, he took a notion that he would not talk to Ned.

I'll say this for my husband: he was grief-stricken, and took to heart the harsh things John R. had said to him. Generally, the old man whom Ned called "Pop" had been tender with his unwise son. Yet Ned, as did most persons who counted on the favor of John R., lived in fear of his father. Nevertheless, something had to be done if the old man was to be saved from some wild rashness. We knew he had to be restrained, and even though Ned was his son this was not easy.

In April, 1916, at our request, there came from Baltimore Dr. Lewellys F. Barker, who made what seemed to be a social call on old John R. The doctor talked of various matters for the purpose of discovering what was the mental status of the patient. Suddenly, to something Barker said, the old man took exception and was fired into a rage. He seized from somewhere a big parchment pile — a million dollars' worth of bonds.

"Money?" screamed my husband's father. "I'll show you what I think of money!" He raised his flabby arms and flung the bonds so that they showered Barker's head. The doctor then returned to Baltimore and made an affidavit: "This is to certify that the behavior of Mr. John R. McLean on April 24, 1916, convinced me that legal measures should promptly be taken to prevent him from endangering himself or his property."

When Dr. Finney and Dr. Henry Parker had made similar reports, and when these had been supported by Adolph Meyer, professor of psychiatry in Johns Hopkins University and psychiatrist in chief to the Johns Hopkins Hospital, we dared to undertake the first steps to exercise control over the person and the derelict estate of John R. His morbid delusions and fantastic suspicions were the basis for our moves in which we had the backing of Dr. John Blair Spencer and of lawyers. The big trouble was that Ned's father was in no mood to admit that his mind was unsound; consequently, we had to move with caution. His valet and his nurse contrived to obey all his orders as if his mind were normal. We deemed it necessary to replace those two attendants. This job the Pinkertons undertook to do when guaranteed indemnity by Ned.

When Meggett left the I Street house to get a breath of air one day in early May, some men joined him; and from that minute John R.'s one-man army was, in effect, a prisoner. Dr. Adolph Meyer, with a squad of hospital orderlies, proceeded into the I Street house — along with Dr. Finney, Dr. Barker, and some others. These men were John R.'s friends, and Ned was his son; but the old man had determined that this was all a plot against his life and fortune. Even in his delirium, he was persuasive and domineering.

All these men walked into John R.'s bedroom. Every half-minute he would hiccough. That had been going on for weeks.

"What is it?" he demanded sharply as he saw the cluster of faces near his bed. Then he began to roar, "Meggett! Where's Meggett?"

"Now, Mr. McLean, you must stay quietly in bed. Everything will be—

"Meggett!"

Literally, the only thing intended was to restrain Ned's father in the I Street house; but he thought worse was planned, I am sure, because he sprang from bed and yelled such profane threats that no man dared to put a hand upon him. He threw the window open up with a force that made the sashweights clatter. There was a cab stand just across the street from the I Street house.

"Cab!" he roared. "I want a cab." He turned from the window when a driver raised a finger to his visored cap. The old man, trembling with fright and rage, pulled on his trousers, a coat, his shoes, and then started out of that house where afterward I was hostess. He spoke to Dr. Meyer with no trace of respect, saying, "Get the hell out of my house, you." An essence of all the power he had wielded in his day was shining in his half-mad eyes and so, completely daunted, they permitted him to go,

John R. took refuge in the little H Street house and from there sent forth a call by telephone to the editor of the *Washington Post* and for his woman secretary. They were uninformed as to our intentions, and obeyed their boss quite faithfully. They accompanied him to Friendship—where I now live. There are almost eighty acres inside the wall; it is a regal holding with lovely gardens, a private golf course, greenhouses, stables, and other instruments of country living. Yet all of this is a piece of Washington.

In the house at Friendship, John R. prepared for siege; he summoned private detectives, a platoon or more. To Ned he sent a painful message—that because his son was trying to poison him he was going to shoot him.

Our own detectives remained on watch, reporting who went in or out of Friendship. In that way we learned there was a plan afoot to operate on the old man. The doctors were not men we knew.

I remember that Dr. Finney came and said: "Evalyn, he is dying. There should not be any operation. If any surgeon tries to operate he is just after a fee. The case is hopeless. John R. is full of cancer."

The next day Ned and I had those doctors come to 2020. There was a stenographer posted behind a screen while we talked. When we said what was on our minds the doctors shrugged and abandoned what they called "the case."

After that I told Ned we simply had to break the siege and, if necessary, to shoot it out with John R.'s guards. He got six Pinkertons and went to the big gates at Friendship, near the clock tower. The gates were closed and just behind the bars some men, with pistols showing, glowered at him.

"See here said Ned, "I am the son of John R. McLean. He's sick—out of his head. His own physicians say that he should be protected from himself. Now, you get out. I'm coming in. If there is the least resistance I start shooting."

"O.K., big boy," said one of those hulking fellows, "we just work for a living. So we get paid, we don't give a hoot." They opened the gates and Ned drove down the graveled drive and made the loop that brought him to the door. Ned fairly ran upstairs to reach his father.

I always say that God was gracious to us then; old John R.'s mind was clear, and he was contrite. He threw his arms around Ned and said to him, "I want Evalyn."

In half an hour I was entering the house—hearing, as I climbed the stairs, the dreadful sound of a man dying, hiccough by hiccough. Ned and I stayed on at Friendship then, and never was there a minute when we failed to hear at least two hiccoughs. He died on the eighth of June.

We held the funeral at Friendship. John R.'s sister, Mildred Dewey, and the Admiral were out of town. A week before, accompanied by John R.'s woman secretary, Mrs. Dewey had appeared at the gates, intending to take her brother back to his home in town. By Ned's orders, this was not allowed.

The sister and the son had not agreed about what was best for the dying man. So, when it was suggested that the funeral ought to wait upon the Deweys' return, Ned said, "Hell, we'll just go ahead without 'em." However, they arrived before the service ended, and Ned's Aunt Millie was in a grief-stained fury. She had really loved her brother. Beside her the Admiral preened his white mustache. His cheeks were red with rage at Ned's affront.

Next day I telephoned Admiral Dewey.

"May I come down?"

"Of course, dear child. You always can come here."

I went, and for an hour I pleaded with him to appreciate our strain, to excuse Ned.

"Evalyn," he said, "I am not angry with you, but I never want to see Ned McLean again, as long as I live. The way he has treated my darling wife!" The old Admiral clasped his blue-veined hands behind his back and paced the floor. He stopped in front of me: "I never have liked him, and now I know I never want to have anything to do with him. Why couldn't he have had the decency to wait for my poor wife to get here? You know she did adore her brother Johnnie."

Well, that was the end of Admiral Dewey being Ned's uncle. He never spoke to Ned again.

What had me wrought up, when John R.'s will was read and understood, was the stunning discovery that the *Washington Post* and the *Cincinnati Enquirer* had been taken from us. You can bet that made me fume. That was when I had the secret exit of the little house in H Street scaled up. I dismantled it of all its furnishings. What I left there was just an office, and it was simply that until 1921 when Jess Smith and Harry Daugherty moved in, at Ned's enthusiastic invitation . . . . But that comes later.

The will provided that the net income of the estate should be paid to Ned, and at his death to the children, the principal not to be distributed until twenty years after the death of that child of Ned's who was the youngest at the time of John R.'s death. The youngest was our second son, Jock, who had been named John Roll McLean. Of course, the income of itself was sufficient to supply the needs and whims of any ordinary spendthrift; but I never knew until a few years ago that Ned's income had thus increased and ranged between $500,000 and $880,000 annually.

It would be difficult to estimate the exact value of the John R. McLean estate. According to newspaper guesses when the old man died, the wealth he left would total $100,000,000. The appraiser was more conservative, and figured it at just about $7,000,000; fixing $3,000,000 (an understatement in my opinion) as the value of the *Enquirer,* and pricing the rest as follows: stocks, $2,701,597.82; bonds, $886,607.50; household effects, $173,555; jewelry, $128,759.75; and books, $471. That item which relates to stocks included, of course, some rich, going concerns for which only book value was put down without regard to earnings. There were a half-dozen modest annuities provided for a couple of distant relatives and a few old servants. Except for these and insignificant deductions, everything went to the American Security and Trust Company. It was a sort of document that lawyers speak of as a "book trust", one that young students of law are apt to find themselves obliged to read. By extending its provisions into the future, twenty years beyond the span of a well-protected baby's life, it neatly skipped the fortune's real power over Ned's life, and mine.

While we were in the midst of a struggle to establish Ned as co-trustee, Admiral Dewey died. That was January 16, 1917; and, day by day, America was getting nearer to a state of war with Germany. At any time, I suppose, Uncle George would have rated an elaborate funeral, but in the country's situation, with the whole world panoplied, it was deemed fitting to have his obsequies conducted in the rotunda of the Capitol.

The following incident is out of order here, but this is the place to tell it: Aunt Millie grew dissatisfied with Arlington. The tomb that sheltered the Admiral's remains was fine enough, we all thought, till the Episcopal National Cathedral's Bishop Freeman, whom I love, went to call on Aunt Millie.

Later in March, 1925, she had Admiral Dewey reinterred in Washington Cathedral. As a former Cathedral trustee he was entitled to such a sepulchre.

CHAPTER XIX

Tragedy

THE war and Ned's preoccupation with it as a journalist kept me in Washington throughout the summer of 1917. I remember that for a year or more I had been in terror of infantile paralysis on account of my children. Some of that old fear returns as I read a letter sent by me to Dr. John Lovett Morse of Boston. After explaining that I had sent my year-and-a-half-old son Jock to Bar Harbor, I wrote:—

Margaret Connelly, one of the nurses you know, is with him. If she should call you on the phone please do not spare any expense to get to the baby as quickly as possible. If necessary get a special train. I will have to spend the summer here and my address is Friendship, Washington, D.C. If you are called to see the baby, be sure to take up some of the infantile paralysis serum, as that is the thing I most dread.

Herbert Hoover and I met in that year; likewise Mr. Hoover met my finest pet, my enormous white caniche, Sartor. We called that prize French poodle "Sarto", and everywhere I went, there also would go Sarto. Of course, just about everything we did at that time was related in some way to the war.

Mr. Hoover, fresh from his relief work in Belgium, was practically a hero, and President Wilson needed one to serve as Food Administrator. Our great hobby then was to get behind the slogan of the diet dictator, which was "Food will win the war." So I gave a dinner for about sixty people, in Mr. Hoover's honor. I used our finest plate, but there were only three Simple courses. It was practically no meal at all. We had finished this skimpy win-the-war meal and I was leading the way out of the dining room, holding onto Mr. Hoover's arm, when we met Sarto and the butler. The butler was feeding the dog about five pounds of raw beef. I looked at Food Dictator Hoover and he looked at me; then we burst out laughing.

My mother was the busy one with war relief work; under her direction 2020 had been transformed into what was practically a clothing factory. Old clothing was made over into decent garments for the destitute women and children of France and Belgium. Mother was helped by a host of her women friends but they were constantly complaining because they could not accomplish more.

Mrs. Julian James had turned her house over to war work; I went there almost every day. One night as I was leaving there I saw a funny little old woman who had arrived with a strange-looking contraption, and when I showed interest she fastened the small machine to a table, threaded into it a string of wool, and began to turn the handle at a furious pace. In practically no time at all she had produced a wool sock that seemed to me to be a much better sock than the lumpy things we women, with our jeweled fingers, had been slowly knitting, by hand. The old woman told me there was a larger machine that would knit a man-size sweater in about fifteen minutes. I told Mother about these machines, and she promptly bought four and had them set up in the reception room at 2020. She bought a number of the sock machines, and thereafter our old home produced a lot of well-made woolen garments. I did what I could, but I must admit that when it comes to that sort of thing I much prefer to work where my sympathies have been involved directly.

I remember at this time I was trying to buy sight for a little blind boy. (Oh, there is no doubt that money is a splendid thing when rightly used.) One day, as I was visiting a hospital in Washington, I saw this thin little boy of five or so. He was crying on a bench beside his sad-faced mother. He was lame and blind. The sight was gone entirely from one eye, and a total of thirteen operations had been performed on the other. Between day and night, for that poor child, there was just the difference of a feeble glimmer.

I got in touch at once with Dr. W. H. Wilmer, who is the best of all eye doctors. A little later, when the child's strength had been built up with proper food and care, Wilmer operated on him and, by his own miracle, restored sight to that afflicted child. I knew that I had never bought a finer thing with any money when, on a certain day, I took the child into our I Street house and in a shaded room, when his bandages had been removed, showed him a bowl of goldfish. That was something to make one weep, that child's delight in seeing moving shapes and natural beauty.

There were times in the succeeding years when that child's sight would have failed had it not been for Wilmer's skill. There were periods when the boy's mother wished to send him back to a school for the blind. I was stubborn about that, and insisted that he should go to a school where he would use what sight he had. To-day he is a man, a great big fellow who has married. At times his eyes are not as good as I should like to have them.

"It would be so terrible if you were to go blind again," I said to him one time. "You would hate me for my interference."

"Why," he chided me, "I won't mind if I have to go back into the blackness again. Just think of what I have already seen with these eyes of mine. I won't forget; and, if I lose my sight again, I shall remember shapes and colors and live in a world of blackness that is at least a bit rational."

One afternoon in late October, 1918, when I had just come home and was undressing, the telephone rang in my bedroom. I picked it up. It was an officer at the War Department. He repeated (thanks to Secretary Baker) a cablegram from General Pershing. This stated that Lieutenant Walker Blaine Beale, Company I, 310th Infantry, died on September 18th from wounds received in action on the same day. He had been buried on the same date in Commune Euvezin, Departement Meurthe-et-Moselle.

Mine was a ghastly job. I had to break the news to Uncle Truxtun and Aunt Harriet. He was their only child, the finest thing in both their lives. I called up the Metropolitan Club and told Uncle Trux to come over.

I poured a tumbler half-full of whisky, and when he came I beckoned him to come beside the sofa where I stood.

"Now, Truxtun, drink this down," I said.

He looked at me sharply and then drank. I think he knew almost by instinct what this was all about. Then I told him, and his knees gave way. Just as soon as he was stronger we went together to his former wife's apartment to tell her.

I have forgotten how many years they had been divorced, but when Aunt Harriet's grief burst forth Uncle Truxtun was about as fine as anyone could be. She went completely mad in her anguish. She tried to jump from the window. To see those two look at each other then and in a glance trace back the years to the time when they were sweethearts, married, with a baby son — why, that was war enough for me.

One afternoon Lord Reading telephoned and asked if he could come to the house. He was a great friend; I gave a dinner for him when he came to America and another when he left. Distress was deeply printed on his face when he arrived on this 1918 summer day. He was pale and greatly shaken. I asked him what was wrong.

"We have just had an inkling," he said, "of a sickening tragedy."

Tears were rolling down his face and for a moment he could not speak. Then he added: "Through our Intelligence Bureau we have just had a curt message that the whole Russian royal family had been wiped out."

I gasped at that. I knew how hideously that crime would wound the Bakhmeteffs. The Lord knows, it did. Uncle George just seemed to wither when he learned the dreadful facts.

Then and afterward our house in I Street was the strangest meeting ground in all of Washington. Once when William Randolph Hearst was attacking everything British in all his publications, I gave a dinner at I Street for about three hundred. Mr. Hearst and Millicent, his wife, came down from New York. She was looking lovely in a white satin dress and her emeralds. Among the Cabinet officers and diplomats who came that night was Sir Auckland Geddes, then the new British Ambassador. He and Hearst were soon together in a corner. They talked for what seemed to be about two solid hours, while most of my other guests stood off and eyed them.

Thereafter Mr. Hearst kept right on attacking England in his papers.

The persons closest to me say that I am fey. I am aware of some peculiar sensitivity in myself that I cannot define; it simply happens to me from time to time that, without being able to say how, I feel I know that death impends for some life that touches mine.

It so happened that I watched the running of the Kentucky Derby at Churchill Downs on a Saturday in May, 1919, without a trace of thrilling interest in the outcome. That spectacle, which should have made me thrill, was reflected in my eyes as part of a pageant without meaning. I heard the pounding hoofs, the burst of yells from fifty or sixty thousand throats, and still persisted in my fixed melancholia.

I had not wanted to leave home for that Kentucky trip. If I say Something told me I should stay at home, I do not believe there is exaggeration in the statement. But it seemed to be of more importance to my children that I go with Ned and do my best to keep their father out of trouble. On April 1st, that year, the convalescent soldiers who had been in possession of the place all winter were moved out of Friendship, and then, on the heels of decorators, we planned to move in; and never, so I thought, could I feel so safe in any place.

Long ago Friendship was a monastery, and the gardens then laid out and cultivated by brown-robed, cinctured monks were designed, in turn, to produce a finer cultivation of the human mind. Each of a hundred sylvan places, long vistas, greenish nooks, was intended to produce a fruit of holy meditation. There was a duck pond; and Ned, the sportsman, brought some captive mallards there and had a wing of each clipped so that they would not fly away in search of other waters. We kept donkeys, goats, and fat, waddling geese as well as ponies, horses, cows and other creatures whose only obligation was to make our children laugh — once in a while. There was a greenhouse, and in this place $50,000 had been spent just for rosebushes. Maybe we were overcharged, but when the roses bloomed only a trust company president would phrase that thought in the rose-perfumed air. There was a fountain, and not far off a stretch of water where water lilies bloomed.

A private golf course was one of the features of the place that would reveal to a stranger that Friendship had ceased to be the habitat of men in holy orders. Otherwise, the country air was as it had been for years past. The proof of that was fixed beyond the need of affidavits, by the presence, in each corner of the wide porch, of a tiny woven nest where hummingbirds, year after year, reared iridescent, honey-suckling families.

My quiet-voiced, sweet-tempered mother at my plea had left her books and privacy to come to Friendship, and only when she came was I content to go aboard our private car for the Kentucky trip. The children meant as much to her as I had meant. My son Ned, born July 28, 1918, was then less than ten months old. Jock, who had been named John R. McLean, was three years plus three months - a precious imp who never moved out of the sight of a heavy-shouldered man below whose armpit there was kept each minute of the day an automatic pistol; by Ned's order that was a forty-five. ("Even a crackpot," Ned would say, "would be knocked down and made limp if struck anywhere by such a ball.") Vinson was guarded by a man who had become a sort of older chum. We sent the children, with their guards, their nurses, and a big proportion of the staff of servants, out to Friendship, to stay under the protection of my mother during the few days Ned and I were to be away.

I want to say a word right here about Ned McLean: Our children had developed what was beyond a doubt his sweetest side. I never heard him speak harshly to a dog, a horse, or a child. With servants he was soft-voiced, too, by habit. When he was not drinking he had charm, or else he would not have had the years I gave him. The children, though, were what we shared as well as we could share anything. Why, I remember one Sunday morning when Vinson had a touch of fever, and how Ned took off his little garments and then proceeded with exquisite tenderness to give his oldest son an alcohol rub. When he was not spree-drinking he often led a most exemplary life; he loved to play with horses and dogs, and concerning golf he became, eventually, so keen that he hired a leading professional, Freddie McLeod, to devote himself to teaching him — at a salary, as I recall it, of $10,000 a year. Of course, there was a Harding twist to that, because a better golf game seemed to be the path, for Ned, to greater intimacy with all who stood well with his friend the President.

I could not understand what made me so blue on those days before we left for Louisville, Kentucky. My depression was complete, and as I interpreted my feelings I was being warned that I was going to die. Something dreadful, of that I was sure, was going to happen to me. I went — for the first time in my life, I think — and made a will. My health was better than it had been during many years, and yet I was feeling worse than at any time I could remember.

I kissed the children and then, just as any other foolish mother, went back to them on some pretended errand — when the truth was all I wanted was to kiss them more.

Almost my final word was to complete an order for two extra guards to keep a vigil out at Friendship. It is not normal for me to be so deeply shadowed by forebodings; but when I am afflicted with a prescient feeling of the kind my woe increases because repeatedly these warnings (or so I call them) have been justified.

Two nights, or maybe it was the night after we left Washington, I sat propped up in bed for hours past midnight as I wrote page after page of a letter to Vinson. In him, I felt, lived all that I had ever wanted to exist in the grandson of Thomas Walsh. He was sweet and preternaturally wise. I told him in my letter what I knew of wealth, and what I felt he ought to do to make himself a worthy man. He was, I told him, the big man of our family. I thought that some day my written message would speak to him, for me, when I was in my grave. We were so closely bound by mutual love that I knew he would obey my letter; and still I grieved. I did not want to leave him, I did not want him to become the motherless prey of sycophants nor to know the other things that are as grasping, taloned fingers attached to excessive wealth. Vinson had been nine in the previous December.

FRIENDSHIP

There was the usual post-race celebration in Louisville, but through it all I moved as in a daze. I felt that, in spite of anything I might do, whatever threatened me would have to happen.

It was early on Sunday morning when Ned answered the telephone. Washington was calling the McLeans at Louisville, Ned came from the telephone to my bed to say that Dr. Mitchell had called him up. It was not important, but Dr. Mitchell wanted to keep faith with me by reporting that Vinson had a mild case of influenza. (They lied to me — in gentleness, of course.)

"Probably," said Ned, and held my hand with one of his, "you will want to go straight home. It isn't necessary, but we will go right away."

"Now? "

"Right away; we'll take the next train out."

As we entered the train shed that day the sun shone brightly, and I had no sensible cause to be afraid until I saw the shortened shadow of the train. Walking toward the rear vestibule of our private car, which was by custom hooked to the last regular car, I noticed on the station platform the shadow of our car and that of just one other. Beyond those two shadows was the silhouette of the steam-snorting engine. There were friends with us then and some perhaps were tenderly conspiring with Ned to make me think this was a needless hurry we were in. But just the instant I saw that the train was short I knew we were traveling out of Louisville as a special. It was not through occult knowledge that I realized from that moment that an awful thing had happened. All my forebodings now were adding up into a fearful worry which had as its sane pedestal one significant fact: a long-distance telephone call from Dr. Mitchell concerning Vinson.

I was alone when a colored servant of the private car staff brought me some coffee. Craftily I sought from him a bit of information.

"This is a special train," I said, and by inflection made that statement into a question.

"Oh, yes, madam," he said, and softly closed the door. That dark-skinned man never knew, I fancy, that his simple answer to my question was to me bad news.

I knew; that is all I can say about the matter. The noises of the train, the sharply curving roadbed on which we were riding through green Kentucky hills, were just a nightmare after that. The day wore on until the train was speeding eastward through a landscape stained with shadows, and then I tried to find comfort in my recollections of my father. I need no photograph to see his features plainly, not ever; on that occasion I even seemed to hear his voice, but rather than court disbelief I simply want to state that when I was told in Washington on Monday morning I already knew my son was dead.

Old John R.'s valet, Meggett, who had become Ned's man, had been looking after Vinson on that Sunday morning. They were walking in the grounds under the big trees.

"Let's go outside the gate," said Vinson, and there seemed to Meggett to be no reason why, on such a lovely Sunday morning, they should not. Across the street they saw an old friend driving a wagon loaded with ferns. The driver was a gardener who had worked for us, a man named Goebel.

"Hello, Goebel," cried Vinson, and hastened across the road — "how are you?"

They chatted merrily and then Vinson, playfully, snatched a few ferns and ran, in fun, back across the road while Goebel: yelled, "Hey, you can't have those."

Vinson had turned to run in another direction, hoping by his dodges to lure his friend Goebel into pursuit. He did not see what was approaching at a slow pace, a Ford of that species which Americans commonly spoke of as "Tin Lizzies." This automobile struck Vinson, but not hard. Meggett said afterward, and this was confirmed by other witnesses, that the machine did little more than push the child so that he fell down. From what I know I should even hesitate to say that the automobile knocked him down. So slowly was it going that the driver braked it to a halt, and it did not even pass over the fallen child.

Vinson seemed to be not badly hurt. They picked him up and brushed from his clothes all traces of dust. Then holding Meggett by the hand, he walked back to the house. Miss Georgiana Todd, whom we always call "Baby", was with him then; and soon he was being fondled by his Grandmother Walsh.

He shrewdly interpreted her deep concern as he heard her order the immediate presence of the doctor.

"Will you tell Mother?" I know he asked the question hoping he would learn that I was not going to be made to worry over his mishap.

"No," Mother assured him, "you are all right."

All the doctors whom I might have brought to Friends had I been there came swiftly to the house. There was nothing left undone. The doctors said there was nothing to be done. If the skull was not fractured, they seemed to feel, would be none the worse for his experience; however, they quite fairly pointed out that there were possibilities in such an accident of serious harm. A bleeding might have started internally.

Later in the day my boy became paralyzed. Once he propounded a question to his grandmother: "Is it wicked for me to love Mother more than God?"

At six o'clock that Sunday night he died.

CHAPTER XX

The McLeans, the Hardings, and Calvin Coolidge

THE one time in our life when I thought that Ned McLean was going to be saved from a disastrous end in dissipation was when he was going around with Warren Gamaliel Harding. Good heavens! I had cause enough for hope, because that friend of my husband, and of mine, became the President and thus possessed not only the power but the will to confer on us some great distinction that would fully gratify the most ambitious appetite for dignity. I have the President's written word that he was alert to recognize becomingly "our valued and devoted friendship."

Yet what happened to us all was just about as tragic as if each one, instead of only I, had worn a talisman of evil. Some died, one probably was killed, one is blind, some went to jail; I suffered humiliation, and Ned lives on, a fancied fugitive, in an asylum where he pretends, with characteristic slyness, that he is someone else who does not know McLean.

In that stage of the 1920 campaign when the Republican candidate was leaving his front porch from time to time to make speeches from the rear platform of his train, and in auditoriums before vast gatherings of cheering people whom he addressed as his "fellow countrymen", Ned and I were with the Hardings for a while and found out that the Hardings we had known as poker-playing friends were quite unchanged. However, out of doors, or any place where others might observe us, Mrs. Harding was clutched by a set of the strangest fears that I ever encountered; and so, to a less degree, was her husband.

I stood beside her one day as photographers prepared to take our picture in a group with several others. I was engaged, at the time, in what for thirty years or more has been one of the least compromising of my habits—I was smoking a cigarette. Suddenly, aware of its smoke, she whirled on me and snatched the cigarette from my lips. She was as much concerned as if its tip had been hovering over a powder barrel.

"Evalyn," she chided me a little later, "you've got to help us by being circumspect. The Lord knows I don't mind your cigarettes, or jewels. You know how much I think of you but you must give a thought to what we now are doing."

"But the Senator smokes cigarettes," I said.

"Not when he is having his picture taken," said Mrs. Harding grimly. "Just let me catch him light a cigarette where any hostile eye might see him! He can't play cards until the campaign is over, either."

"But he does smoke tobacco?"

"A pipe, cigars, yes; but a cigarette is something that seems to infuriate swarms of voters who have a prejudice against cigarettes. He can chew tobacco, though." When she added that bit of information Mrs. Harding grimaced with a twinkle in her cornflower-blue eyes.

I learned that golf was something else that seemed to upset the stomachs of great masses of the voters; of factory laborers, of farmers, and of others who dwelt by myriads in those states where the campaign would be won or lost. Altogether the candidate had to shape himself, or seem to, just to fit the convolutions of the voters' minds.

What caused them constant worry was a fear that crafty James M. Cox, the Governor of Ohio who was the Democratic candidate, would plant some spy to watch them in their relaxed hours. Mrs. Harding used to shake her head from side to side and cluck just like a hen as she sought to convince me that Jimmy Cox was apt to do almost anything to win. (What seems strangest to me now is that we never saw that the simplest recipe to foil a rival politician is to live free of all hypocrisy.)

I began to understand how sincere Warren Harding had been when he told us one time when we played poker that he really did not want to run for President.

"I'm satisfied with being Senator," he said. "I'd like to go on living here in Washington and continue to be a member of the world's most exclusive club. I'm sure I can have six years more; I may have twelve or eighteen. If I have to go on and live in the White House I won't be able to call my soul my own. I don't want to be spied on every minute of the day and night. I don't want secret-service men trailing after me." He meant it, and it is my conviction that his wife meant it, too, when she said she preferred that they should be to the end of their days Senator and Mrs. Harding. The one who nagged and coaxed them to change their course was Harry M. Daugherty.

I remembered that Mr. Cox, who owned a newspaper in Dayton, Ohio, and one or two other small city newspapers, came to see us in Washington almost before the campaign was under way. He wanted to make sure that Ned would put the *Cincinnati Enquirer* wholeheartedly on the side of the Democratic party — and Cox. The *Enquirer* always had been Democratic.

"We've got to make up our minds," said Ned. "We're for Harding, you and me, but the readers of the Enquirer and the Post may be less ready for a shift than we should like to have them."

The fact is, I suppose, that old John R. would have walked the earth as Hamlet's father did, if he had known how lightly Ned was flipping back and forth with the idea of altering, overnight, the political complexion of two big, money-making papers. The question was especially vital with the *Enquirer*. Under Washington McLean, as I recall it, that paper during the Civil War had been referred to by its enemies as a Copperhead sheet. Always under John R.'s direction it had been devoted to the Democratic party, which was natural since he himself was a party boss out in Ohio.

Just what to do came to me clearly in the night! Harding was going to win hands down, and everybody loves a winner. I put it plainly up to Ned, and he to me; we convinced each other (and I think so still) that as between Harding and Cox for President my choice to the end of time would be Warren G. Harding. There was no open break with the party, but Ned made it clear that he wanted nothing printed that would interfere even a little with the success of the Harding campaign.

There came a time when the Hardings expressed fear that Cox's adherents might manage to get some detrimental story into the *Enquirer*. Mrs. Harding used to say, "You don't know that man Cox; there isn't any trick of politics he doesn't know." We remembered that in his early days Governor Cox had worked on the *Enquirer* as a reporter. Ned took steps to make doubly sure that his instructions would not be violated by stealth late some night when the editor was taking a night off.

What awful hatreds boiled just below the surface of political ambitions in Ohio were beyond my comprehension then. On Cox's side, in secret, were some Republicans who hated Harry Daugherty so much that they would have been quite willing to defeat Harding by any instrument, for the sake of being revenged on Harding's Warwick; that sort of treachery was really hard to comprehend. Nevertheless, I had the convincing behavior of Mrs. Harding to persuade me that she really was afraid of some vile act, a threat that was real and not a phantom.

One day we got word in Washington of an astounding story. Some slanderer out in Ohio was offering to give to newspapers facts about the ancestry of Senator Harding. The charge was being made that in his veins there coursed a strain of Negro blood. We knew then, and I know now, the story could not be true; yet we were frightened by the possible consequences to his campaign. Mrs. Harding, so we learned, was red-eyed from weeping.

Ned, in the first flare of indignation, jumped to the conclusion that the Democratic party was responsible for the circulation of this false statement. At first he wanted to use that situation as an excuse to change the newspapers to open Republicanism; but he was dissuaded from this course. However, he arranged with an employee of the *Washington Post* to go to the White House and discuss this dreadful business with President Wilson's secretary, Joseph P. Tumulty.

Mr. Tumulty told his caller, who reported back to Ned, that certain "proofs" about Senator Harding's history had been submitted to him. He said he had reported this to Mr. Wilson, and that Woodrow Wilson had directed him to act toward Senator Harding in the very same way that he would want Harding to act if the situation were reversed. That was a noble application of the golden rule.

We learned directly from Harry Daugherty that the last thing Warren Harding wanted was to have anything printed with reference to the Negro blood story. A denial would reveal to millions, so it was explained to us, that such a charge had been made, and taint their minds; consequently, Mr. Harding's friend would ignore the slander. We knew that some unidentified conspirators had paid thousands of dollars to print and mail copies of the fiction. Thanks to President Wilson's quickacting decency, those abominations were taken from the mails and burned. Even so, the report spread swiftly—but not so swiftly as such things are spread by print.

Judge then what must have been our concern when we learned that white-haired Mrs. Heber Votaw, Senator Harding's youngest sister, was scheduled to address a meeting of colored people in Washington. She was then a policewoman in Washington and had for eight years been a missionary in Burma.

I made sure of her intention to attend this meeting, and then called Mrs. Harding at Marion by long-distance telephone. When I told her, and she had grasped the meaning of my words, I heard a harsh and grating sound; Mrs. Harding was gritting her teeth. Then she spoke peremptorily.

"Get that sister of Warren Harding to come out to Friendship—if you love us. Keep her there! Do not let her make that speech if you have to lock her in your cellar."

I promised, and soon after that the Marion long-distance operator was calling Ned. Senator Harding wanted to speak with Mr. McLean. He was quite as exercised as his wife had been. He implored Ned to prevent his sister from making the speech and gave him complete authority in the matter. At a half-hour after midnight a man in Ned's employ started out to find the candidate's sister. He found her, and let her read (but not keep) this letter:

Dear Mrs. Votaw:—

Senator Harding has just gotten through talking to me on the' telephone and wishes you to receive a message of imperative importance from Mrs. McLean before you go to your office this (Saturday) morning.

My wife had a slight automobile accident yesterday or she would come to see you. We are living at Friendship and will send a machine for you any time you wish or will send one to show you where the place is.

With very best regards, I remain

Yours very truly,

EDWARD MCLEAN.

P.S. For reasons which Mr. Brown will explain to you I am asking him to return this letter to me.

Well, Mrs. Votaw came and we persuaded her to remain with us for dinner. We kept her with us until we learned, through one of the *Post* reporters, that the meeting had been held and that the audience had dispersed. After that, Mrs. Votaw was put aboard a train and shipped to Marion to stay for the remainder of the campaign.

One time in the White House, when he was President, Warren Harding grew expansive about that slander. It had been used against him in every campaign; when he ran for Lieutenant Governor and won, when he ran for Governor and lost, and when he defeated old Joe Foraker in the Republican primaries for the senatorial nomination. The thing grew out of a village quarrel that occurred long before he was born.

The Hardings were Abolitionists and their farmhouse at Blooming Grove, Ohio, was a station on the Underground Railroad by means of which runaway slaves were helped on their way northward from Kentucky and Virginia into Canada. Some of the Hardings' neighbors resented this and called them "nigger-lovers." One day at the country school the Appleman children, neighbors, appeared with faces scabby from what was known as "buckwheat rash." The Harding children jeered at them and called them "lousy." The Appleman children retorted, "We may be lousy, but that comes from having to associate with you Harding niggers."

The school board had to settle the schoolboys' feud that grew out of that exchange of words; and then, sometime later, a blacksmith in another county married a Miss Harding. He, too, quarreled one day with a customer and, when this man evened up their score by saying the blacksmith had married "one of them Harding niggers", he picked up from his anvil a heavy sharp-edged tool and flung it with a deadly aim; the steel clove through the victim's skull. He died, and what he had said was repeated as evidence at the blacksmith's trial. In that way the slander lived.

In the sweet way of politicians out in Ohio (and perhaps in other states), when this old slander was repeated against Warren Harding a fake ancestral tree was charted to make the story more convincing. This supposed "proof" fixed the paternity of a half-black child on Harding's great-great-grandfather, Amos Harding. The chart was easily shown to be a fake. What should have been the most convincing thing of all was the blue-eyed faces of the Hardings who dotted the country towns and villages in Ohio.

Just about a week before election Ned had a letter from Mrs. Harding and all her fears had shriveled. She wrote:—

The trip was wonderfully satisfactory; we faced immense throngs everywhere. It does not seem there can be a Democrat left anywhere, and yet I want to pitch in harder than ever. We must win—Big.
Give my dearest love to Evalyn.

The overwhelming victory of the Republicans in November, 1920, meant first of all to Ned and me that we were going with them on a vacation celebration down in Texas at what we thought of as a God-forsaken place called Point Isabel.

"But why do we have to go way off to Point Isabel?" I asked Ned.

As he explained it, the newspaper correspondents who had been with Senator Harding throughout the campaign had been told by him that in the event of his election they could choose the place for the vacation that was sure to follow. Then Ed Scobey came up from San Antonio as the escort of R. B. Creager, a sharp-thinking man of business who was the Republican National Committeeman from Texas, sometimes called "the Red Fox of the Rio Grande Valley." This red-haired Mr. Creager and his wife owned a summer home at the most southerly spot in the United States—a fishing village called Point Isabel, near the mouth of the Rio

Grande. It was inhabited by about a hundred and fifty Mexicans and, possibly, by one hundred who were white. The nearest town, some twenty miles away, was Brownsville, Texas. Mr. Harding had told Scobey and Creager of his promise, and they had gone into the back-yard bungalow where the newspaper correspondents had a headquarters, to make them think that Point Isabel was a Paradise where even apples could be freely eaten.

The tarpon fishing was described; deer, ducks, quail, wild turkeys were mentioned. Each man was assured of at least one tarpon, and furthermore there were references to the nearness of Matamoros in Mexico, with its supply of gambling houses. Consequently, so Ned told me, when Senator Harding called for a vote the newspaper correspondents, as one man, exercised their suffrage on behalf of Creager's place at Point Isabel.

The Scobeys and the Hardings were real old friends; to each other they invariably were "Ed" and "Warren" and "Florence." Years before, Scobey had been the sheriff of Marion County; and when Harding had presided over the Ohio Senate while Lieutenant Governor, Scobey had been the clerk of that body. Then he had developed tuberculosis and, to save his life, had moved to San Antonio. There he had recovered his health and prospered in the storage warehouse business. Besides a rumbling voice, he had a double chin, bushy gray eyebrows, and an inner compulsion to be the life of any party of which he was a member.

Well, as a persistent hostess I could understand the eagerness of the Creagers to capture, as their guests in Texas, President-elect and Mrs. Harding; but I could not comprehend why they had failed to appreciate the size of their hospitable undertaking. Probably they had their minds fixed on their Texas neighbors. Mr. and Mrs. Harding were no longer just one couple. There were other guests, of course: Mr. and Mrs. Malcolm Jennings years before had been partners of the Hardings in the Marion *Star*. Dr. and Mrs. Charles E. Sawyer were there as friends, but also because it was not ever safe for Mrs. Harding to go far away from Sawyer. Others in the party included Senator Harding's three playmates of the Senate: Davis Elkins (brother of my friend Katherine) of West Virginia, Fred Hale of Maine, and red-faced Joseph Freylinghuysen of New Jersey. Those four senators were bound together not as an oligarchy but simply because they were a constant golfing foursome with a complete nineteenth-hole understanding of each other. But necessarily there were many, many others in the party. All told, there were three railroad carloads.

At Brownsville we had to leave our private cars. The only railroad line to Point Isabel was a narrow-gauge equipped with rolling stock that in Europe would be rated as fourth-class. We went in automobiles. The Creager cottage was a comfortable summer dwelling, but there was not sufficient room in it nor in the adjoining house to take care of all the party. The overflow had to be accommodated in a hotel that, until our coming, seemingly had been abandoned. It was unscreened against mosquitoes.

There was no dining room, nor any service whatever. George Christian, the young women stenographers, the Secret-Service men, all the reporters and cameramen, and some of the Hardings' closest friends had to find shelter in that dismantled old red brick structure. Most were sleeping on army cots. Ned and I were in a cottage and Ned, because he was so tall and heavy, rated the bed that had been assigned to us. I slept on a cot, and once when I tried to roll over in the night I landed, plop, right on the floor—I hope on some mosquitoes.

For food, all but a chosen few who ate with the Creagers depended on the ham and eggs of the lunchroom counter, which was the only open restaurant in the community.

Ned had supposed there would be plenty of hunting as well as tarpon fishing. There were no bird dogs, that he could discover, for miles around. The tarpon fishing was first-class, but tackle of the kind used in that sort of fishing had been made available only for the Hardings and about two others. Loud squawks were heard in private; and the newspapermen's were not so private—their peevish outbursts resulted finally in the appearance of Mr. Scobey and Mr. Creager at the ex-hotel.

The kickers were almost speechless when they tried without profanity to set forth their complaints that they had been grossly misled when they chose to come to Point Isabel. The final straw upon the load of their indignation was that they could not even hire a boat in which to cross the Bay to see the President-elect at play; both launches there had been chartered by Mr. Creager. Ned listened at this meeting and he heard Scobey exclaim, in the tone of one who has seen a vision, "Why, Red, I know what these fellows want: they want a boat."

Senator Harding caught a few big tarpon; it was thrilling to watch such a creature, all silver, leap clear of its element to shake its head and try to throw the hook from its mouth. I caught one or two, aided by Davis Elkins, and Mrs. Harding hooked a prize and then alternately coaxed and scolded Fred Hale as he played it for her.

A howling norther—what I would call a blizzard—swept down upon us in our unprotected state. How we shivered! Several members of our party got tight through their efforts to get warm. We were marooned for several days and spent all our time playing poker. Well, of course, the bitter weather compelled us to abandon Point Isabel and retreat to Brownsville. The roads were too deep in mud (remember, that was 1920) for any automobile to get through; so, wrapped in blankets, we all went aboard the train, which was made up of roller-coaster cars or something very like them.

The point of this is that I find excuse for any President who chooses to accept the hospitality only of those who own big yachts or who are in other ways equipped for the special sort of entertaining that presidents require. The Creagers, the Scobeys, indeed, none of us, quite realized in December, 1920, just what had happened to our friend Warren.

The constant adulation of people was beginning to have an effect on Senator Harding. He was, more and more, inclined to believe in himself. He cherished an idea that when a man was elevated to the presidency his wits, by some automatic mental chemistry, were increased to fit the stature of his office. We, his friends, could see him, during that vacation, as a young Aladdin testing experimentally the terrific power of the mighty engine called the presidency.

"Hey, Ed," we would hear him call in a loud tone, as a king in olden times called for a jester. He really loved Ed Scobey; and it was fun for Harding to be able to announce to him that he should become the Director of the Mint, and to know that what he promised would, by reason of his great power, come to pass.

It was the same with Dr. Sawyer. C. E. Sawyer was a frail hundred pounds of whiskered country doctor. He was a wizened little man, soft-voiced, with thick glasses to enable his kindly eyes to make sound diagnoses. In Mrs. Harding's judgment he was the one and only doctor who could keep her alive despite the defects of her kidneys. He watched her diet and kept her nearly well. Several times in previous years he had performed major operations on her. Just outside of Marion, he had a paying sanitarium that had all the attributes of a rich man's country estate: wide shady lawns; a herd of blooded cows. He was by no means easily persuaded to leave that well-organized establishment to follow a single patient to Washington. The patient, positively, was not Harding, but Mrs. Harding. How could Dr. Sawyer be made to change?

I sometimes wish I might have heard Warren Harding break the news to Dr. Sawyer that he was going to give him the rank of brigadier general. I should have known that he was jesting in a small-town way, but that also he was doing something finer. He wanted Sawyer in Washington for Mrs. Harding's sake, and I honor him for the lengths to which he went to keep her, "in sickness and in health."

Ned, before long, was to learn that he had been made Chairman of the Inaugural Committee, which would have full charge of all arrangements for the celebration in connection with the ceremony whereby Woodrow Wilson would relinquish power and Warren Harding take it. A few other acts of powered graciousness were revealed to us on that trip, or just a few weeks later, as, one by one, all of Harding's well-liked friends received some kind of title. Dick Crissinger, for example, had been Harding's playmate when they were barefoot country boys. He grew up to be a Democrat of consequence in Marion, but it was his old pal Harding who made him Governor of the Federal Reserve Board. These were not bad appointments; as good, no doubt, as needed for the jobs; but it seems significant to me, now, that they were made as they were — because Warren Harding had received the presidency by chance, without having expected until late in life that he had even, as he might have said, a Chinaman's chance to win the office. The office of president was hardly a subject that he had studied. I think it was a thing he had merely dreamed about, as we all dream when we wish we had power to fix everything. It is my opinion that Warren Harding, if he could have looked ahead when he was young and seen a vision of the time when he would be selected to go and live in the White House, would have lived quite differently. As it happened, he was a loyal friend who was, unhappily, loyal sometimes to the wrong people.

Those old folktales that harp upon the theme of tragic complications coming in the wake of wishes too easily granted are merely patterns of my husband's story and my own. There are those who would believe that somehow a curse is housed deep in the blue of the Hope diamond. I scoff at that in the privacy of my mind, for I do comprehend the source of what is evil in our lives; but I can see no way to filter out the blackness from the magic that oppresses us. I am helpless in my plight as a Chinese woman who contemplates fashion-bound feet and yearns to run with fleetness. The hamperings I wish to overcome are, I think, the natural consequences of unearned wealth in undisciplined hands. But even so, I have had my fun. The kind of life that Alice lived in Wonderland is what I expect and want; indeed, it should be obvious by now that I like to be fantastic. It is only when the thing I buy creates a show for those around me that I get my money's worth. We live but once, and of all things in this world I hate boredom most. Wealth is the key to this cipher I am trying to decode. Whatever change in our lives my husband or I ever wanted either one of us could bring about; we were as two wizards in one family—and that made the greatest complication. I say that because if a whim occurred to either one of us that whim was gratified. From Ned's angle, I suppose, some of mine were foolish; his were more than foolish to me.

One day, to cite a case at random, I started out with my little girl to buy her a small white poodle. We went to place after place, but there seemed to be not a single poodle for sale. We were riding in the Rolls-Royce, just a little one with two seats at the back. The chauffeur sat up front; he spoke to me over his shoulder to say that he knew where there was a dog, the champion of all champion St. Bernards. We went at once to see the dog. Gosh! My Great Dane, Mike, who nowadays sleeps beside my bed, would seem as a puppy beside that monster of a dog. The price was $5,000, and I scribbled a check. We put the dog beside Evalyn and I rode home beside the chauffeur. I simply can't tell how big that dog was unless I say his lolling tongue was like a whole boiled ham. Ned rolled his eyes to heaven when we came up to the door at I Street.

Because of our wealth, the rich scenes in which my husband and I moved were peopled with the great, and the powerful, of our generation. When any one of these might wish to meet his kind at play around Washington, a likely place to make the contact was our country estate—my home, which we call Friendship, and which has been a piece of the Capital.

A mad place, truly!—with a monkey in my bathroom, a llama on the lawn, and our corridors shrill with the curses of our parrot (learned from a diplomat). In the stables when my children wished to play at being grown-ups they could find there midget horses and the coach, brightly painted, that had once belonged to General Tom Thumb. The cellar was as richly stocked with wines and spirits as if the sale of these were the first concern of the owners. The kitchen was a place as artful in its cuisine as any hostelry.

Some of our acres had been remolded into a golf course where the grass was far more costly than any kind of Oriental rugs; and, partially, this is why our country home became the playground of President Harding and all those who wished to win from him some inch or two of official stature.

Guns, dogs and horses were the instruments with which my husband had much of his fun; a duck blind on a raw and foggy morning was for him a place rich with excitement, and I think he liked nothing better than to see some horse he owned, such as the Porter, racing—out in front. However, when Senator Harding was elected Ned took up golf. He was well equipped to play at poker, but not so well equipped as the President-elect at bridge. Upon deciding to become a better golfer Ned did not merely buy a book; as I have said before he hired the full-time services of a first-rate professional, Freddie McLeod. When that was done we had at Friendship all the appurtenances of a splendid country club; but this was a club where none paid dues, nor any other fees—except we two McLeans. We had our money's worth in providing entertainment for those who came. As for me, there was an added value in the chance I seemed to sense that Ned McLean would stir with fine ambitions as he watched our friend, President-elect Harding, wield power and change the destinies of other men.

Certainly, when Harding started in to pick his Cabinet some of his selections were of a kind to make other men envy him his power. Charles Evans Hughes, Herbert Hoover, John W. Weeks were names that aroused my enthusiasm when I heard they were slated for the Harding Cabinet. There was a special thrill for me in those choices, because one afternoon during his post-election vacation at Brownsville, Texas, Senator Harding talked to me about that first big job he had to do.

"I want to have a really great Cabinet," he said. Saying this, he was looking out the window of our private car. His shaggy brows were knit, and under them his blue-gray eyes were tender as he let them peer beyond the flatness of the Texas landscape until he took into his mind some concept of the whole of that country of which he had become the leader. Even there and then, however, one might have seen that troubles were in store for a man so easygoing with his friends. He was, himself, a loyal friend, and could not think that treachery could mask itself behind the eyes of those he looked upon as friends of his. Unhappily, for many persons he had become something other than a friend; he was to all of these no less a thing than Opportunity. In consequence, if he talked alone with one man for five or ten minutes some others became uncomfortable, fearful of losing an expected favor.

Among those who came to Brownsville on that post-election vacation trip and who joined us in poker games in our private car was Senator Albert Fall of New Mexico. I liked Albert Fall and so did Ned. He showed me his six-shooter one afternoon; he carried it always, a habit of frontier days. He wore a black slouch hat, and the cigar that stuck forward from his angular jaw was about the size of a lead pencil and as poisonous as a cobra. At that time, so we understood, Senator Fall, who had been Senator Harding's seatmate in the Senate chamber, was not among those under consideration for the Cabinet. However, what was most interesting to Ned and me as the party left Brownsville and rolled along the Gulf toward New Orleans was the fact that Ned was expected to become the chairman of the committee in charge of the inaugural celebration. The Hardings and the bulk of their party went on to Panama, but we came back to Washington and with us was the journalist, Mark Sullivan.

Ned went to considerable personal expense in connection with the inaugural plans. What he wished to have was an affair about ten times as lively as a Fourth of July celebration combined with the ending of a victorious war. There were to have been fireworks displays, bands by the score, and all manner of excitement to mark the passage of the executive power from Wilson's hands to those of Harding. Then Senator Borah and some others began to squawk about the cost of all this to the Government. Some man sent off to Harding a telegram of several thousand words of protest concerning Ned's authority, and signed himself "CHAIRMAN EXECUTIVE COMMITTEE HARDING AND COOLIDGE REPUBLICAN LEAGUE NO. 1."

The President-elect had Harry Daugherty try to straighten out the mess. His instructions were to "see this party and pour oil on the troubled waters if possible." Because of this bickering, and complaints in Congress about extravagance, it was decided finally that there would be no celebration.

Poor Ned! I think he never had worked so hard to develop any project. Not long ago I found among some papers at my house a copy of a message sent to Marion, Ohio, by telephone. It had been, I think, what Ned intended as his resignation from the Inaugural Ball Committee. It was simply a statement to be relayed by an employee of the *Washington Post,* giving Ned's opinion of everybody at the Harding headquarters in Marion. They were, he wished to have them told, a lot of sapheads.

When the plans for an Inaugural Ball were abandoned, we determined that the McLeans would provide a celebration anyhow, and pay the bills without regard to penny-pinching Senators; that was our attitude. Moreover, we felt like celebrating; our home town was going to be a gayer place because two friends of ours had skyrocketed to power. What I proceeded to arrange was an enormous dinner at the I Street house. I invited the new Cabinet members, the Justices of the Supreme Court, the diplomatic corps, the Senators and, as guest of honor, the new Vice-President, Calvin Coolidge. That was our first meeting with the Coolidges, who became our good friends.

When it was time to go in to dinner that Fourth of March night and I took the arm of Mr. Coolidge, I was astonished to discover that he was shaking. I forgot his trembling for a little while as my mind filled with all my problems as a hostess. In the ballroom I had provided three tables, each about a hundred feet long. There was a gold service on each of the two outside tables; on the center table there was a silver service. With the Barberini tapestries on the walls, with the great wood carvings that John R. had prized, and with the masses of flowers, I had contrived a scene that I found immensely satisfying. That is, it was satisfying until I observed that my guest of honor, Mr. Coolidge, was eating none of his dinner. Several courses had been placed before him and taken away untouched. I saw that now and then he was looking out of the corners of his eyes at the glitter on my hands and arms, but I could not believe that he was disturbed by jewels. What could be troubling him? At last my feelings overcame me.

"Mr. Vice-President," I whispered, "you have not eaten anything. What is the matter? Is anything wrong?"

"Yass," said Mr. Coolidge. "I have the most terrible stomach-ache."

That was something I could fix. I sent at once for bicarbonate of soda and stirred half a teaspoonful into a glass of water until it was dissolved, and then I made him drink it. Through-out that gay evening he was a side-line guest who drank glass after glass of soda. Mrs. Coolidge was perfectly delightful then, as always. From that night on, I was devoted to them; and I know they counted me among their friends.

As it turned out, it was I who transformed Mr. Coolidge into a golfer.

President Harding and his foursome friends of the Senate— Fred Hale of Maine, Davis Elkins of West Virginia, Joseph Freylinghuysen of New Jersey— came often to play golf at Friendship. They were a jovial group and florid. Their mood at Friendship was always one of mirth, and was told by the President that he dared unbend at Friendship as he might not do elsewhere. By that he meant that he could simply be himself at our country place; he could laugh aloud, behave generally as a free and independent person. It was a kind of sanctuary. Elsewhere, his life had in it some of the elements of the pampered year accorded by the Aztecs to the victim selected for sacrifice. Outside our walls I often saw President Harding overwhelmed by those who reached for his hand as if there were some potent charm in such a touch. He was unfailingly gentle, warm, and unhurried with the swarms, yet each day's end found him more tired and packed just a little tighter with a sense of care.

Once, just before a snowy Christmas, a stream of threatening letters poured into the White House. A sort of final warning was delivered in which some mysterious enemy boasted that on Christmas Day the thing would happen. Mrs. Harding said to me, "Evalyn, we want to spend that day somewhere else." She was wearing at her throat a diamond buckle ornament that I had selected as her Christmas present the year before; it was excuse for a black velvet band that neatly hid her aging neck.

"You come and stay with us," I said. (We were living in the I Street house.)

They went to church and then drove to our house. We had lunch, then sat around and talked until dinnertime. After dinner we put the President upstairs in a sitting room connected with my bedroom. Up there, we all decided, would be the safest place.

Weeks, Harry Daugherty, Ned, and Charlie Curtis kept him company at bridge or poker. Downstairs, Mrs. Harding and I had a private picture show—Mary Pickford in "Little Lord Fauntleroy." I know that Harding's mind was quite at ease. I heard him laugh a time or two, and threaten what would happen to his friends when he held better cards; but Mrs. Harding twitched and jumped about. She was convinced that at any instant something of first-page moment would happen to them. Outside our house secret-service men were watching, inside the house were others. I always felt a good deal safer when those men were around.

Suddenly, somewhere in the house there was a loud crashing. Mrs. Harding half-screamed and almost slid from her chair. There was no comedy about her fears; they were too real. A servant came in response to my loud calls and apologized because a door had slammed.

About two in the morning the Hardings left, and drove home to the White House. Mr. Harding, shaking hands with me, amusement in his eyes, said, "I'm very grateful to my assassins for a very pleasant Christmas Day." Of course, he had not worried for a minute.

Amusement was the sort of precious stuff we tried to mine from all our hours at Friendship. So, when it was revealed that on a certain afternoon that Calvin Coolidge was coming out expressly to learn the game of golf, some other golfers decided they, too, would play that day and have an extra bit of fun.

My recollection is that Mrs. Oscar Underwood played with me. I recall that Mrs. Coolidge took her knitting from a bag and smilingly announced that she was going to spend the afternoon in the shade, on our veranda. The fourth person in the foursome I had arranged was McLeod, the professional. We waited, and then Vice-President Coolidge arrived, having come directly from the Senate over which he then presided. I was astonished when I saw him. All our other golfers, such as President Harding and Senators Elkins, Freylinghuysen and Hale, were mighty dressy on the golf course. So were Ned, George Christian, and William Gibbs McAdoo (who at that time was being paid $3,000 every quarter by Ned for legal services. I have forgotten just why he had been retained). Well, as I say, those golfers and most of the others were usually attired as if they were about to pose for some fashion plate to demonstrate what should be worn on the golf course. Plus fours that year were flaring much wider than women's skirts; the men golfers wore hose woven in designs of chessboard checks or dizzy alternating circles; and their caps were so generously made that I used to ask them please not to let the breeze waft them up into the trees.

Calvin Coolidge was a different sort of golfer. He had a bag of clubs when he arrived; he had played before, of course, but not enough to justify his playing with the Harding foursome. That day of which I speak he fixed himself for playing by simply taking off his coat. At that moment, in long pants and suspenders, he was almost ready to take a stance on the first tee. His other act of preparation was to take from his golf bag a white cotton hat, lined with green. Its brim was turned up closely, saucer fashion. He was quite solemn, and both remembered and applied the morsels of advice tossed to him by the pro. I think he himself did not speak one word, however, until we reached the seventh hole. It was there he addressed himself to me. "Your dress is wet in the back," he said. "Thought you ought to know it." I thanked him.

As we approached the last hole I heard a lot of noisy chatter, and then I saw President Harding and a half-dozen of his companions lined up as a gallery. I heard them commenting gaily on Mr. Coolidge's suspenders, as if to tease him. They had no luck at that; and finally I heard the President confess that he, too, wore suspenders.

CHAPTER XXI

The Distaff Side

EVENTUALLY, through his practice out at Friendship, Mr. Coolidge became a quite fair golfer. Mrs. Coolidge would always bring her knitting and sit on the front porch. When we could induce them to remain for dinner we were delighted.

When our lawns were turning brown with fallen leaves that autumn I had to give up golf myself because, in the early winter, I was going to have another child.

My fourth child, and only daughter, was born a little more than four months later, on November 16, 1921. When she was about six weeks old I had her christened; she had a little bonnet with a pink plume, and a very long pink chiffon dress made by Hickson, a perfectly lovely thing. The ceremony of baptism was held in the ballroom of the I Street house; I had an altar built in there, and the child was baptized by the Bishop of Washington, the Right Reverend Alfred Harding, right on the scene of so many of our splendid parties; however, this affair was a party, too. President and Mrs. Harding were the baby's godparents, and there were a score or more of others present, including Secretary of State and Mrs. Charles Evans Hughes, Secretary of War and Mrs. John W. Weeks, and Mr. and Mrs. James B. Duke.

That was a feat—to get the society-dodging Mr. Duke to Pay us a visit. However, Nannie Lee Duke and I had been such good friends that I persisted until she succeeded in persuading her husband to come. It was cold and snowing when I went to the station to meet the train to which their private car was attached; and when Mr. Duke stepped down I discovered he was in a tough humor. As I extended my hand to greet him his first words were, "I was a fool to come, and I'm going straight back home."

Mrs. Duke is beautiful —beyond comparison I think. Her hair is black and her features perfect. It was a lovely eye she winked at me there on the station platform. She wished to stay, of course.

"Now, Mr. Duke," I coaxed, "you just come on out to dinner—"

"I hate this society game," said Mr. Duke, "and I am not going to begin now." I began to suspect that I had stepped into the middle of an argument. He kept on talking, saying, "I'm going to have the car hitched to the next train going North."

"That will be all right, Mr. Duke," I conceded; "but just come on out to dinner, see the people, and then, if you don't like it, you can go back."

In my automobile he made a sort of explanation of his grumpiness by saying, "My feet are hurting." He was Nannie Lee's second husband, and far from young.

I put them in the little H Street house. (It had been refurnished by Ned to make a temporary home for Harry Daugherty and Jess Smith when they came to Washington, and when they moved elsewhere I began using it as a guest house. Among others whom I sheltered there were Millicent and William Randolph Hearst.) The H Street house was beyond the zone of any noisemaking by my children, and so Mr. Duke found it soothing.

As it turned out, he loved the party.

Right after dinner I began a picture show and when that was over the first to come to speak to me was Mr. Duke. He wanted to know all about my projection machine. I could tell him, because for a long time it had been my hobby to make motion pictures of all my friends. David Wark Griffith had helped me transform a part of the basement of the I Street house into a movie workshop. Down there are developing rooms, containing vast reels upon which I supervised the drying of just about eighty miles of film that I exposed before I wore the newness off the hobby. I was really good at picture-making. Experts taught me, experts sent by Griffith. I learned how to set up the tripod in the tonneau of an open car and then, with tires half flat, to crank at a measured pace while riding Past some scene I wished to take. I bought the finest cameras and all the other instruments of that craft. Some of my enthusiasm about the movies boiled out of me that night when I discovered that Mr. Duke was happy as a child at having discovered that the movie way of telling a story was so enchanting.

"I am going to get a couple of those machines for each house," he said—and added, That will be eight. This solves my problem. Hereafter, when we have a dinner party I'll know how to fix it so we won't have to sit around and talk."

Because of his delight with the picture show I arranged another for the midday following, to precede the christening. That was primarily for the children, and as a result of it I think we worked a further change in the Duke establishment.

My old maid and friend, Maggie Buggy, had married Ernest Bauer, formerly my father's secretary. Alice and Ernest, their two children, were playmates of my sons. This arrangement was explained to Mr. Duke as these children arrived for the show, and he then and there declared: "By George, that is what we are going to do for Doris. I am sick and tired of seeing that child by herself. I know who could play with her. The gardener has a lovely child. She ought to make, for Doris, a real playmate." I have forgotten whether he did fix upon the gardener's child, but I know he carried out the plan with some child. Nannie Lee was furious with me; when she went to Europe that summer with Doris she had to take that playmate child along. Moreover, from the time of that visit to our house, Mr. Duke was a constant movie fan. He could hardly bear to wait for the guests to finish dinner, so eager was he to drag them into his private picture shows.

Right after the Bishop left that afternoon we started playing bridge. President Harding, Mrs. Duke, Secretary Weeks, and I played. Mrs. Harding felt, and said, that her husband had a job to do over in Pennsylvania Avenue. She spoke of this to me and then she spoke to him a time or two.

"Warren," she said, "you should be getting back to work." He played an ace with table-banging force, but said no word. Presently she spoke again, "Warren, you really ought to be going back to work." I watched the faces of my guests, the calm, the lovely, unperturbed features of Mrs. Duke, the twitching of Mrs. Harding's lips, and the President's black brows that were becoming tightly knit.

"Five spades," said Secretary Weeks.

"Warren!" Mrs. Harding spoke with undisguised sharpness.

I passed, and then the President turned his head and declared himself. "I am going," he said, "to play all afternoon. Five spades doubled."

The baby's great-aunt, Mildred Dewey, had urged me to name the child for her. I had refused, saying that she should be named for Mummie McLean. Aunt Millie tried to have her way by saying she would leave all her money to the child, but I still refused. When my daughter was twelve or thirteen, she turned against her name and declared she must have another. She kept after me to change it until at last I gave consent; and so she is no longer called Emily Beale McLean. Her name, by law, is recognized as Evalyn.

With diplomats and admirals of all the nations gathered in Washington for the Arms Conference, I turned some of my attention from my infant daughter to a scheme I had for giving a great big party. President Harding and Secretary Hughes had just astonished everybody by proposing to destroy battleships and limit future naval building in the interests of peace. It seemed to me that was sufficient excuse for an entertainment.

Pale gold sateen with an overcloth of yellow lace was what I ordered for two of my three long dinner tables; each of them was seventy-five feet long. The third table, placed in the middle, was covered with a silver cloth and lace; that one bore the silver service with its great candelabra given me for a wedding present. On the tables with the cloths of gold I placed, on one, the golden service left to us by John R., and on the other the golden service of the Walshes. My father had had that one made to his order, and in the center of each gilt-encrusted plate there is a camp bird fashioned out of gold. When those tables were set, and the Barberini tapestries covered the I Street ballroom walls, the scene was much more lovely than can be imagined.

Ned was proud of the great dinner I had planned, but he was not a bit of help. Baby Todd, my social secretary, was my right hand; Grafoni, the butler I inherited from Mummie and John R., was a worker of miracles. That man could be a maître d'hotel anywhere he might choose to go. But Ned laughed at Miss Todd and me, saying, "You make so much work out of this; let me put these place cards around." I was delighted to have him take an interest, so I vanished to attend to some other chore, leaving Miss Todd to supervise his help. Afterward, I learned that Ned actually placed cards on one whole table before he wearied and called out,

"Totten!" Totten was a member of the household staff, a carpenter. He came in answer to Ned's call, leaving some decorations hanging from a ladder.

"Totten," Ned inquired, "are your hands clean? 0. K., You take the rest of these cards and put them around on these other tables." At this social sacrilege, Baby Todd almost screamed; she took back the cards.

At most parties people hardly knew whether Ned was present. He had good manners for such occasions; at least he had surface manners, but he did not enjoy big dinners. To me he would whisper, "Who am I to take out to-night? Who is my dinner partner?" I would tell him; then he would grumble, "What, that old bag of bones?"

This Arms Conference dinner was the one at which I showed Griffith's movie of the Gish sisters in "Orphans of the Storm." That was the night Alice Longworth sat on a gilt sofa between Senator Borah and Balfour. Hidden in his pocket, Balfour had a souvenir that I had given him. Just before we left the dinner tables so that they could be cleared away, he and Lord Lee of Fareham came and subtly flattered me. They asked what cloth it was that shone with such a yellow luster; it seemed to be, with all the lights turned on, something woven out of Camp Bird ore.

"It's just ordinary sateen," I gladly told them.

Balfour let his scholarly blue eyes review the cluster massed at the doors; most of the men that night wore handsome uniforms, not olive drab but richly ornamented fabrics, their breasts bright with jeweled decorations.

Lord Lee fingered the yellow cloth and murmured that he would try to remember that the word was "sateen."

"You shan't have to think about the word," I said, " because I'll let you have a sample."

A servant brought a pair of scissors and those two British gentlemen stood popeyed as I whacked off for each of them a square of yellow cloth. When I explained how inexpensive sateen really is, Lord Lee said that he would have something to tell his womenfolk when he got home.

In the story of her life Alice Longworth commented on the contrasting reactions of Balfour and Senator Borah to this moving picture "Orphans of the Storm." The scenes of the French Revolution were lurid, as Alice says, and the cruelties of the French nobles portrayed something that I know does not exist in the United States. With Alice for my reporter, I know that as the picture story was unreeled Balfour murmured near her ear from time to time, "Very moving; very moving." Borab, on the other hand, she says, behaved as though the scenes had been taken on the spot. She describes him as blazing with indignation at the cruelties.

Well, something else came from Mr. Borah that night, something that I want to have in my book. The Senator from Idaho stood there in the ballroom in his somber evening clothes, surveyed our guests, our servants, and the rich furnishings of the I Street house. Then he spoke aloud, and according to my friends what he said was, "This sort of thing is what brings on a revolution."

I made up my mind that, for a while at least, I would not subject Senator Borah to such a hazard. The next time I had a party I wrote a note to Mrs. Borah saying I knew her husband did not like dinner parties and evening clothes but that I should be delighted to have her come.

In the first days of our acquaintance Mrs. Borah had come to one of my parties and was standing right near me, unaware of my presence. I heard her say my name and then add, "She is right sweet-looking, and I suppose she would be all right if it wasn't for that awful voice of hers." Just then she saw me and turned another color. I walked over.

"Mrs. Borah," I began as sweetly as I could, "you know I come from the West, a mining camp; so what can you expect of me? I ain't a lady."

Poor Mrs. Borah! I was only teasing her. The truth is, I do not care what people say about me, if only they tell the truth; and, after all, that voice of mine is kind of rusty.

Later in that winter of the Washington Arms Conference my husband and I were at The Breakers in Palm Beach, awaiting word to proceed with another sort of entertainment we were planning for the President. We had the *Nahmeoka* under charter. She was the property of H. N. Baruch (a brother of Bernie); she was a houseboat with four double staterooms. In Washington, President Harding was no less eager than we to be off on a coastal canal and river cruise in Florida. We had tempted him with comments on the golf courses and the freedom from the constant pressure at the White House.

On February 10, 1922, Ned read aloud to me this letter:—

My dear Ned:—

I have just been having an interview with our mutual friend, the new Ambassador to Belgium [Henry Fletcher]. We are clinging to the hope that it will be possible to come South for the houseboat trip for a week. It does not seem possible, however, to make this trip before the end of the first week in March. The Secretary of State [Charles Evans Hughes] is leaving on the 15th for Bermuda and will be absent for at least two weeks. There is no possibility of the Under Secretary [Henry Fletcher] getting away during his absence. It would be rather difficult, certainly disappointing, to make up a party without him. Of course, there is the chance that the whole thing will go by the board, but I wanted to tell you we are still hoping, and I felt that if I told you I was sure we would not come before March 6th you could probably be making other plans for the house-boat trip meanwhile. I hope you are having a very delightful time of it.

Please give my very best regards to Evalyn.

Very truly,

WARREN G. HARDING.

On March 8, 1922, President and Mrs. Harding with a small party of friends left Washington and when they arrived in Florida joined us aboard the houseboat, tied

PRESIDENT HARDING AND MR. MCLEAN

1920 HOUSEBOAT PARTY INCLUDING THE HARDINGS, MCLEANS,
HARRY DAUGHERTY AND JESS SMITH

up at St. Augustine. The others in the party were Attorney General Harry Daugherty, Undersecretary of State Henry Fletcher, General Sawyer, Speaker of the House Frederick Gillett, and George Christian. To my notion it was not highly successful as a party, but I think the men enjoyed themselves. Mrs. Harding was not really in good health at any time I knew her. We two spent most of our time aboard the boat cruising ahead while the men, after their golf, would follow in automobiles, coming aboard the boat in time, usually, for dinner. Mrs. Harding's meals were supervised by Dr. Sawyer; he kept her on a strict diet. Generally in the evenings we all played poker.

After Palm Beach, Ned and I returned to Washington for just a little while, and then went to Bar Harbor. Consequently we saw but little of the Hardings till fall.

On an evening in September, 1922, as I hastened along a White House corridor, I remember seeing a wall clock with its black hands showing half-past nine. As I paused outside a wide door, some impulse of the clock mechanism made its long hand jump a trifle so that I was startled. The movement gave me a melancholy feeling that there was not much time left for me or Mrs. Harding.

She was ill. The news had come to me at Bar Harbor and, after an exchange of wires with Sawyer and a long-distance talk with Harding, I had started for the Capitol on a special train. We broke all records into Baltimore, and at Washington I was met by Doris Christian in a White House car. I was taken directly to the office of the President. Secretary Weeks was seated with him there. Mr. Harding had his arms stretched out before him on a big desk blotter.

"I am afraid Florence is going," he said.

"Surely," I protested, "there is something we can do. We can muster all the doctors —"

President Harding shook his head. "Finney and Mayo are here. They say her only chance to live is in an operation. Sawyer won't have it. Suppose you talk to him."

"Let me talk first with Finney."

I found Finney and Dr. Mayo, for both of whom I have profound respect, shaking their heads over the state of affairs.

"She won't live," said Finney. "Dying now, I think." There is no surgeon in the world whom I rate higher than Finney.

"Are you certain?" I asked, and he nodded.

Mayo was downright mad because the little whipper-snapper, Sawyer, was standing pat. He said he was so disgusted he was ready to go home.

"Let me go to work on Sawyer," I said.

So I saw Sawyer. I found him pacing up and down the floor just outside the bedroom where Florence Harding was lying, quite out of her senses from the effects of self-generated poisons. He was wearing russet-colored puttees on his thin calves; his uniform tunic was buttoned across his hollow chest. It seemed to me that he was trying to take power through the silver stars on his shoulders, to make them testify afresh each minute that he was, after all, a General. He was so pitiably small of body that there was something ridiculously birdlike in his striding.

"Now look here, General, I began, "do you realize the load of responsibility you have taken on yourself? You are standing out against Finney and Mayo. Good heavens! Think who they are."

"Evalyn," he said, and paused to emphasize his words. He was squinting behind his thick glasses. "I realize much more sharply than you can just how the country will think of me if Florence— if anything happens to her." It almost seemed as if he had the reluctance of a savage to name the thing he feared. Then he went on: "Finney and Mayo are great men; but let me tell you this: they are not going to operate on her unless they do it over my dead body!"

His voice was a trifle shrill. He pressed my arm with his fingers. There were tears in his eyes.

"I have pulled this woman through many and many a time. I know her constitution. I know what she can stand, and I know she cannot stand another operation. She lived just through luck or God the last time she went under ether. I was the surgeon then; I know. I am gambling my reputation—I am facing ruin, almost —just because I am convinced that if her heart holds out the kidney stoppage will open up. I tell you, I'm their *family* doctor."

He brushed his palms across his eyes, that small-town doctor from Ohio, and all of a sudden I wanted very much to hug him. He took me on tiptoe to the side of Mrs. Harding's bed. As I looked I thought, "She must be dead." But she was not, and in the morning she showed a trace of improvement. Slowly she eliminated poisons and slowly she began to mend. In the space of weeks she was being pushed around on a wheel chair. She lived because of Dr. Sawyer's skill and courage.

Mrs. Harding used to rely on me to select her clothes. While she was getting well I took her a boudoir cap of lace shaped like a crown. She was deeply concerned just then because Warren had lost so much sleep during her illness. Time after time each night the nurses had to attend to her; and every time they did, of course, the President was disturbed. That went on for weeks; and by day he worked at one of the hardest jobs in the world. No wonder he grew tired.

Our last long time with the Hardings was in March, 1923. It was another vacation party on a houseboat we had chartered, *the Pioneer,* with seven staterooms, one with two beds and four with double berths. Our preparations were under way at Palm Beach in February when a letter came from the White House. It was dated February 15th.

My dear Ned —

Christian has shown me your letter, presumably written on the 13th, which arrived this morning. Our present plans are to leave here on the forenoon of the 5th and go directly to Ormond in accordance with the plans which we discussed when I last saw you. We ought to arrive at Ormond on the forenoon of the 6th and after proper salutations we ought to be able to look forward to a game of golf over the Ormond Beach course. When that is out of the way we can proceed on a leisurely journey southward. No change has been made in any way concerning the personnel of the party. General Dawes will meet us at Ormond. You understand that Lasker and Speaker Gillett are to be in the party. You talked to me about General Daugherty and Mr. Smith. I think the General is making such progress toward recovery that be will be able to come, and I have no doubt he very much desires to have the Southern vacation, and I think it is a fine thing for him to have it if he is able to make the trip. I saw him briefly yesterday but did not discuss the matter with him. I understand from General Sawyer that he is figuring on being a member of the party and, of course, this is highly agreeable to us as I understand it will be to you. Of course, you are counting on General Sawyer and Mr. Christian and I assume that Mrs. Harding must have her maid, and I will be glad to have Brooks come along if it is possible to take care of him. He can adjust himself to any arrangement either on or off the boat which is necessary. I think I ought to tell you about one party whom I think would like an invitation. At one time his inclusion in the party was discussed. I refer to Secretary Weeks. Nothing has been said to him, however, and the extension of an invitation will be wholly left to your wishes in the matter.

Mrs. Harding wanted me to write about a matter that she is deeply interested in. She wants the privilege of sending my horse and the one you placed at her disposal out to your Virginia farm for an early Spring recuperation. She would like to send an attendant along so that the horses might be properly housed at night and be given the out-of-door life during the day. Of course I will be very glad to cover all expenses if your situation at the farm is such that the addition of two animals will not embarrass the management. Please let me know frankly concerning the matter.

We are looking forward to the trip with the most delightful anticipation. Mrs. Harding is getting herself in form so that she may fully enjoy it and counts upon making a great improvement. She has been out of doors in the South grounds of the White House every day that weather permits and we are confident she is going to find great satisfaction in the trip.

Please give my very best to Mrs. McLean, and be assured of my continued high regard,

Very sincerely yours,

WARREN G. HARDING.

I have a pencil-written scrap of paper that Warren Harding apparently tucked inside the envelope that carried the letter. This reads,

The Weeks matter is wholly up to you and Mrs. McLean. Of course I am referring to him alone, since I understand the party is stag— outside of Evelyn [*sic*] to look after you and the boss to keep me right.

That trip was much more pleasant than the one we had the preceding winter. Harding, Dawes, Lasker, and McLean were generally the foursome, as I recall it; but sometimes George Christian played with them and once or twice they took along some professional.

What happened in the next few months to change our friend Warren Harding into a weary, heartsick man? I am sorry to report that an illness of my own here compels me to drop a stitch or two of yarn.

One day at Friendship, Ned watched me sharply as I moved about my room.

Then he called to Miss Todd and asked her if she had noticed a swelling of my throat. She had not, but when I stood before a mirror and Ned pulled back my hair could see a faintly bulging line just above the place where my blue diamond touches me. Soon after that I went to Baltimore to see Dr. Finney.

"Yes," he said, after feeling with his fingers and making other tests, "it's goiter."

I took that calmly. For a while I thought I should prefer to have it taken out by Dr. Crile of Cleveland, but he refused to operate in my bedroom. Finney did not want to, but when I coaxed he consented.

"How are you going to do it?" I inquired on the appointed day.

"Give you gas," he said, "and you won't know a thing about it."

"You don't know me," I said.

He clucked when he took my pulse and remarked that it was thumping; then he added that I had an even chance.

"Of course it thumps," I complained, "when you tell me I'm about to die."

I was chewing gum and trying hard to keep myself calmed down. My bedroom was as crowded as a theater lobby with nurses and doctors all in white, with rubber-coated hands held carefully aloof from everything I treasure there in my boudoir.

"We're going to give you gas right on this table," someone said. I walked over, thinking that soon the world would be over as a play is over when the curtain falls. Then I asked myself a question: "How shall I know if I am dead?" As I reclined, with help, upon the table, I saw the bluish globe of a chandelier above me, and decided to remember that as a kind of landmark. Then I stuck my chewing gum on the underside of the so gosh-darned-sanitary table and announced a rule. I said to Dr. Hardin, "Now if I press your hand three times, you will know I'm conscious and you must not begin to cut."

He held my hand; in a minute I heard somebody say "all ready," and I nearly squeezed his fingers off. So they waited and then, in blackness, I felt a feeble thought rise up through my mind as bubbles in thick fluid. None of my normal contacts with the universe seemed to be working, but at last I managed to command myself a little and one eye must have opened, for there above me was the bluish light; then, and only then, I knew I was alive.

In the same spring that I was operated on, Harry Daugherty was verging on a nervous breakdown. I suppose I missed a lot by being in seclusion. On May 19, 923, Ned showed me a letter from Jess Smith, who was staying in Ohio. Smith reported: —

I came to Columbus to-day to see Harry [Daugherty] and do a little shopping. I have not seen him yet but will later in the day. He is making steady improvement and is less nervous, think, and looks much better. He is dieting and holding his weight down. He has had a lot of callers but evades most of them tho they try to run him to death. He is taking things comparatively easy.

There is another paragraph I want to quote, because Jess W. Smith really was a kindly fellow whatever else he may have been. He wrote: —

I miss seeing you [Ned] very much. You have always been so nice to me and I have such a deep affection for you that I really get homesick for you. I hope you are all right and still reducing your weight and going along good. I sincerely trust Mrs. McLean is also continuing to improve and will soon be able to be about. Kindly give her my regards, and also my regards to the children. I want you to know how much I appreciate your kindness to me in every way. I probably will never be able to repay you but I am always willing and ready to do anything I can for you at any time.

Ten days after we had read Jess Smith's letter from Columbus, our telephone rang one evening; we were down at Leesburg on our 2,600-acre farm. Ned answered.

"It's Jess Smith", he told me. "He wants to know if he can come down here for three or four days."

"Oh damn" I said, "I don't feel good; but tell him all right. I will have my meals up in my room; I should anyway, the way I feel."

A while later, about ten in the evening I should say, the phone rang once more. It was Jess Smith again, calling from his apartment in the Wardman Park. He told Ned a big storm was drenching Washington. He would be at the farm in the morning.

At midnight, or thereabouts, the phone rang again. Ned was asleep. I answered it. Jess Smith was on the wire again.

"Hello," I said. "How are you?"

"I am fine but rather nervous."

"Now, now," I said, "what's wrong with you?"

"Oh, I'm just a little upset. Ned's asleep, you say?"

"Isn't Mr. Daugherty with you?"

"No; the Chief sent for him to come to the White House."

"Well, you get a little sleep now and you'll feel better."

"I'll be at the farm at seven," he said.

"You can stay as long as you like," I told him.

"I am so glad I can come," he said.

I went to sleep right after that, and woke up about noon. My son Jock, who then was twelve, was standing wide-eyed beside my bed, "Jess Smith is dead," he said. "He shot himself, the paper says."

There was no postmortem examination of the body. I have often wondered why.

Once when I talked with President Harding that year I chided him about new traces of tenderness that he was showing for the League of Nations. My tutor in high politics was our friend, the Ambassador to the Court of St. James's, Colonel George Harvey.

"If you're not careful," I said, "you will swing us into the League, and then you won't get four more years in the White House." I had spoken almost playfully, but his face tightened swiftly.

"Evalyn," he said, "I wish to God I could walk out and slam the door and never go into it again."

Few of our old crowd were going West with the Hardings on the Alaskan trip.

General and Mrs. Sawyer were going; also George Christian and his wife, Speaker Gillett, and. Mr. and Mrs. Malcolm Jennings. Most of the others were rather less well known to us, such as Albert Fall's successor as Secretary of the Interior, Dr. Work and his wife, Secretary of Agriculture Henry C. Wallace, and Secretary of Commerce and Mrs. Herbert Hoover. They were a Western crowd.

My physical condition was such that summer of 1923 that, although the Hardings urged us to go with them to Alaska, Dr. Finney told me he must forbid my making such a trip. We were at Bar Harbor when we got the first news that Mr. Harding was ill. Then we heard that all he required was rest: as we were in receipt of frequent bulletins, relayed from the *Washington Post,* we were not worried, and really supposed he was soon to be himself again. Consequently the news that he was dead came as a clap of thunder. We hurried back to Washington and I was with Mrs. Harding at the White House during those first oppressive hours in what had ceased to be her home.

Right in the middle of the August night, at one-thirty, Mrs Harding decided that she was lonesome for want of her husband's companionship. He was downstairs in the East Room of the White House, in his coffin. I held her arm, soft and dropsical, as we descended the curving white marble staircase. She was being game with all her might. Through all that time I never saw her shed a tear.

George Christian, with a grief almost as deep as hers alertly watched for any sign of weakness, of collapse; there was no such sign.

"Put back the casket lid," she said to him, and he obeyed at once.

In the nighttime what was no longer the President appeared quite alive; rouge and lipstick touches, that in daylight were, ghastly, with a softer illumination made him seem almost himself. Then I began to shiver, because I heard Mrs. Harding talking to her husband. The heavy scent of flowers cloyed my nostrils as we stayed on and on and Mrs. Harding talked. A chair was placed for her and she sat down.

"Warren," she said, her face held close to his, "the trip has not hurt you one bit."

That poor thing kept right on talking, as if she could not bear to hear the silence that would so poignantly remind her that he could not speak to her in turn.

"No one can hurt you now, Warren," she said another time. That one remark helped me to understand how she was weaving strands of comforting philosophy out of grief. I know how she had feared that some crank might do him harm; I too sometimes am conscious of a feeling of warmth when I think that my own dead are now beyond the reach of harm.

Before we left she looked about at all the flowers, the costly sheaves of roses, the wreaths and the usual collection — oversize of course — of those stupid fabrications that the florists make, and then buy back, withered, from cemeteries for further use. Somewhere in those mounds she saw something that she wanted, and she stooped down as if she were in a growing garden to pick it up— a small bouquet of country flowers, of daisies and nasturtiums. These she placed directly on the coffin after she had told George Christian to close the lid. It was three o'clock in the morning when we started back upstairs.

Ned went out to Marion on the train with Mrs. Harding and the body of her husband. The doctor would not let me go. That same night the Coolidges came out to Friendship and brought the Stearnses along. We five had dinner; that was arranged by Mr. Coolidge because, I fancy, he was being too much hectored at the Hotel Willard. I looked at him that night and wondered at the swift change that had been wrought. How had it all happened?

I asked Brooks. He was Harding's valet, a colored man with the dignity of an Othello. He was a major in the National Guard.

"Brooks, please tell me what you can. How did it happen? You should know a lot."

"Mrs. McLean," said Brooks, "if he had turned back when he was first told to . . ."

"How about that awful sunburn in Kansas City when he rode around under a broiling sun on a reaper in a wheat field; when his lips were so swollen?"

"That wasn't due to sunburn," said Brooks. "That was caused by his heart."

Then he said some more: "We were on that transport and had a slight collision. Remember? They called out, 'All hands on deck.'

"'Brooks,' the President said, 'what's happened?' He was lying down with his face hidden in his hands. I told him it was not serious, but that everybody was ordered on deck. Then he spoke again.

"'I hope the boat sinks.' That's what he said. And two hours later they had him dressed up once more, reviewing a parade."

When Mrs. Harding had supervised the packing of all their personal belongings, when she had burned a mound of souvenirs and papers, given his dog away, and performed a lot of other chores of widowhood, she lifted up her chin in a characteristic gesture. Then she walked out of the White House and came to Friendship. I myself was preparing to return to my children, at Bar Harbor. Cicadas were singing with their wings as we walked beneath the trees that shade the lawn.

"Now that it is all over," she said, "I am beginning to feel it is for the best. I could not, could not wish him back to all that strain."

The next time I saw her was in Marion. She was staying at Dr. Sawyer's sanitarium. Many of the patients were mental cases. Sawyer was the one who had been keeping her alive; but Sawyer by that time was dead. I persuaded her to come down to the private car in the railroad yard and have dinner with us. When she was leaving in the middle of the evening, to drive back to the sanitarium farm, she spoke with finality.

"I will never see you again. Good-bye."

"Now, now," I chided her. "You are going to get better and visit me— see all your friends in Washington."

"Evalyn, this is the end."

It was, indeed. With General Sawyer dead, her shield was down. She died November 21st, 1924.

CHAPTER XXII

Oil and the First-Page McLeans

My husband, and our way of living, became first-page news in 1924. Hot on the trail of bribery and graft in connection with the leases upon the Naval Oil Reserves in a wilderness called Teapot Dome, the United States Senate's Committee on Public Lands and Surveys ran Ned to earth as a minor accessory after the fact.

In this tricky matter of the Teapot Dome and the Elk Hills Oil Reserves, designed to fuel the Navy, Ned's only part was that he lied to help a friend. That friend was Albert Fall.

After Fall's resignation as Secretary of the Interior had taken effect on March 4, 1923, he went abroad, and into Russia on an oil development mission for Harry Sinclair (who by intimates is always called "Sinco"). Fall was, we always understood, an expert oil man. He traveled overseas with Colonel Zeverly, another one of Sinclair's men. Then President Harding died, on August 2d. In the autumn there were stories published of some impending scandal. My recollection is not clear as to when we learned that Albert Fall was being accused of having taken a large bribe in return for leasing the Naval Oil Lands on a basis that excluded competition. In October, Fall had testified before the Senate Committee of which Senator Walsh was such an able member. I remember that, in a little more than three months after President Harding died, all of our friends in Washington were wondering where Albert Fall was; it was no secret that he had been drinking heavily. Then, early in December, when Ned and I were preparing to start for Palm Beach, there came a telegram from Fall. He was in Chicago and asked if he and Mrs. Fall might come to Friendship for a couple of days. Ned wired for them to come, but we heard nothing more for a week or so and then I was called on long distance by Mrs. Fall. She was talking from Atlantic City. (Her name is Emma.)

"So glad to hear from you," I said. "Where is Al?"

"He's here," she said, "very sick; and he wants Ned to come over."

"We are ready to start for Palm Beach. Is it very important?"

"A matter of life or death," she said, and something in her tone caused me to believe her.

The next morning Ned left Washington in the private car "Enquirer" for Atlantic City, and returned late the same day.

"I found Al in a terrible condition," Ned told me. "He's been in such a state for days and days." Ned told me that Fall had asked him to do him a favor, to say that he had loaned him the $100,000 which the Senate Committee somehow had heard about. He told me that Fall had assured him that the Committee was "barking up the wrong tree", adding further that the money in question had nothing to do with Harry Sinclair or Teapot Dome. That Sinclair was the one with whom Fall was involved had been inferred theretofore, because Fall had resigned from the Cabinet to take what we all had understood was a fine job in Sinclair's employ.

We started for Florida on December 20th. As we traveled, Ned was exchanging telegrams with his personal employees, John Major and William Duckstein. What Ned became concerned with chiefly on that journey to Palm Beach was a scheme to set up a private telegraph wire to link our cottage down there with the *Washington Post*. The one who advised us to spend about $1,500 every month for that wire and a couple of operators was Francis Homer, a Baltimore lawyer who had been the close friend and last adviser of John R. McLean. There was so much spying, back and forth, that this seems to be as good a place as any to reveal that at that very time a man who had access to all our things, Ned's papers and my own, was being paid money by a man named Gaston B. Means. I still keep as a souvenir of that mad time an affidavit later made by this man, in which he confesses that he worked for Means that winter at the same time we were paying him. Means, maverick detective, had fallen out with Harry Daugherty, and was preparing to do his best to compromise the Attorney General. That was his reason for making, as he would say, a "contact" with one of our most trusted household employees.

Bascom Slemp, a former Virginia member of Congress who in September, 1923, became secretary to President Coolidge, was a friend of Ned's. Three days before Christmas he left Washington for Palm Beach, where we saw right much of him.

On Christmas Day in Palm Beach, Ned wired John Major in Washington that he had a tip saying he was going to be subpœnaed before the Senate Committee; he referred to the same committee that was investigating the leases of the Naval Oil Reserves. Ned instructed Major to get A. Mitchell Palmer to represent him if he should be subpœnaed. (Palmer had been: Woodrow Wilson's Attorney General.) On that same Christmas, Day, Ned sent a wire to Albert Fall:

PLEASE WIRE ME WHERE YOU WILL BE SATURDAY STOP WANT MY SECRETARY TO SEE YOU FOR IMPORTANT BUSINESS MATTER THAT DAY STOP MRS MCLEAN JOINS ME IN WISHING YOU AND MRS FALL A MERRY CHRISTMAS STOP WIRE ANSWER.

The day after Christmas Ned began his foolish actions whereby he tried to lure old Senator Walsh of Montana off the scent of graft. Ned sent a wire to his man Major, instructing him to see A. Mitchell Palmer and tell him (so that he could tell the Senate Committee) that the only thing that might remotely connect him with the investigation before the Committee would be that in 1921 he had loaned Fall $100,000 on his personal note. Of course, Ned never had loaned any such sum to Albert Fall; in saying that he had, Ned was doing what a field lark does when she pretends to have a crippled wing, and thus leads those who pursue away from her nest of eggs. It was the day after Ned arranged for Mitchell Palmer to tell that fabricated story to the committee that Fall himself informed the Committee that he had received $100,000 from Edward B. McLean. (I almost think that Ned was having fun right then.)

Then the Falls joined us at Palm Beach. They came at Ned's telegraphed suggestion, arriving on the last day of the year. For the first time in my life, I saw a man crumble right before my eyes. Albert Fall used to sit on the hotel porch gazing out to sea, and his face was a mask of tragedy. We really loved the Falls; and I used to beg Albert to tell the truth and get his life straightened out.

"I can't tell without bringing ruin to some others," he would say; "but I tell you I have done nothing wrong."

Drinking had changed him from a virile, sharp-witted man into a trembling wreck. Night after night, I tried to get Albert Fall to make a clean breast of what he knew. He was sick and weak, but his lean jaw would tighten at the thought of talking to his former colleagues of the Senate.

I was provoked with Ned for getting deeper into the mess. I told him it was time to call a halt.

Ned said, "I won't go back on Al Fall."

"You've gone far enough," I said. "This Committee will root back through all your papers until they prove you're lying. Who believes that story, anyway? Somebody gave Fall the money; let him say who it was."

For hours every night there would be a steady exchange of telegrams, most of them in weird codes. Ned had, besides the badge that identified him as an agent of the Department of Justice, a copy of its secret code. Some of his messages were in that code; some were in hastily devised new ones. Many of the communications were unimportant. However, there was confusion in our cottage on the day we got a wire saying that Senator Walsh was requesting Ned to appear before the Committee in Washington on January 7th.

Poor Ned! Short months had worked a change in his position; he was no longer one to whom men appealed when something was to be fixed up. There, in that rich playground at Palm Beach, he was being ordered as an ordinary culprit to come North prepared to tell the truth. We were scared.

Ned got his doctor, who was also treating Bascom Slemp, to say his sinuses were in such a state that he could not travel safely. To our dismay, we next heard that Senator Walsh was coming down to Palm Beach to take Ned's statement, under oath.

When I heard that news I was taking care of my little girl, then two years old. I was breaking her in to a new nurse. Well, I just threw her to the nurse and went, flaming mad, to see Albert Fall.

"Now look," I said: "If Ned McLean gets up before Senator Walsh and perjures himself, nobody can save him. I'm not going to have the father of my children sent to jail on your account."

I was so wrought up and frightened that poor Albert tried to comfort me. He showed me a telegram he was sending to Edward L. Doheny. This was my first inkling that Doheny was the one who had loaned him the $100,000. We talked some more; I argued and I pleaded. Finally I said, "If you don't release Ned from his promise, I'm going to tell Senator Walsh just what I know."

We settled it there and then: he would tell the truth. But that afternoon Ned appeared before Senator Walsh and told a lame story about having given Albert Fall his checks for $100,000, adding that these were never cashed. Senator Walsh thereafter established that Ned did not have sufficient money to cover checks for that amount in the banks on which he said the checks were drawn.

Subsequently Albert and Emma Fall, two broken people, went to New Orleans and there met Doheny, who agreed to reveal that he had given Fall the money. Doheny did; he told the Committee how his son (since murdered by a maniac) had carried a black satchel, containing $100,000 in bills, to Washington and there delivered it to Secretary of the Interior Albert B. Fall. I did not understand it then; I do not now. It seems to me that Fall, who had been so greatly loved when he was in the Senate, must have lost, if not his mind, at least his point of view when he accepted that money.

In March, Ned went North and appeared before the Committee; thanks to a childlike manner when responding to questions, to a squad of high-priced lawyers, and to some other factors, he succeeded in avoiding punishment and finally heard Senator Walsh say, "That is all."

A few months after the unhappy oil mess had ceased to get so much attention in the newspapers, Ned hired a new editor for the *Washington Post.* He did it in the kind of mood that would send me forth to buy a jewel. The one he hired at a salary of $75,000 a year was George Harvey, who was giving up his post as Ambassador in London. I wrote the agreement that they both signed one night at Friendship, on a sheet of my monogramed letter paper. Harvey was a fascinating character; to have him at work for one was something like having a tiger as a pet - a most flattering arrangement as long as the tiger likes his keeper. Once the hating mechanism of George Harvey got in motion, it never seemed to stop; but he was to the McLeans the warmest kind of friend.

"I miss you both like the very devil," he wrote to us in that summer of 1924. We were at Bar Harbor and he was staying in the White House with the Coolidges, who were then in mourning for their son - Calvin, Jr. That had been a tragedy that shadowed Ned and me, because it made us feel again the pangs of little Vinson's death. Both Calvin and John Coolidge had been accustomed to come often to Friendship when they were out of school. They sometimes used our swimming pool. Calvin, Jr., was the sweetest kind of lad, who would have been, I always felt, a splendid man. What President Coolidge was going through that summer, George Harvey helped me realize. On White House stationery he wrote:—

As the days pass I realize more fully the change in him -he is still very tired. Though quite brisk as a rule, every once in a while his face suddenly goes gray and pitiably sad and it is with distinct effort that he fetches it back... He feels lonely naturally and seems to hanker for somebody or something to lean up against once in a while.

CHRISTMAS TREE PARTY

At the I Street House

I think it was shortly after we received that letter that George Harvey joined us at Bar Harbor, his brow wrinkled over the problem of producing an acceptable 1924 campaign slogan for the Republican Party. One night on our porch he burst out, "Evalyn, I've got it."

"You've got what?"

"The campaign slogan. Listen!"

"I'm listening."

"Coolidge or Chaos."

Well, it sounded pretty flat to me—quite disappointing as the product of a week of cerebration by Harvey, who so often said smarter things on the spur of the moment. Sometimes in the intervening years as, in the role of client, I have sat across an office table and watched the calm, strong face of John W. Davis I have wondered at the impudence of suggesting to the nation that his name could be a synonym for "Chaos." However, in 1924 I was for Coolidge; and if he were alive to-day I think I'd be a partisan of Coolidge still.

Before we left for Palm Beach I had a sweet note from Grace Coolidge, written on Christmas Day, thanking me for a fan that I had sent her. They were to have four years more in the White House, but I could tell how the time would be flavored for her as I read,

I hope you will all have a merry, merry Christmas and in your family circle I know you count, as we do, the boy who is singing his carols in Heaven.

With my love,

GRACE COOLIDGE.

The only favor I ever asked of President Coolidge was to have Mrs. Edward Hutton presented at Court, in London.

I had not seen Mrs. Hutton in a great many years until we encountered each other at Palm Beach, and she reminded me that she was a boarder at the Mount Vernon Seminary when I was a day pupil. That had been when she was Miss Post of Battle Creek. She had been married, divorced, and married a second time. (Since then she has been divorced from Hutton.) We became very friendly in Florida. One day she came up and said, "Evalyn, I want so much to be presented at court -on account of my daughter."

The next time I saw President Coolidge I asked him, and he agreed to fix it. Then it developed that Mrs. Hutton and her daughter wished to be presented at the same time. A bit later Everett Sanders wrote a letter to Ned saying: —

I am quoting from a letter I have just received from Ambassador Houghton at London:

"In regard to the presentation of Mrs. Hutton and Miss Hutton next year I am bound to tell you that we have been compelled to establish a definite rule that only one member of a family can be presented. There are, as you know, scores of applications embracing requests from mother and daughter. The number, however, that we are permitted to present is so limited, that we have found it necessary to establish the rule just mentioned. The rule, of course, can be broken, and if the matter is of enough importance, it will be broken. But in view of our practice, I wish you would let me know when I am in Washington whether so marked an exception should in the case of the Huttons be made. My only fear is that if we make one exception, the pressure next year for many more will be pretty severe, which would result in practically cutting the presentation list in half."

In view of what the Ambassador says I wonder if it will not be satisfactory if we advise him to arrange the presentation of the daughter alone. Please let me know.

Nannie Lee Duke was offering me a hundred to one that the thing could not be done, but I was determined. I wheedled and pulled strings until at last Ned got an angry message from President Coolidge, the essence of which was, "I wish she [meaning me] would not annoy me. We are doing everything we can." However, in 1928 Mrs. Hutton and Miss Hutton were presented.

One night at the I Street house Mr. Coolidge spoke to me in an undertone, saying, "There's a lady here who is going to lose five dollars."

"Whom do you mean?" I asked. "And how?"

He told me and then he said: "I heard her bet some friend five dollars that she could get me to talk. Well, I'm not going to open my lips all evening."

I watched and had a lot of fun. The lady would chatter at him archly, then fire a question, then retreat before his grunt. Sometimes he nodded, sometimes he shook his head, but he did not talk. Contrary to legend, however, usually Mr. Coolidge really liked to talk.

I never have figured out why he did not stand for re-election. When he came back from his trip to the Black Hills in 1927 I went to the White House for dinner and chided him at my first opportunity for having said, "I do not choose to run."

After my usual habit of saying what is in my mind, I went on: "It was a foolish statement because we need you here in Washington. I hear people saying it's because you're sick."

I saw the muscles of his face grow taut, which was his common reaction to annoyance, and he fairly snapped at me, "That's absurd. I am not sick at all. I never felt better in my life."

Time goes by so fast! It seems as yesterday that I was being introduced to Andrew Mellon at the White House soon after he came into the Harding Cabinet; and then I see myself with him again during a Sunday morning gathering at Friendship, as we strolled toward the swimming pool, talking of things we had seen and heard in Washington under Harding, Coolidge, and Hoover. It seems to me we laughed again that day as we recalled the time that Babe, our long-tailed monkey, snatched from a table on the porch a tall glass of lemonade or something and scampered up the side of the house by clutching vines and projections; and then, how everybody had forgotten about the little beast until it dribbled the contents of the glass down on the striped flannels of President Harding. That same little brute stowed away one day in the automobile of Mr. Mellon and rode from

Friendship clear to the Treasury Department before it was discovered.

The monkey was an almost human creature. At first, when it was young, I kept it in my bathroom and every morning, due to its nightlong researches, the place was inches deep in broken glass, pink bath salts, powder, perfume, and cold creams. So, in spite of all its drolleries, it had to be banished out of doors. Thereafter it had the run of the place and scampered up and down our trees and callers indiscriminately. When I would place my daughter on the lawn it would rush at her and snatch away her orange juice. If workmen on the place brought luncheons in a box, they would have to watch, or the monkey would make off with all their food. It had one trick that astonished everybody: it would swim underwater the length of our garden pool.

All the puppies and other young pets got their adolescent training in my bathroom, so that sometimes the second floor at Friendship was like a zoo. I remember once when I was sick I heard a clatter and a clicking as of small hoofs on hardwood floors. I thought: "That *can't* be that white llama Ringling sent us!" But it was, as I discovered when my boudoir door swung wide and my little daughter, in the saddle, rode the woolly animal to my bedside. A horse kicks, a dog bites, a cow hooks, but a llama spits. One of those things will spit you right over on your back. I was nearly petrified, because already I was in a nervous state that had the doctors worried. Little Evalyn made the llama put its head down on my pillow. I stroked its chinchilla-soft ears and told myself I had better make no sudden move else I'd be blown right out the window.

"Now," I said to little Evalyn when I felt stronger, "will you kindly ride this thing into some other room?" Her bodyguard was with her. He led it out as gently as you please. After that we sent the llama to the zoo; it is there to-day, but I don't believe the Sunday visitors who stare through the fence that pens it in ever suspect that once it was our house pet.

The one continuing problem in my life has always had the shape of just one question: What amusing thing can I do next? It is not only me it bothers, so I notice; it afflicts all my friends except those who have their noses deep in work. Nick and Alice Longworth used to help us solve that problem with their musicales. Nick really loved music, and played on his violin with entrancing skill. Moreover, his music was always rich with fun; he would write amusing parodies on popular songs, and sometimes Gypsy, the wife of Senator James Hamilton Lewis, would sing to Nick's accompaniment. Sometimes the star performer at one of Nick's evenings would be the Hungarian Minister, Count Széchényi, who used a felt covered mallet to play upon a saw. The Count could play divinely, too, on the theremin, an electrical gadget which gave off tones of highpressure oscillations which the player would shape into melodies with gestures of his hands.

In thirty-eight years swarms whom I have known in Washington have died, so that, for me, it is more thickly populated by ghosts than by living friends. One I shall never cease to miss is Nick. When he was being taken back to Cincinnati a blanket of roses placed on his casket, in the station, was from me.

EVALYN B. McLEAN
Daughter of Mrs. McLean

In our married life together I gave Ned some queer surprises. One was when I let him go without me to Cincinnati, when the Porter was racing at Latonia, and then just as soon as he had gone began to make my plans to fly out there and join him. That was 1926, when such occurrences were far less commonplace than now. I called up New York and told them to send me the biggest plane they had, and with it their best pilot and best mechanic. The plane they sent was a three-motored Fokker. I asked the pilot to come out to the house. I wished to discover if he was sober, and in other ways all right; he proved to be very nice and quiet. His name was Wilmer Stultz. Alice Longworth wouldn't go; she said it would not be fair to her Paulina.

"Well, Alice," I said, "I'm going to leave my three and fly. God will take care of me."

My maid, Inga, went along. We were in the air six hours and at Cincinnati Ned had discovered what I was up to just about the time our communication with the ground was interrupted. He was in the office of the *Cincinnati Enquirer* when I walked in. I heard him swearing at all who had a hand in my adventure. Then he saw me, safe, and was so mad that he walked right past me without speaking.

Another time when I was in a humor for amusement I rounded up some of the oldest men I knew in Washington: old justices and others of distinction who had long beards and walked with canes. I had them out for dinner to meet my friend Fanny Ward, the rejuvenated actress. She shows no wrinkles, not a line.

That night she displayed creamy round arms and shoulders in a low-cut, baby-blue taffeta dress. She wore a wig of yellow curls held close by a bandeau of blue ribbon. It seemed to me her face had been lifted so effectively that I promptly knew that when the time came I would have mine lifted too. It was a treat to watch those feeble guests of mine when they saw Fanny and were told that she was more than seventy. I hear that Fanny sits up all night, and rarely goes to sleep. She does not, so she says, take any exercise. I've never been a Girl Scout, but I knew that I had done my good deed for weeks and weeks when I saw those old fellows, clustered around Fanny, perk up and glow with the realization that, after all, they were not so old.

Another act of mine that ought to be on record concerns the time I returned home with the forlorn mother of an injured girl-acrobat of the circus. That time Ned met me at the door. When he saw the sniffling woman, he spoke as if to one I could not see, asking, "God, please tell me what she is going to bring into our house next?"

A few days previous at the circus I had talked with John Ringling, of whom I am very fond. He had told me about a distressing accident that had happened the night before. A girl, standing on her head at the top of a tall and limber pole supported on the shoulder of a strong man, had lost her balance and fallen to the sawdust far below. When I asked if she would live John Ringling shrugged. So, after that I went to the hospital, had the girl moved into a private room, arranged for a nurse, and had Dr. Jim Mitchell X-ray her skull and spine. About the time the girl was recovering consciousness her mother arrived from Vermont, and to me she appeared as if she had never been away from Vermont before. A minister had given her the money for her fare. She was the one I brought out to Friendship.

I am not a social case worker, but I began to think that my handling of that woman's case was going to be better than first-class. In her youth she, too, had been an acrobat but after years she began to look as though she had spent most of her time in kitchens. I brought the convalescing daughter out to Friendship and she wore, anchored with some string, a gaudy bracelet I had given her. It was the only imitation thing I owned, but she prized it so much that she was getting well, she said, just so she could show it off around the circus. At last I spoke my mind to the mother.

"Look," I said, "I've been studying you, and you could be made over. You've had hard luck and lost your husband but that does not prevent another try. You come along." I took her downtown then; first to Émil, who is the best hairdresser on my list. Her hair was gray-black and long when he began. When he finished it was smartly bobbed, permanently waved, and red.

"Now," I told my protégée when I had her dressed in lacy underwear and a smart dress, "I'm going to get you married."

I took her back to Friendship; and when she walked, transformed, into the room where Ned was sitting, he asked, behind his hand, "Who's that?"

In a week the daughter was going to rejoin the circus, but it had been a week of sniffles from the mother. I supposed her tears flowed from her gratitude, until at last she told me that she simply had to confess.

"You ought to know it," she began. "The fact is, I've been married several times, since I lost the husband I spoke about. Right now I'm happily married. I hope he'll like me the way you've fixed me up, and I hope you'll forgive me for what I made you think."

That poor thing had been worried for fear I had another husband all picked out for her and waiting with a ring. When I forgave her she set out for Vermont, delighted with her new finery.

CHAPTER XXIII

Private Problems — and Public

How strange it is that I could spend a few dollars on a woman's hair and clothing, and patch her life up neatly, although with all my money and all of Ned's we could not fix our own. I think our lives were spoiled for us when we were little. His mother, and his father too, believed that the way to make him happy was to give him what he wanted. They never gave him any taste of discipline, because they could not bear to see his tears or hear him wail. We went apart for keeps in 1928. I went back to him one time when he was ill, but just to nurse him.

There is a lesson in all this, I rather fancy, for those persons who suppose that life would be entirely smooth if only they had money. Well, we had money! And yet, what did we buy except the stresses that broke up our home? Lest anyone should think that he, or I, with money, can evade the consequences of that rupture, I want to set down here a poignant line Ned wrote, from some place far away, to our young daughter: "I hope my darling girl is happy and that you never in your life be *lonesome*." Unhappily, a broken family always goes on being lonesome.

There is a question in my mind as to how much I ought to say about our private troubles. I ought to show that Ned McLean's wild behavior was at last revealed to be a progressive madness caused by dissipation. I say I should tell this, because from day to day I have to teach my sons and daughter how, with money, their father bought all his trouble.

My own story has not ended, but there is little more to tell about my husband. At intervals I get reports from a Maryland hospital concerning a patient there who has morbid preoccupations and lives in a state of mental exile, shut off even from himself. If he is addressed by his right name he grows excited and swears he is not McLean.

Outside of 2020 Massachusetts Avenue a blizzard wind was howling and the noise of it seemed to take the shape of words I'd heard about people starving and freezing in the parks. Alice Longworth was staying with me. As neither of us could sleep, we were in my sitting room before a fire. It was after midnight.

"Alice," I said, "I simply can't stand this. I am so worried about those people suffering. I am going out to investigate, to see just who is sleeping in the park with newspapers wrapped around them."

"Evalyn, you can't do that," said Alice.

"I can and I am; I am going to take my little pistol and sally forth."

"As I'm your guest I'll come," said Alice; "but none too happily."

We first stopped at Franklin Square. Alice got out of the taxicab and walked around with me. We saw no one there. Then we went to the Pension Office Park. This time she would not get out of the cab. I did and saw two figures huddled on a bench and started toward them. They seemed to duck their heads as I came closer, and I suspect they thought from my determined manner that I was a policewoman. The girl was wrapped, not in newspapers, but in a fur coat.

"What are you children doing out here in this blizzard?"

"Lady," said the boy, "we've got no other place where we can find privacy." The girl spoke up to say that it was crowded at her home.

"Here's three dollars," I said. "Go to a nice restaurant and enjoy yourselves."

Leaving them agape, I entered the women's restroom. I had been told such places were crowded with female victims of the depression. There was a three-hundred-pound chocolate colored woman in that one, and no others.

"What are you doing?" I asked her and saw her eyes roll white with fright.

"Oh, lady, I ain't doing any harm. I just stopped in here on my way home."

"You're sure you've got a home?"

"I have a nice home with lots of children, and a husband waiting for me."

That was all I could find of starving people in a park, so I went back to Alice and said that I was going to the Salvation Army place. I crawled up a steep staircase there, and asked if they had empty beds. They said they had some in case I wanted to send any poor to use them. We saw some other empty parks and then I went to Precinct One. Alice did not leave me, but she continued to sit in the cab. The police that night had rounded up a lot of poor men who were shooting craps, so that I had half a mind to stay at Precinct One. It was after two when Alice and I went into Childs' for something warm.

About that time my own system of living was undergoing change. I was not poor, of course; but I was no longer spending at the rate I like to spend. Only a few months before, there had expired the second ten-year period of trust in which, voluntarily, I had left my half of my father's fortune. I had grown dissatisfied with the arrangement and so, escorted by Judge A. A. Hoehling, I had gone to the American Security Trust Company and demanded everything of mine they had. When it had been accounted for, bond by bond, it was wrapped into a bundle, and with this I had started across the street toward the National Metropolitan, Judge Hoehling's bank. He was greatly agitated, and protested: "You can't do this. We'll be held up. You've got more than a million dollars in your hand."

"Don't be timid," I counseled him. "Nobody knows why we came here."

Most of those bonds that I then carried across the street had to be turned into money to pay off debts; I owed about $800,000, and five-eighths of that was for Ned's debts. However, none of my real estate was mortgaged for a dollar. In that, I had the bulk of what my father left me. Another asset, not so good, was an order of a District of Columbia court instructing the trustees of the estate of old John R. to pay me $7,500 a month. Already, though, they were shrugging their shoulders and trying to maintain as fact their notion that they could not pay out money even though the estate included two big newspapers, the Rosiclair mine, bonds, stocks, Friendship, and the I Street house.

One day when I was blue from all the trouble of making million-dollar ends meet, I remembered my old prescription for that state of mind, went to New York, and asked Cartier to show me something fine. He then dazzled me with a ruby and diamond bracelet—one that owed its existence to the Depression.

"That principal diamond," said Cartier, "was placed in our hands by a well-known family that owned it, but on the condition that their name would not be revealed. The stone was always known as the Star of the South. It is almost sixteen carats. There are sixteen rubies and sixteen other diamonds." Cartier held it up before my eyes, and I could only utter just one question—"How much?" He told me $135,000.

I thought it over carefully for about a day; and then I sent him an offer of $50,000 cash and the balance to be paid in monthly sums spread over two years. Cartier telegraphed me "YES."

That is the way I always get into trouble when I have some money in my hands. I seem not to be able to do otherwise than spend it. However, it is no use for anyone to chide me for loving jewels. I cannot help it if I have a passion for them. They make me feel comfortable, and even happy. The truth is, when I neglect to wear jewels astute members of my family call in doctors because it is a sign I'm becoming ill.

My mother died on February 25, 1932. She had sent for me when she was in great pain. I promptly brought in doctors, who discovered she had cancer of the lungs. However, my mother would not accept treatment from the doctors and insisted on having a religious healer, one she had known for years. I brought the woman from Chicago to Washington and let her do precisely as she wished for a while.

One morning Mother whispered a request for me to close the door. Then she said, "Please give me something for this pain and don't let her come near me any more." From that time my mother had morphine whenever she required it; I made sure of that until the day she died.

My mother left all her property to me, in trust; at my death to go outright to my children. So 2020 Massachusetts Avenue became mine, likewise other real estate, more bonds, and varied possessions, along with that fresh sorrow.

It was while my grief was sharpest that the Lindbergh baby was kidnapped from its crib in its parents' isolated house in New Jersey.

Why should I have tried to get the Lindbergh baby back to its mother? Well, for one thing I had lived more than a score of years haunted daily by the fear of just what had happened to the Lindberghs. So many people were then wishing they might save the baby and revenge the crime that I wonder why so many persons now ask me what prompted me to involve myself in the hunt. It should be obvious, I think, that I tried to do what millions wished they might try to do. In my case the wish was harnessed, just as a carriage, to my money. I wished and, presto! things began to happen.

On Friday, the fourth of March, 1932, I sent for Gaston B. Means. I found out how to reach him through Mrs. May Dixon Thacker, who sometime before had repudiated the book that she had written based on his fanciful and wicked story of the death of President Harding. I telephoned to him asking, "Means, can you come to see me?"

"Yes," he said, "this evening."

He came at half-past eight. He stood before me in my drawing room—a fat and deeply dimpled scoundrel, who was, I thought, precisely what I needed as an instrument to get in touch with the kidnapers. William J. Burns had said this man was the best investigator he had ever known. A New York County prosecutor had said he was the cold-blooded murderer of a rich widow, but a small-town North Carolina jury had held him innocent. Means had served, in the Federal prison in Atlanta, a sentence imposed on him for being a grafter. I had no illusions about Means except that I supposed the chance to act as go-between in the ransoming of the Lindbergh baby would seem a bigger prize to him than any other chance he might discern in his dealings with me.

I wanted Means for precisely what he was—for the lack of straightness in his smartness. (I still think that Means was just the sort of man I wanted, even though he failed me.) Before very long the Lindberghs themselves had adopted a similar notion—that the way to make a contact with the underworld is through someone linked with it. Means told me, plausibly enough to convince me, that he wanted nothing more than to re-establish himself, for the sake of his own son and Mrs. Means. He hoped by such a coup as finding the Lindbergh baby to restore himself to favor. With just one deed, he could remake his world.

"Means," I asked him, "do you know where the Lindbergh baby is?"

"I do," he said, and then proceeded to tell me a highly colored yarn that was easy to believe. Means had been sent to Atlanta by the Federal Government for taking bribes from men engaged in the illicit liquor traffic, and for weeks after the Lindbergh baby was stolen the theory common to most police officials, and held by the Lindberghs and the Morrow family, was that bootleg criminals were the kidnapers.

Means told me the kidnapers wanted $100,000 ransom. By placing a short-term mortgage on the Oxford block, I raised the money and then gave the $100,000 to Gaston Means. A foolish thing to do? I was as wild to get back the child as if it were mine; and twice Colonel Lindbergh acted on a hope no less vain than my own, and paid out cash on such a trust. And on doing this I was acting with the full consent and co-operation of Colonel Lindbergh.

Night after night I waited out at Fairview, outside of Washington. That had been my mother's home. At the time I tell about, the house was tightly shuttered, the graveled drive neglected, and in the gardens weeds were showing. This estate that was now among my possessions had been chosen by Means, from a list of suggested places, as the ideal rendezvous where we should meet the kidnapers and get the Lindbergh baby back. Each night I waited there, and through the darkness tried to see along the paths my mother's feet had made. Each dawn was just another disappointment; but with sunrise hope would grow again.

I would think how fine it was that I should be engaged in something really useful in the world. In my Irish blood, which Tom Walsh gave me before he had a bit of gold, there was a compulsion pumped from my heart making me undertake that quest. I may spring from peasant stock, but that was a stirring, after years of luxury, of *noblesse oblige*. This is why I feel no chagrin whatever for having failed in an impossible undertaking. I did my best, paid out good money, and wanted no reward except a glow of satisfaction that I hoped to experience in my heart.

Well, Means had the cash, but there was no baby; yet my disappointments were no more difficult to account for than those that had to be explained away each of those days in the Lindbergh household. This fellow Means was kept informed, of course, by reading all the newspapers; but thanks to his understanding of the half-world of crime he could interpret what he read in such a manner as to make it seem to me that he had predicted some of the happenings. When March was two-thirds gone, I gave him another $4,000 for expenses and agreed to go to the house at Aiken, South Carolina, that I had leased for the season while my son Edward, Jr. was down there in school. Means said that would be a first-rate place for the meeting with the crooks.

At Aiken, a doctor friend loaded for me a special fountain pen. Its barrel was filled with a deadly poison, disguised as ink. From that time on, if anybody had tried to make me write under duress, I should have been prepared with a mild-looking device about as harmful as a cobra's fang.

Once I clutched that fountain pen in the middle of the night when I awoke in a bed that shook and trembled. I heard the melancholy screaming of a railroad engine's whistle, and realized with a sharply focused mind that again I had dug myself deeper into a desperate situation by acting on impulse. Means had persuaded me that the criminals were ready to play fair with me at El Paso, Texas. So I had consented to go, taking with me my trained nurse and my maid, Inga.

In El Paso I registered in the hotel as "Mrs. Lane", and each instant I kept in sight of the nurse and Inga. I was growing more and more suspicious about everything Means told me; and yet, the baby still was missing. Means swore the criminals were close at hand, ready to deliver the child to me now that they could so easily cross the international line and be fairly safe from capture. Then, a few hours later, Means came to explain to me that the kidnapers were already across the line, but would not give up the baby except in Mexico. Then I knew as plainly as though a rattlesnake had buzzed its tail that I was in mortal danger; right now

I feel sure that had I crossed into Mexico I should have been destroyed. However, I instructed the nurse to stay behind to get the child if possible—and then I started back to Washington.

It was after these adventures that Colonel Lindbergh in New Jersey identified the remains of a child's body as that of his little son.

I sent Father Hurney, a Roman Catholic priest, to Means to demand my $100,000. Father Hurney had been selected earlier as an appropriate person to receive the baby, and had helped me all he could.

The record of all Means's yarns and explanations would fill endless pages. His final statement was that he had permitted some associates to take the $100,000 to be used in a whisky deal in which they expected to double the amount within the space of a few days. Well, after that I had Means and his confederate, a man named Whitaker, arrested. I testified against them, and Mr. Means was given twenty years; at his age, I think that means life. I am sorry that I failed, that I was tricked; but I shall always be glad that in my heart there was something that compelled me to try my best to take part in the effort to ransom the Lindbergh baby.

CHAPTER XXIV

Depression Days

THE bank was going to foreclose the mortgage on the Oxford corner. I tried to make them hold off, but the only concession they would make was an agreement to "wait until Friday." None of my pleading had counted for a darn. I went on home and said, "To the devil with them; I've got to have a hundred thousand dollars."

I paced the floor a bit. Then I went behind a big heavily upholstered chair. I ripped out the back and pushed my arm deeply into a sort of squirrel's nest until my groping fingers found a cache of jewels there. With those stones I set out for New York, accompanied by a woman friend and my young daughter. One pawnbroker let me have $50,000 on the stones taken from the chair; another, Simpson's, 91 Park Row, gave me $37,500 on the Hope diamond.

Sometime later, when I had the money to redeem them, I went back with my same escort of one woman friend and one little girl. I pushed my cash across the counter, and when the stones were brought I stuffed them into my dress. When I went back to Simpson's after the Hope diamond it was in their original shop, downtown in the shadow of Brooklyn Bridge. Down there, the pawnshop men exclaimed as I started into the noisy street; they thought I ought to have detectives along.

We went uptown for luncheon, but lingered too long. We jumped into a taxi, and then ran through the station so fast I thought I would be shaking the stones out of my bosom at every step. We just managed to step into a baggage car as the train began to roll. I was in a lather; but I was happy to be going back with all my jewels.

On a day in June, 1932, I saw a dusty automobile truck roll slowly past my house. I saw the unshaven, tired faces of the men who were riding in it standing up. A few were seated at the rear with their legs dangling over the lowered tailboard. On the side of the truck was an expanse of white cloth on which, crudely lettered in black, was a legend, "BONUS ARMY."

Other trucks followed in a straggling succession, and on the sidewalks of Massachusetts Avenue where stroll most of the diplomats and the other fashionables of Washington were some ragged hikers, wearing scraps of old uniforms. The sticks with which they strode along seemed less canes than cudgels. They were not a friendly-looking lot, and I learned they were hiking and riding into the Capital along each of its radial avenues; that they had come from every part of the continent. It was not lost on me that those men, passing any one of my big houses, would see in such rich shelters a kind of challenge —2020 was a mockery of their want.

I was burning, because I felt that crowd of men, women, and children never should have been permitted to swarm across the continent. But I could remember when those same men, with others, had been cheered as they marched down Pennsylvania Avenue. While I recalled those wartime parades, I was reading in the newspapers that the Bonus Army men were going hungry in Washington.

That night I woke up before I had been asleep an hour. I got to thinking about those poor devils, marching around the Capital. Then I decided that it should be a part of my son Jock's education to see and try to comprehend that marching. It was one o'clock, and the Capitol was beautifully lighted. I wished then for the power to turn off the lights and use the money thereby saved to feed the hungry.

When Jock and I rode among the bivouacked men I was horrified to see plain evidence of hunger in their faces; I heard them trying to cadge cigarettes from one another. Some were lying on the sidewalks, unkempt heads pillowed on their arms. A few clusters were shuffling around. I went up to one of them, a fellow with eyes deeply sunken in his head.

"Have you eaten?"

He shook his head.

Just then I saw General Glassford, superintendent of the Washington police. He said, "I'm going to get some coffee for them."

"All right," I said, "I am going to Childs'."

It was two o'clock when I walked into that white restaurant. A man came up to take my order. "Do you serve sandwiches? I want a thousand, I said. "And a thousand packages of cigarettes."

"But, lady—

"I want them right away. I haven't got a nickel with me, but you can trust me. I am Mrs. McLean."

Well, he called the manager into the conference and before long they were slicing bread with a machine; and what with Glassford's coffee also (he was spending his own money) we two fed all the hungry ones who were in sight.

Next day I went to see judge John Barton Payne, head of the Red Cross, but I could not persuade him that the Bonus Army men were part of a national crisis that the Red Cross was bound to deal with. He did promise a little flour, and I was glad to accept it.

Then I tried the Salvation Army and found that their girls were doing all they could. I asked the officer in charge, a worried little man, if he would undertake to find out how I could help the men. With enthusiasm he said he would, and the next day he came to my house to tell me that what the Bonus Army leaders said they most needed was a big tent to serve as a headquarters, in which fresh arrivals could be registered. At once I ordered a tent sent over from Baltimore. After that I succeeded in getting Walter Waters to come to my house. He was trying to keep command of that big crowd of men. I talked to him and before long we were friends. I sent books and radios to the men. I went to the house in Pennsylvania that Glassford had provided for the women and children. There was not a thing in it. Scores of women and children were sleeping on its floors. So I went out and bought them army cots. Another day I took over some of my sons' clothing, likewise some of my own, and dresses of my daughter. One of the women held up one of little Evalyn's dresses and examined it on both sides. Then she said, "I guess my child can starve in a fifty-dollar dress as well as in her rags."

One day Waters, the so-called commander, came to my house and said: "I'm desperate. Unless these men are fed, I can't say what won't happen to this town." With him was his wife, a little ninety-three-pounder, dressed as a man, her legs and feet in shiny boots. Her yellow hair was freshly marceled.

"She's been on the road for days," said Waters, "and has just arrived by bus."

I thought a bath would be a welcome change; so I took her upstairs to that guest bedroom my father had designed for King Leopold. I sent for my maid to draw a bath, and told the young woman to lie down.

"You get undressed," I said, "and while you sleep I'll have all your things cleaned and pressed."

"Oh, no," she said, "not me. I'm not giving these clothes up. I might never see them again."

Her lip was out, and so I did not argue. She threw herself down on the bed, boots and all, and I tiptoed out.

That night I telephoned to Vice-President Charlie Curtis. I told him I was speaking for Waters, who was standing by my chair. I said: "These men are in a desperate situation, and unless something is done for them, unless they are fed, there is bound to be a lot of trouble. They have no money, nor any food."

Charlie Curtis told me that he was calling a secret meeting of Senators, and would send a delegation of them to the House to urge immediate action on the Howell bill, providing money to send the Bonus Army members back to their homes.

Those were times when I often wished for the days of Warren Harding. Harding would have gone among those men and talked in such a manner as to make them cheer him and cheer their flag. If Hoover had done that, I think, not even troublemakers in the swarm could have caused any harm.

Nothing I had seen before in my whole life touched me as deeply as what I had seen in the faces of those men of the Bonus Army. Their way of righting things was wrong— oh, yes; but it is not the only wrong. I had talked with them and their women. Even when the million-dollar home my father built was serving as a sort of headquarters for their leader, I could feel and almost understand their discontent and their hatred of some of the things I have represented.

I was out in California when the United States army was used to drive them out of Washington. In a moving-picture show I saw, in a news reel, the tanks, the cavalry, and the gasbomb throwers running those wretched Americans out of our

EDWARD B. McLEAN, JR. AND JOHN R. McLEAN
Sons of Mrs. McLean

Capital. I was so raging mad I could have torn the theater down. They could not be allowed to stay, of course; but even so I felt myself one of them.

After that, I concluded it was high time the family of Tom Walsh went back to work.

How shall a woman in my fix train her youngsters to become useful members of society rather than leisured playmates of society? Well, I turned on discipline as one turns on a faucet. My friend Mary Roberts Rinehart, the mother of three sons, says now that I am too strict with mine. When one son was arrested for speeding, I took away his car—no fooling. When the other, while in prep school, stayed out too late, I induced a detective to scare him with a gun. In showing my two sons just what a man's lot is, I have had a great deal of help from Admiral Mark Bristol who is now retired from the United States Navy. He is a fine man and by court appointment acts for my husband in all business matters. That makes it simple for me to seek sound conclusions when I plan for my sons and daughter.

Jock, my elder son, at the age of eighteen went to work in Cincinnati in the counting room of the *Enquirer,* the newspaper his great-grandfather founded. Jock started at the bottom. He was paid $15 a week, on which he lived, in a boardinghouse, until he had earned a promotion. A bit later there will be a job for Ned. I have every reason to believe my sons and daughter will inherit wealth. The point is, I have learned that with riches one inherits obligations.

I would not undertake to say how great a change has been worked in me. However, in the spring of 1935 I went to dinner at the home of Senator and Mrs. Hiram Johnson. (In Washington we always call her "Boss.") Senator and Mrs. Key Pittman were there; just a few others. As I came in Attorney General Cummings leaned toward Hiram Johnson's ear to ask, Who's that?" At dinner I sat next to Mr. Cummings and expressed surprise that he had failed to recognize me.

"But there is something different about you, Mrs. McLean," he said "Something I can't quite define."

"Well, Mr. Attorney General," I replied, "as your department contains all the G-men, you are supposed to be the nation's greatest sleuth. And you tell me you can't figure out the change in me?"

"I really can't," he said, "and I'm amazed."

"Mr. Attorney General, the last time you saw me my hair was jet black, and now it's pink."

Even so, I dare to tell myself sometimes that there really has been a change and that it goes far deeper than hair dye.

I suppose that many have read this with envy, some with amazement, others with anger, that money, so powerful in this world, so desperately necessitous in their own households at times, should be given beyond all need into such hands.

Well, money is power—power for good, power for evil, accordingly as it is used Power is a test—the test—of character. I want pity from no one, do not want to seem preachy or sorry for myself, but, as any woman, I should like to be understood a little. Unless you have been put to the test, don't be too sure that you would have made a better mark than I have. He jests at scars who never felt a wound.

If Ned McLean and I had been born into average-income families and normal environments, given just what we were born with, we probably should have been average citizens to-day, leading normal lives, with normal faults and virtues, reading this story with the same emotions You have felt. Character or environment? The world never has settled that argument. I think we each had enough character to have met the negative tests of such an environment. The very circumstances of normal life encourage self-discipline, punish self-indulgence.

Not all the moral tests of life are tied up with money or the lack of it, but only the rich may be reckless, foolish, ignorant, and snap their fingers at the consequences. If you are not rich, the piper is at the door with his bill in the morning. The rich can defer their payments; they may easily delude themselves that they are not paying at all.

I said that money is power. You may believe that you know this quite as well as I. That I doubt. It is not something you can know by hearsay. Money and electricity are much alike. Both are stored energy. Living amidst electricity, using it constantly, you take its presence and its utility for granted. Treated with respect, it is constructive, tireless. Treated with disrespect, it is destructive, vicious. It will light your way, pull a twelve-car train from Washington to New York in a bit more than four hours, kill you or burn your house alike. Electricity is insulated, though, and children are not permitted to play with it.

Those who make money rarely are reckless with it. They know its values from having made it. They know that it takes at least as much gumption to keep it, to use it wisely, as it does to create it in the first place. If they misuse it badly now and then, it is in the full knowledge of their folly and with a reservation not to make a habit of it. Yet they assume often that to their children this will be sense as plain as that a hot stove burns and pins stick.

They bring their children up surrounded by wires charged with the high voltages of wealth, thinly insulated with "Naughty! Naughty!" commands. If they are generous of heart, they will want to share the bounties of wealth with their own. If it is easier for any parent to say "yes" than "no", how much easier for those whose yes involves no sacrifice, or inconvenience even? If they have known hardship and denial, they will wish to spare their own.

In this eagerness to give their children the things they themselves did not have as children, to save these children from what they themselves did have, they innocently deny their sons and daughters the very incentives, the aids to character and ambition which impelled their own successes. This is instinct in most parents, rich, poor, or in between. You may see the impulse operating under nearly any roof, but those who do not have money are in little danger of softening their children with money.

There is nothing noble or virtuous, as such, about poverty and discomfort. If a man in his own youth broke the ice in the water pitcher of a winter morning, it isn't necessary to deny his son a radiator. If a woman walked barefoot to a dance, carrying her shoes, it won't corrupt her daughter to ride in a car or to own five pairs of shoes. But if it was good for the man to earn his own spending -money as a boy, it will be good for his son. Twenty-five cents a week may have been enough for the father; five dollars may not be enough for the son. Times change, and the value of money, but boys and girls and first principles don't.

Or if parents are mean-spirited, I have seen them dangle riches tantalizingly before adolescents, not to discipline them to moderation, but teasing them with the scraps of wealth. If they have pride in their own achievements, they may easily communicate the pride, without the achievements, to their sons and daughters. Surely the greatest responsibility of all that money brings is the responsibility to keep it from distorting your children's lives.

Yes, money was our devil, but it was not money's fault.

I can hear my father talking now of "clean money." His came directly from the earth, not from other men, whether fairly or unfairly. He took pride in that. A generous man and one who liked people, he taught me that there was no true generosity in giving money if the giver has much money; that unless I gave something of myself as well, it cost me nothing; therefore meant nothing. This I have tried to practice, hope to practice more. That he did not teach me more, I cannot find it in my heart to reproach his memory. He had not, after all, experienced the evil side of money. He knew little of weakness. A strong character himself, it would have been natural for him to take for granted the strength of his children, to fail to realize the different circumstances of money earned and money inherited. It is myself I reproach; most of all, because he would be disappointed in me.

I best can make amends by teaching my children what I had to learn the hard way, and late. I am teaching them; be sure of that. As for myself, I am pretty nearly broke now. I hope my acquaintances— I won't say friends—are satisfied. The Hope diamond, and every other jewel that I have, have been in and out of New York pawnshops in recent years. There is a spot three feet square where the plaster has fallen from the ceiling of my bedroom at Friendship. Its repair is indefinite and I think of hanging pink ruffles around it.

With care, if times improve, there will be enough salvage from the two estates to provide what still will be a fortune for each child. I think they will give a better account of their stewardships than their father and mother have. It won't be for lack of a bad example or for ignorance of that example, if they do not.